Demand My Writing

Liverpool Science Fiction Texts and Studies

General Editor DAVID SEED

Series Advisers
I. F. CLARKE, EDWARD JAMES, PATRICK PARRINDER
AND BRIAN STABLEFORD

1. ROBERT CROSSLEY, *Olaf Stapledon: Speaking for the Future*, ISBN 0–85323–388–8 (hardback)
2. DAVID SEED (ed.), *Anticipations: Essays on Early Science Fiction and its Precursors*, ISBN 0–85323–348–9 (hardback), ISBN 0–85323–418–3 (paperback)
3. JANE L. DONAWERTH AND CAROL A. KOLMERTEN (ed.), *Utopian and Science Fiction by Women: Worlds of Difference*, ISBN 0–85323–269–5 (hardback), ISBN 0–85323–279–2 (paperback)
4. BRIAN W. ALDISS, *The Detached Retina: Aspects of SF and Fantasy*, ISBN 0–85323–289–X (hardback), ISBN 0–85323–299–7 (paperback)
5. CAROL FARLEY KESSLER, *Charlotte Perkins Gilman: Her Progress Toward Utopia, with Selected Writings*, ISBN 0–85323–489–2 (hardback), ISBN 0–85323–499–X (paperback)
6. PATRICK PARRINDER, *Shadows of the Future: H. G. Wells, Science Fiction and Prophecy*, ISBN 0–85323–439–6 (hardback), ISBN 0–85323–449–3 (paperback)
7. I. F. CLARKE (ed.), *The Tale of the Next Great War, 1871–1914: Fictions of Future Warfare and of Battles Still-to-come*, ISBN 0–85323–459–0 (hardback), ISBN 0–85323–469–8 (paperback)
8. QINGYUN WU, *Female Rule in Chinese and English Literary Utopias*, ISBN 0–85323–570–8 (hardback), ISBN 0–85323–580–5 (paperback)
9. JOHN CLUTE, *Look at the Evidence: Essays and Reviews*, ISBN 0–85323–820–0 (hardback), ISBN 0–85323–830–8 (paperback)
10. ROGER LUCKHURST, *'The Angle Between Two Walls': The Fiction of J. G. Ballard*, ISBN 0–85323–821–9 (hardback), ISBN 0–85323–831–6 (paperback)
11. JEANNE CORTIEL, *Demand My Writing: Joanna Russ/Feminism/Science Fiction*, ISBN 0–85323–614–3 (hardback), ISBN 0–85323–624–0 (paperback)

Demand My Writing

Joanna Russ/Feminism/Science Fiction

JEANNE CORTIEL
Department of English and American Studies,
Universität Dortmund

LIVERPOOL UNIVERSITY PRESS

First published 1999 by
LIVERPOOL UNIVERSITY PRESS
Liverpool L69 3BX

British Library Cataloguing-in-Publication Data
A British Library CIP record is available
ISBN 0–85323–614–3 cased
ISBN 0–85323–624–0 paperback

Typeset in Meridien by
Northern Phototypesetting Co. Ltd., Bolton
Printed and bound in the European Union by
Redwood Books, Trowbridge, UK

Table of Contents

Acknowledgements

How many more than two are there. If they heard it at once and at once was as afterward whom would they have to mention. And leaves. This makes them wish—Gertrude Stein, *A Novel of Thank You*

As customary and appropriate for a project of this size, which is necessarily indebted to the minds of many people, I will make an attempt to express my gratitude for the help and support I have received during the long process of writing this book. I participate gladly in this ritual because it positions me in a relation of thankfulness to a number of people who have been important in different ways during the past five years of my life.

Helga Kellner's enthusiasm for the embryo version of the book helped me believe in its merit. I am thankful for the comments of Julie Linden, Kerstin Holzgräbe, Jackie Vogel and Christine Gerhardt on individual chapters and the project as a whole. Jackie's dog Clyde with his uninhibited zest for life cheered me up during a time when I thought the book would never materialize. Lawrence Kane and ricki wegner patiently read an early version of the manuscript and gave me invaluable suggestions for revision. Judith Marco and Peter Cortiel helped me with numerous details regarding my research, including tracking down difficult-to-find texts by Joanna Russ. The critical suggestions of the reader at Liverpool University Press helped me reconceptualize the project in significant ways. Finally, Christine Gerhardt and Stephen Watt meticulously proofread the last version of the manuscript and forced me to clarify passages that my chaotic mind had left obscure to any reader other than myself. Special thanks go to Elisabeth Kraus, my first teacher of science fiction, and Walter Grünzweig, who has taught and supported me far beyond the scope of this project.

The list continues and this public statement of gratitude as any other must remain incomplete in more than one way.

For Christine

Introduction

One moves incurably into the future but there is no future; it
has to be created—Russ, *On Strike Against God* (85)

The struggle on the page is not decorative—DuPlessis, 'The
Pink Guitar' (173)

Joanna Russ published her first science fiction story 'Nor Custom
Stale' in the popular *Magazine of Fantasy and Science Fiction* in 1959,
when she was 22 and in her second year at the Yale School of Drama.
'It is Miss Russ's first story—' wrote the editors in their introductory
note to this text, 'first, we are confident, of many' (75). Joanna Russ
has since not only written many stories, she has also accomplished a
few things that the editors might not have expected from this young
woman. Together with writers such as the French author Monique
Wittig, James Tiptree, Jr., Marge Piercy, Ursula Le Guin and others,
this promising young 'Miss' Russ would become one of the forces
which revolutionized the genre in the 1960s and '70s. This revolution transformed science fiction from a bastion of masculinism to
one of the richest spaces for feminist utopian thinking and cultural
criticism.

Although Russ published two poems when she was 15 and went on
to study play writing, she chose narrative rather than poetry or drama
for most of her work. In an interview which Donna Perry conducted
with her in the early 1990s, Russ said that she had abandoned the
'bare art' of drama for narrative because 'Too much of what I write is
internal' (293). However, most of what Russ writes also reverberates
with a consistently radical political voice and is as much concerned
with its external effects as it is with exploring 'internal' spaces. The
title of this book, *Demand My Writing*, echoes this political urgency of
Russ's fiction. Her writing always intensely engages with its audience
and specifically with the individual reader. One could call this
approach didacticism, but I prefer to call it political responsibility.
Russ's concern with the reader correlates with her interest in writing,
particularly women's writing. I stole the phrase I use in my title from

Rachel Blau DuPlessis's essay 'The Pink Guitar', from which I once heard her read at a lecture. However, I had misunderstood what DuPlessis had actually said and it is this misunderstanding which makes the phrase so appealing as an emblem for my reading of Russ's work. The passage in DuPlessis's essay reads as follows:

> I am not a writer, as such. I am a marker, maybe that is a way to say it. All the signs that emerge on the page (I put them there, they came here through me) (some were already there, in the weave of the paper, no tabula rasa)
>
> demand my reading. The responsibility for making words is the responsibility for reading. The practice of writing is already a reading, of the writing already written, of the saturated page,
>
> smitten with that already-written, in
>
> language, anguage. I am some character in a little folk tale, call me 'a-reading-a-writing'. (173)

'Demand my writing', as I had heard it, addresses not the signs on the page, but the imaginary readers who urge the production of these signs. Thus, the interrelation between my misunderstanding and the original text crystallizes the ways in which Russ's work interweaves the processes and political significance of reading and writing. Like DuPlessis's essay, Russ's fiction expresses no anxieties over the influence of the author's reading; indeed, this reading is not so much an influence on, as it is a precondition for, writing. The following chapters will identify and analyse some of the multiple intertextualities in Russ's work. As a reader and writer, Russ is also part of twentieth-century feminism. This book provides a narrative of Russ's development as a writer and analyses the ways in which her work reads/writes itself into the discourses of Western feminism. As a consequence, my interpretations rely largely on comparison. The two major points of intersection relevant for these interpretations are speculative fiction and feminist theory. The remainder of this introduction will outline how these points of intersection become productive in my reading of Russ's fiction.

Intersection: Speculative Fiction

Few critics feel comfortable with clear-cut definitions of science fiction. When called upon to define what is meant by the term, writers tend to seek refuge in roundabout vagueness. Ursula Le Guin in her introduction to *The Norton Book of Science Fiction* addresses this issue, asking: 'Why are all the answers to that question either brisk evasions or labored partialities?' (20) Some critics have tried to get away with flippant statements, such as the by now classic quip of Damon Knight, which Ursula Le Guin also comes back to: 'science fiction is what [I'm] pointing at when [I] point at it' (21). Probably more so than any other genre, science fiction defies definitional closure, if only because the transgression of genre boundaries is already part of its unique tradition. Fantasy, romance and elements from other forms such as utopian writing have always been used by science fiction writers.

However, genre criticism has developed a terminology to deal with these blurred distinctions. For the purpose of this study, four terms seem to be particularly useful. I use the term 'genre fiction' whenever I want to refer to popular forms such as science fiction, fantasy, utopian fiction, detective fiction and romance, which have all been appropriated by feminist discourse.[1] Implied in this definition are the characteristics which these forms all share: they are immensely popular and their readership is diverse, which makes them particularly useful for 'propagandistic' purposes. Marleen Barr in her early work, together with other scholars in the field, prefers the term 'speculative fiction', which provides a more focused categorization and a slightly different emphasis. In speculative fiction, according to Barr, political appropriation of genre conventions is not only a potential, but a conscious practice, extrapolating as it does from a critical analysis of the power relations in contemporary society (*Alien to Femininity*, xii). The term as Barr defines it includes feminist utopias, science fiction, fantasy and sword-and-sorcery.

Although Russ's own speculative fiction does not always honour the boundaries between 'fantasy' and 'science fiction', she makes clear distinctions in her critical work. Russ's concise and accessible provisional definition in 'The Image of Women in Science Fiction' (1971) will also serve as the basis for my discussion here:

> Science Fiction is *What If literature*. All sorts of definitions have been proposed by people in the field, but they all contain both The What If and The Serious Explanation; that is, science fiction shows things not as they characteristically or habitually are but as they might be, and for this 'might be' the author must offer a rational, serious, consistent explanation, one that does not (in Samuel Delany's phrase) offend against what is

> known to be known. ... If the author offers marvels and does not explain them, or if he explains them playfully and not seriously, or if the explanation offends against what the author knows to be true, you are dealing with fantasy and not science fiction. (79, italics in original)

Thus, although both genres use the speculative potential of the human imagination, science fiction works within the constraints of the scientific episteme. Traditionally, the plots of fantasy stories are populated by creatures from pre-Enlightenment folk lore, such as ghosts, vampires or dragons. Science fiction, on the other hand, generally positions its narrative worlds and protagonists in the future or in outer space. Russ's definition—like her fictional practice—allows for broader conceptualizations of both genres. Since less empirically rigid sciences, such as psychology or the social sciences, entered the realm of popular knowledge, science fiction has opened its doors to explorations of 'inner spaces' and social relations. Particularly feminist criticism of science and society became part of 'what is known to be known' in feminist science fiction.

Such definitional openness in science fiction criticism also reverberates through categorizations of Russ's fictional writing. Science fiction and genre scholarship has placed Russ's work in a variety of different, sometimes overlapping genre categories. The majority of critical work focuses on Russ's novels, most of which are primarily science fictional. Such criticism consequently reads her predominantly as a science fiction author. More comprehensive appreciations of her work, however, categorize it in broader terms as genre fiction or speculative fiction, acknowledging her as a writer of fantasy—particularly in her short stories—as well as of science fiction (Delany 1976, 1985; Hacker 1977; Lefanu 1988). In placing particular emphasis on Russ's largely neglected short fiction, I will reassess these categorizations. Russ's short stories span a rich variety of different sub-genres, such as sword-and-sorcery, horror, ghost and vampire fiction, elements of which also become instrumental parts of her novels. These distinctions therefore become important in my readings of Russ's fiction primarily to demonstrate the specific ways in which her work transgresses genre boundaries.

Russ's definition, which I quoted above, reveals a slightly higher regard for science fiction than for fantasy which is particularly characteristic of her earlier critical work. As Russ stresses in 'The Wearing Out of Genre Materials' (1971), science fiction for her occupies a special place within genre fiction and may not even properly belong to that category, since it has a potentially infinite supply of new conventions from new scientific knowledge and is therefore less likely to become fossilized in petrified narrative routines (53–54). However, this assessment is convincingly contradicted by Anne Cranny-Francis's study *Feminist Fiction: Feminist Uses of Generic Fiction* (1990). Cranny-Francis suggests that feminist writers have successfully revolutionized each of the popular genres. The detective novel, for example, announced dead by Russ in 'The Wearing Out of Genre Materials' (53), has been remodelled and reactivated for feminist purposes. Feminist genre fiction has found a supply of 'new materials' at least as vast as that of science in its reinterpretations of women's life stories, of culture, history and mythology. Russ's own fictional work has taken part in these reformulations and has created alternative images of women that carry the imprint of women's material existence (Lefanu, 13–14). Science fiction has also changed drastically since 1971 when Russ critically surveyed the then largely male-dominated field in her essay 'The Image of Women in Science Fiction'. The essay concludes: 'There are plenty of images of women in science fiction. There are hardly any women' (91). However, feminist speculative texts have generated more than just images of women that female readers can recognize and identify with; they have resisted the reproduction of the stories patriarchal societies tell about women and instead envision stories that thoroughly displace them.

I have so far used the term 'feminism' as if it were a homogenous discursive ground. However, my readings of Russ rely on the many-levelled contentions that exist among different feminist positions. One such distinction separates feminist theoreticians, who devote their energies to thinking about philosophical questions, from feminist activists, who are primarily interested in changing the lives of 'real' women. This is also a question of access to privileged knowledges. Recent feminist theory has been criticized for its inability to address the needs of non-academics in a language accessible to people who do not have a Ph.D. in philosophy. Feminist work influenced by poststructuralism, especially, is largely incomprehensible to people who are not at home with the rhetoric of Western philosophy. Although this dichotomy between 'theorists' and 'activists', or 'theory' and 'politics' simplifies the complexity of the issues, it does delineate major lines of confrontation. Feminist writers have used genre fiction to challenge these dichotomies as they have challenged patriarchal constructions of reality. Their stories counteract sexist manipulation in the areas where it is most effectively perpetuated: popular culture and the media.

Speculative fiction, and specifically science fiction, thus has the potential to break down distinctions between feminist theory, feminist fiction and feminist practice, exploring as it does complex theoretical concepts in the terms of popular fiction. Feminist theory becomes part of the 'science' in science fiction while feminist practice motivates the text. In *Alien to Femininity* Marleen Barr uses the image of two horses pulling together: 'Feminist Theory and Speculative Fiction appear in the critical arena pulling together as a team' (xxi). Barr's objective is to form a link between feminist theory and speculative fiction, so both can work together against the limiting and restrictive social roles of women in patriarchal societies. Pointing out that we live in an age in which primarily the mass-media reproduce our realities and values, Barr also has a political message for literary critics and educators: 'We must give women critical tools to resist pervasive sexist media images' (xx). At a historical moment in which feminism is confronting the breakdown of the category 'woman' while none of the basic political objectives of feminist 'identity politics' have been sufficiently achieved, feminist speculative fiction may offer discursive possibilities unavailable to other genres. For at its best, speculative fiction can be a popular platform on which issues related to such diverse fields as technology, science, social theory, reproduction and ecology combine with feminist concerns to call into question the social and ecological policies of (post-industrial) capitalist patriarchy.

Intersection: Feminist Theory

> When there is a respectable, academically acceptable 'feminism' that has split completely from what women's studies used to be—Florence Howe once called us the academic arm of the women's movement—we will all be the losers. Once a radical politics (or literary criticism) is limited and diluted to the point where it can safely become part of the establishment, it can also be dispensed with. (Russ, 'On "The Yellow Wall-Paper,"' 166)

Another major cluster of contentions that engenders diversity in feminism corresponds to the confrontation between younger feminists and their predecessors and teachers. Although there are many other types of diversity in feminism, and Russ's writing is not coextensive with its feminist politics, the historical development of Western feminism is crucially relevant for an appreciation of Russ's fictional work. The historiography of feminism generally identifies three 'generations' in twentieth-century feminism. Julia Kristeva in her influential and much-cited essay 'Women's Time' (1981) differentiates these generations based on their respective concepts of time. The first of her phases presumes a linear temporality as unquestioned given, while the second rejects this notion of time as inherently patriarchal, superseding it with a circular temporality. The third phase, then, reveals both concepts as discursively constructed and historically specific. The phases of feminism in her categorization thus either embrace, reject or deconstruct the idea of time as linear, teleological entity. In this delineation of feminism, Kristeva uses both the language of history, that is linear temporality, and that of spatial relations to represent developments in feminism. This choice of metaphor is particularly useful for an analysis of speculative fiction, since it disrupts monolithic temporality without completely negating the functionality of its logic.

Kristeva begins her survey of feminism, in which she focuses on the radical exponents in each 'generation', with the early Western women's movement. These early feminists strove to gain access to the process of history and focused on the political and social equality of women. European and American suffragists in the nineteenth and early twentieth centuries and—in a so-called 'second wave'—existentialist or materialist feminists in the 1960s and '70s put forward specific, political demands directed towards achieving an equal status for women in society. In so doing, they identified with the dominant logic of their respective cultures, globalizing the problems of women under the label 'Universal Woman' (Kristeva, 18–19). In other words, women—as members of a trans-national and trans-cultural sex-class—sought to become men's equals within the social order created by patriarchal culture and to be recognized as agents in the historical process. This feminist moment has the strongest narrative force in Russ's early work, particularly in her short story sequence around the character Alyx. Kristeva associates this moment with a linear concept of time. This position establishes causal relationships between historical events based on the notion that time has a certain direction, a telos towards which history progresses. Linear temporality, therefore, informs the materialist project.

This linear concept of time, according to Kristeva, was rejected by a second generation of feminists, who, as a consequence, distrusted the political dimension and demanded recognition of an irreducible female identity without equivalent in the 'opposite' sex (19). While the first generation of feminists fought for economic, political and professional equality, this second current in feminism focused on the question of sexual equality, or rather difference (21). This position, which assumes an immutable female essence, has also been called 'cultural' or 'essentialist' feminism. Although there is as much diversity within this generation as in both of the others, these feminists generally celebrate sexual difference in the search for the specificity of the 'Female' and of each individual woman. Reclaiming women's cultural heritage as a distinct historical category, this strand of feminism repudiates linear History and dis-covers Herstory identified with a cyclical temporality. In the attempt to recover and reconstruct a separate sphere for women and to found a distinct women's counter-culture, these feminists rejected the patriarchal 'symbolic order' as inherently oppressive (see also Moi, *Sexual/Textual Politics*, 12). The central strategy for this feminist generation is forging political, emotional, and erotic bonds among women. Without giving up her materialism, Russ's work in the 1970s puts a new emphasis on this 'essentialist' position.

The third generation, then, locates the dichotomies man/woman and feminine/masculine in the realm of the metaphysical (Kristeva, 33). This generation sees both the concept of gender and the concept of time as historically and culturally specific constructs (today, one might add biological sex as well). Particularly criticism from non-white and/or non-middle class feminists has been instrumental in identifying the interests of the dominant culture in the call for a universal, all-encompassing 'sisterhood'. Challenging the notion of a singular social and sexual identity, which had been at the centre of both previous moments, these feminists focus on the 'multiplicity of every person's possible identifications ... the *relativity of his/her symbolic as well as biological existence*, according to the variation in his/her specific symbolic capacities' (Kristeva, 35, italics in original). In the 1980s, particularly in the short story collection/novel *Extra(Ordinary) People* (1984), Russ's emphasis shifts towards this deconstructive feminist stance.

This brief survey indicates the ways in which Russ's work has participated in the major transformations in Western feminism. The remaining chapters will substantiate this assertion. Although feminism is not the only concern in Russ's writing, it does structure Russ's development as a writer. While Kristeva could not completely foresee the feminist developments in the 1980s and '90s, her basic distinctions are still valid and will help me to identify major strands and developments in Russ's writing. It is important to note that Kristeva's stages of development do not supersede each other in neat succession. Kristeva points out that her 'usage of the word 'generation' implies less a chronology than a *signifying space ...*' and notes that this definition 'does not exclude—quite to the contrary—the *parallel* existence of all three in the same historical time, or even that they be interwoven one with the other' (33, italics in original). Since I put more emphasis on the idea that these strands in feminism are inextricably linked and depend on the interrelations with each other, I prefer to use the term 'moments' rather than 'stages' or 'generations'.

My reading of Russ's work suggests that these moments may be even more intimately interwoven than Kristeva's categorization admits. In Russ's writing these three moments appear to be inseparable, each deriving its specific force from the presence of the others. These moments correspond to three major concerns which run through and structure Russ's fiction: (1) women's agency, (2) female sexuality, and (3) the indeterminacy of both of these categories. Even though feminist theory seems unable to find common ground for these concerns because of the perceived fundamental clash between 'determinism' or 'essentialism' and 'deconstruction', my interpretations of Russ's fiction demonstrate that combining all three moments is not only possible in, but an intrinsic part of most of her work. In other words, although identifying and naming distinct moments in the history of twentieth-century feminism suggests separation, breakage and opposition, the fictional work of Russ as examined in this study focuses on the continuities. Russ's work links the radical materialist ideas of the late 1960s and early '70s with the separatism of the late '70s and early '80s and also anticipates the poststructuralisms of the late '80s and '90s.

I have organized my readings in this book around major thematic clusters in Russ's writing rather than in correspondence with the chronology of her work. However, as I have said, Russ's writing has gone through major shifts in emphasis since the late 1950s when she started to publish her fiction. Since these transformations are motivated by the three major concerns which I identified above—agency, sexuality and indeterminacy—the three parts of this book also roughly correspond to three phases in her career as a writer.

Part One, 'Agency', focuses on the materialist aspect of Russ's work and underlines the way in which she creates images of women who demand access to the symbolic order and to the process of history. The chapters here read selected novels and short stories along with Shulamith Firestone's work, which analyses woman's relation to reproduction as constitutive of the gender dichotomy. Firestone defines 'woman' not as a natural category, but as a sex-class. The stories of agency Russ tells are based on such materialist concepts and operate within the logic of linear temporality.

Part Two, 'Sexuality', highlights the characters in Russ's texts who claim their sexuality and their body as their own and seek connections to other women in their lives and in history. Particularly lesbian sexuality provides a space in which the woman's body is freed from male proprietorship and the debasing meaning attached to her by patriarchal discourse. In associating with women in texts such as the Bible or the *Nibelungenlied*, the stories about women examined in Part Two implicitly reject the notion of linear temporality and replace it with a cyclical notion of time. These chapters will explore the intersections of Russ's texts with radical separatist feminism and (feminist) psychoanalysis.

Part Three, 'Indeterminacy,' analyses how Russ's texts reformulate the (post)modern crisis of the subject. Her writing always also subverts the notion of a singular identity which is implicit in both materialism and separatist feminism, without however, nullifying these positions. The fractured, multiple self in Russ does not negate the self as member of a sex-class and the self reaching out to other women, but supplements them. The new, fluid subjectivity created by the simultaneous presence of a unified identity and its disintegration, contains the (desire for a) utopian space beyond gender antagonisms.

Since these readings work with texts from diverse phases and political affiliations and feminism is far from being a homogenous discursive field, a number of preliminary terminological distinctions are indispensable. I will, of necessity, use the simplifying term 'oppression', with which I refer to any position of disadvantage in a social structure, not just overt suppression of human potential. Similarly, I use the term 'patriarchy' to refer to a society in which women are oppressed and subject to male domination. However, as I have indicated, my readings of Russ's fictional work will also require reference to feminist concepts that reach beyond these clear-cut categories and make the opposition between 'oppressor' and 'oppressed' unstable.

More recent feminist work has examined the categories 'woman' and 'man' and has extensively theorized the classic terminological distinction between 'sex' and 'gender'. At the same time, however, there is also a great deal of vagueness and uncertainty about the outlines of and the distinctions between these two terms. Although all signifiers are unfixed and shifting, words like 'sex' or 'sexual' are particularly slippery and shift over a variety of different signifieds, which is why it is virtually impossible to pinpoint these terms even for the moment of analysis. Since my focus is on textual analysis of fictional writing, my definitions are based on how these two categories operate in written texts. 'Sex' in this study therefore refers to textual representations of the male or female *body*, which I take to be historically and culturally specific. This category is distinct from 'gender', which signifies those aspects of the *performance* or role of a character which belong to a set of characteristics that her/his culture (or fictional world) identifies with masculinity or femininity. Although sex and gender of a character are not entirely separable and both are produced and reproduced in culture, a feminist reading of Russ's work requires clear terminological distinctions. Janet, for instance, a central character in Russ's novel *The Female Man*, has a female body but is—at least partially—gendered masculine. Although the text implicitly refers to her body as female, she is not a woman. Although her sexual relations are exclusively with other female characters, one can argue that she is not a lesbian either.

In order to locate Russ's complex oeuvre in the discursive field of feminism, *Demand My Writing* explores intersections between specific representative texts in feminist theory and Russ's fiction. It is not my intention in this study to scrutinize how certain aspects of feminist theory 'resurface' in Russ's texts. Feminist writing in my reading is not a matter of 'reflecting' or 'illustrating' political theory in fiction. Feminist science fiction as a self-consciously political practice is part of the feminist struggle, not its 'reflection.' I will re-examine radical ideas of early 'second-wave' feminists such as those of Shulamith Firestone as well as the work of 'cultural feminists' or 'essentialists' such as Mary Daly or Adrienne Rich. Examining the recent history of feminist theory in relation to the developments in speculative fiction, I will formulate connections, without, however, establishing exclusive causal links between texts or events.

Joanna Russ was one of the first and one of the most radical writers in feminist speculative fiction. Her work demonstrates how feminism can indeed become part of what the 1960s and '70s called the 'establishment', without at the same time becoming apolitical and therefore dispensable from a feminist activist point of view. Furthermore, her texts engage an analysis of the ways in which feminisms are part of the dominant culture, and how feminists may make this troublesome role politically useful. Experimenting with empowering ways of transforming subjectivity, Russ's fiction stands as a challenge to feminist theory. The way in which she uses speculative fiction lends itself to dislocating accepted ways of thinking, since it displaces the individual by having it venture into alien outer space and explores the alienated inner space of the individual mind, defamiliarizing our most familiar categories. A careful reading of Russ's texts may reveal new strategies for radical feminist theory, which can propel it beyond the sex/gender antagonisms into a yet unthinkable new utopian space.

> Scholars don't usually sit gasping and sobbing in corners of the library stacks.

> But they should. They should. (Russ, *On Strike Against God*, 91)

PART ONE
Agency

Introduction to Part One

The story of feminism as told by Julia Kristeva in 'Women's Time' begins with the utopian vision of 'Woman' as a self-knowing subject who acts as an equal to all other individuals in the social system. This is also the point where my exploration of Russ's work will take off in Part One, tracing the materialist feminist moment through her short stories and novels. The main site of intersection between Russ's fiction and radical materialist feminism lies in both discourses' desire for women's agency and knowledge of self. The epigraph for this chapter from Monique Wittig crystallizes this impulse. However, Russ—like Wittig—also *challenges* fundamental assumptions of materialist feminism such as the notion that 'woman' constitutes a stable, universal social class.

In this context, 'agency' signifies the power and ability to effect changes in the process of human history, combined with the recognition by others that the agent is indeed the origin of that change. In other words, I am an agent, if I do something and society (which includes myself) acknowledges the products of this activity as effected by me. This concept builds on two premises: first, that the actions of an individual constitute her identity and second, that agency is prerequisite for human existence within the cultural context. If I am denied this capacity, I do not exist as part of society. My point here is not that agency is essentially and necessarily the basis of identity, but that it has this function in a materialist feminist analysis of society. From this materialist feminist perspective, a patriarchal society is a society which fully or partially denies women agency. The desire for agency underlies issues such as voting rights and reproductive rights, as well as images of women in literature and the visual arts—most of which are as relevant today as they were 100 years ago. This feminist moment, therefore, strives to create an equal existence for women (and by extension all members of society) and to transform the socio-economic framework.

In Russ's fiction, agency as a political concept operates in complex ways. Its availability or non-availability governs not only women's stories in Russ's fictional worlds but also the ways in which the protagonists relate to the acts of narration and writing. Therefore, authorship, narration and reading as sexed and gendered acts figure prominently in Russ's writing. Another, related concern of Russ's work is to explore how fictional representations of women's lives correlate with the actual life stories and material bodies of women—specifically white American women—outside the text. This correlation is not one of simple equivalence.

Part One will analyse how women's agency—or its lack—functions in specific texts, such as 'My Dear Emily' (1962), 'Life in a Furniture Store' (1965), the sword-and-sorcery short story sequence *The Adventures of Alyx* (1976; 1983),[1] or the novels *The Female Man* (1975) and *The Two of Them* (1978). In these readings, I rely on the humanist, stable concept of agency outlined above in order to position Russ's texts within the context of early second-wave materialist feminism. This approach is based on the belief that to identify and explore the intersections among different feminist texts, one needs to keep these texts' own logic intact for the moment of analysis. Therefore, the readings in these chapters partially suspend the fundamental indeterminacy that governs more recent feminist thinking. Instead of emphasizing breakages between the feminist 'generations', I will highlight the continuities.

CHAPTER ONE

The Act of Telling: Who is the Subject of Narrative Action?

What can a heroine do?

What myths, what plots, what actions are available to a female protagonist?

Very few.—Russ, 'What Can a Heroine Do' (83)

One way to conceptualize agency in narratological terms is to assume a homology between the linguistic structure of a sentence (subject-predicate [-object]) and the structure of human behaviour (agent-action [-object]). An agent (subject) performs an action which may affect an object. A similar homology exists between the logic of a narrative text and the stories of people's 'real' lives (or rather the ways in which people construct/invent their own lives as stories). Without this structural similarity (which does not suggest complete identity), narrative texts could not be comprehensible.[1] It is this analogy which renders stories plausible. Conversely, the stories an individual creates about her (or his) own life will be shaped in complex ways by the narratives available to and permissible for this particular individual in a given culture.

It is at this juncture that Russ's writing becomes identifiably materialist. The stories of women's agency created in her texts are not politically significant in and of themselves, but rather in how they strive to relate to the material existence of women outside the text. The act of reading connects the flesh and bones of real women to the acts of writing and narrating as well as to the acts performed by characters in the narrative world. Accordingly, Russ's early short stories develop three levels of narrative agency: (1) the agency of the characters in the narrated world; (2) the agency of the narrator; and (3) the agency of the (fictional) author. All of these concerns remain relevant in her later work.

In this delineation, the stories around Russ's sword-and-sorcery heroine Alyx, collected in *The Adventures of Alyx*, occupy a threshold position, presenting as they do a woman who positively asserts her ability to act as an independent individual. The radiantly assertive character Alyx represents a straightforward assault on the male bastion of heroism. By contrast, the stories published before the Alyx sequence concentrated on making women's *lack* of agency tangible. A reading of two short stories, 'My Dear Emily' (1962) and 'Life in a Furniture Store' (1965), will illustrate the ways in which the characters' (lack of) agency interrelates with the narrator's agency and (in the case of 'Life in a Furniture Store') with the agency of the fictional author.[2] These early texts employ comparatively sophisticated narrative techniques to conceal their hidden agenda of empowerment, while *The Adventures of Alyx* makes agency a conspicuously visible structural element of the text.

Designs of Becoming a Destiny: 'Bluestocking'

> ... there is one and only one way to possess that in which we are defective, therefore that which we need, therefore that which we want. Become it. (Russ, *The Female Man* 139)

In the iconoclastic short story 'Bluestocking' ('The Adventuress'[3], 1967), the first story in *The Adventures of Alyx*, Russ introduced the character Alyx, who was to permanently change the possibilities of imagining women in speculative fiction. Alyx, a 'small, gray-eyed woman, ... a neat, level-browed, governessy person' (9), lives in a sword-and-sorcery world whose social structure is a form of pre-capitalist, feudal patriarchy. However, one aspect of this society which clearly sets it off from other male-dominated societies makes her emergence as an exceptional woman plausible: Alyx's world tells an alternative myth of creation, in which the first man was shaped from 'the sixth finger of the left hand of the first woman' (9). In this world, in spite of male supremacy, women do have the advantage of having been created half an hour before men. The first woman was also the first human. She does not give *birth* to the first man—the text avoids the conventional reference to Mother Nature—but, in an ironic reversal of the biblical story, relinquishes an extraneous part of her body.

Alyx is an exceptional woman in the terms of her own society and even more so by the standards of present-day patriarchy: 'Small women exist in plenty—so do those with gray eyes—but this woman was among the wisest of a sex that is surpassingly wise' (9). She is independent, sensuous and as willing to enter violent physical confrontations as she is to enjoy sexual pleasures. According to the myth of her own society, she is as complete as the first woman (human) before the creation of man: 'The lady with whom we concern ourselves in this story had all her six fingers, and what is more, they all worked' (9).

'Bluestocking' ingeniously blends two standard literary motifs, one clearly patriarchal and the other potentially anti-patriarchal. The primary story line borrows from a standard patriarchal pulp template which Delany in his introduction to *Alyx* refers to as '*Beat up villain: get girl*' (xvi)[4] Specifically, this template is the adventurous rescue of a young, virginal woman from an undesirable marriage. The relationship between rescuer and rescued develops and matures in the course of a series of adventures which they face together. In the end, the two fall in love and live happily ever after in a marriage marked desirable by convention. The problem with this plot for the story of Alyx, who takes the position of the rescuer, is obvious: the hero in the original is clearly gendered masculine (the conventional gender of agency) and must be male to be able to supply the mandatory deflowering of the virgin in the end. 'Bluestocking' finds a way out of this impasse by overlaying this patriarchal plot with a version of what Elaine Marks has called 'the Sappho model'.[5] In this model, an emotional and erotic relationship develops between an older woman, who may act as or be a teacher, and an uninitiated young woman. In variations of the story, one of the two is the seductress. The relationship between the two is generally analogous to that of a mother and a daughter (Marks, 274). I will discuss this paradigm, which is one of the central themes in Russ's fiction, in more detail in Parts Two and Three. At this point, it is sufficient to say that although explicit lesbian sexuality remains subdued in 'Bluestocking', an erotic and emotional relationship between Alyx and Edarra, the young escapee, does develop.

What is more, the rescued maiden in this story is from the outset clearly not the passive victim of action, but takes the initiative herself, resisting the position of the demure quasi-daughter and student. Alyx, who makes her living as a pick-lock, is employed by 17-year-old Edarra to help her escape her home, the City of Ourdh, where she is to be married to a rich, considerably older man. Throughout the story, Edarra does not shy away from violent confrontations with her rescuer. When the two have to traverse a sea teeming with monsters, pirates and other deadly dangers to get from Ourdh to the other, unspecified shore that represents safety, Edarra resists Alyx's claim to a position of leadership and complains about the discomforts of travelling on a run-down dirty little boat. The tensions between them, marked with strong erotic overtones, develop into a physical fight:

> With a scream of rage, the Lady Edarra threw herself on her preserver and they bumped heads for a few minutes, but the battle—although violent—was conducted entirely in the dark and they were tangled up almost completely in the beds, which were nothing but blankets laid on the bare boards and not the only reason that the lady's [Edarra's] brown eyes were turning a permanent, baleful black. (16)

At the climax of this quarrel, their relationship receives a symbolic equivalent in a sea monster which threatens their lives and turns out to be a mother itself: 'It held its baby to its breast, a nauseating parody of human-kind' (17). Alyx faces the female monster, who is also a skewed mirror-image of herself, and kills it, Edarra remaining in the background, paralysed with fear. This encounter with the monster as alter-ego of the protagonist indicates that this and the following adventures represent dream-like externalizations of the psychological tensions within and between the two women. To realize her independence as an individual, Alyx escaped domesticity, leaving her own daughter with her husband. When she faces and kills the mother-monster, she also transforms her relationship to Edarra. The rescue operation is revealed as more than simply removing a paying client from physical danger and becomes more explicitly maternal; Alyx now takes responsibility for Edarra's education. She cuts Edarra's long red hair, which is beautiful but a hindrance in a physically active life, and teaches her to fight with two short swords.

The second transformative adventure confronts the two women with three hostile males. Alyx effortlessly kills two, while Edarra follows her teacher's lead by putting a sword in the third. Again, their relationship changes. Edarra now fully accepts Alyx as her elder and teacher, and becomes almost demonstrative:

> Now it was Alyx who did not speak and Edarra who did; she said, 'Good morning,' she said 'Why do fish have scales?' she said, 'I *like* shrimp; they look funny,' and she said (once), 'I like you,' matter-of-factly, as if she had been thinking about the question and had just then settled it. (20, italics in original)

The third and final test of their relationship and their agency comes in the shape of a fire on the boat, in which Alyx is severely wounded. Edarra takes charge of putting the fire out, mends the hole in the boat (which was made to extinguish the flames) and nurses Alyx back to health. Their relationship remains equivalent to that of a mother and a daughter, but is also already beyond this analogy:

> 'Creature,' said Alyx, 'I had a daughter.'
> 'Where is she?' said Edarra.
> Silence.
> 'Praying.' said Alyx at last. 'Damning me.'
> 'I'm sorry,' said Edarra.
> 'But you,' said Alyx, 'are—' and she stopped blankly [*sic*] She said 'You—'
> 'Me what?' said Edarra.
> 'Are here,' ... . (23–25)

Edarra, however, does not want to play the part of Alyx's lost daughter. Resisting the role of Alyx's 'little baby girl', she emphatically and violently demands recognition as a sexually mature adult by using the skills and knowledge acquired in her training with Alyx. When Alyx refuses to amend the omissions in Edarra's sexual education, the young woman exclaims furiously: 'I'll kill you if you don't tell me' (25).

Having transformed the relationship between the two women, at this point the story also changes their interactions with male characters. Alyx discovers an approaching ship with an unspecified number of men, who are now potential sexual partners, and dresses up for the occasion: 'severe, decent, formal black clothes, fit for a business call' (24). Alyx's preparations for the encounter with the males—who are *marked* as unmarried by a sign on the boat, like American women were *marked* unmarried by the title 'Miss' in 1967 when the story came out—are so remarkable because she does not turn herself into a sex-object and remains the agent of the (potential) sexual act. The men are neither greeted as protectors nor potential husbands, but solely as sources of sexual gratification.

The sexual encounter itself is not object of the text, but placed beyond the ending. The two men appear precisely when the emotional involvement and the erotic tension between the two women has increased to a point where a sexual act between *them* would follow if the sapphic model was allowed to run its full course:

> Alyx reached out and began to stroke the girl's disordered hair, braiding it with her fingers, twisting it round her wrist and slipping her hand through it and out again. (25)

An explicitly positive and successful lesbian encounter is still unrepresentable in 1967 science fiction (although there was an increasing presence of lesbianism and lesbian writing in other genres), so the *dea ex machina* supplies two males of appropriate age out of nowhere to stand in for the act.[6] The two men are merely mute players in the performance; the primary relationship remains the one between the women.

In merging two basic plots, rescue story and sapphic model, 'Bluestocking' makes it possible for a female character to successfully appropriate the traditional rescue story template which was coded male. It is crucial for this act of appropriation that Alyx's 'masculinization' does not carry a negative valence. The masculine woman is not a new creation as such, but she traditionally always pays the price of complete de-sexualization. For the heterosexual paradigm requires that those women, who assume characteristics associated with masculinity, have no sensuality and no access to (permissible) pleasurable sexual acts. To the contrary, Alyx's masculinity, as I have demonstrated, rather than depriving her of erotic pleasures, enhances them. The text represents Alyx as knowing who she is and what she wants: 'Alyx had ambitions of becoming a Destiny' (10). However, unlike in Russ's later female protagonists, Alyx's ability to exert the agency that was reserved for males is encoded in her body from birth. Still in possession of the sixth finger, which other women lack because (according to her culture's myth of creation) the first male was created from it, she encompasses and transcends both. Russ's later texts will call into question both the validity of such stories of exceptionality as political strategy and the possibility of becoming a self-knowing subject.

Russ herself attributes a watershed position to the stories around her character Alyx. In an interview, which appeared under the title 'Reflections on Science Fiction' in the feminist quarterly *Quest* in 1975, shortly after the publication of *The Female Man*, Russ declared:

> Long before I became a feminist in any explicit way (my first reaction upon hearing Kate Millet speak in 1968 was that of course every woman *knew* that but if you ever dared to formulate it to yourself, let alone say it out loud, God would kill you with a lightning bolt), I had turned from writing love stories

about women in which women were losers, and adventure stories in which the men were winners, to writing adventure stories about a woman in which the woman won. It was one of
the hardest things I ever did in my life. These are stories about
a sword-and-sorcery heroine called Alyx, and before writing
the first I spent about two weeks in front of my typewriter
shaking and thinking of how I'd be stoned in the streets,
accused of penis envy, and so on (after that it is obligatory to
commit suicide, of course).

It was shifting my center of gravity from Him to Me and I
think it's the most difficult thing an artist can do—a woman
artist, that is. It's OK to write about artist-female with feet in
center of own stage as long as she suffers a lot and is defeated
and is wrong (the last is optional). But to win, and to express
the anger that's in all of us, is a taboo almost as powerful as the
taboo against being indifferent to The Man. (42, italics in
original)

In this passage, Russ graphically describes her development as a
writer from male-centred narratives to female- (or self-)centred ones
as chronologically moving through three distinct phases: (1) stories
in which women are losers by definition (pre-Alyx); (2) stories in
which women win (Alyx); and (3) stories that are explicitly feminist
(e.g. 'When it Changed', *The Female Man*).

While such a chronological categorization based on the development of feminism is useful in a reading of Russ's complex oeuvre, my
readings place more emphasis on the ways in which Russ *participated*
in the formulation of second-wave feminism rather than how her
texts were influenced by it. In particular her early stories show
implicit links to the so-called first wave—the eighteenth and nineteenth century women's movements—while they simultaneously
help to shape radical late twentieth-century feminist thinking. A
reading from this perspective shows that many of Russ's earlier texts
werc not as 'male-centred' as the quote above suggests. What makes
Alyx a breakthrough character in genre fiction, then, is not so much
her victory, but *how* she wins. The following two sections examine
two such earlier short stories, 'My Dear Emily' (1962) and 'Life in a
Furniture Store' (1965), demonstrating that to read them in terms of
'failure' and 'success' alone does not do them full justice.

Oh Dear, One Bite Too Many: Vampire meets Emerson

> Autonomy brings with it fear, guilt and a sense of loss. The creation of a desirous female subject—outside of utopias—necessitates contradictions. (Lefanu, 84)

'My Dear Emily' first appeared in *The Magazine of Fantasy and Science Fiction* in 1962. Reprinted in the collection of short stories *The Zanzibar Cat* (1984), it is among Russ's most interesting early texts. 'My Dear Emily' is a vampire story squarely in the tradition of nineteenth-century gothic fiction, yet it also moves beyond this tradition in significant ways. Even though Russ's texts did not become explicitly feminist before the late 1960s, the story's implicit engagement with nineteenth-century women's fiction forms a connection to feminist literary historiography. The following section will explore an intersection with one of the most important early feminist studies on nineteenth-century women's writing, *The Madwoman in the Attic: The Woman Writer and the Nineteenth-Century Literary Imagination* (1979) by Sandra Gilbert and Susan Gubar. One of the central concerns of their study is the significance of authorship as expression of agency. Positioned in relation with Gilbert and Gubar's expansion on the classic interpretation of *Frankenstein* as a romantic rewriting of Milton's *Paradise Lost*, 'My Dear Emily' emerges as a displaced and unsettling response to Mary Shelley's novel, speculative fiction's mythical ancestor.

This reading suggests that speculative fiction may be regarded as a particularly productive discursive space for an exploration of links and continuities between early and contemporary feminism. For both American feminism and speculative fiction acknowledge crucial impulses from Anglo-American romanticism. 'My Dear Emily' harks back to this period in American cultural and literary history in form and in the narrative world it projects, transforming both the conventions of speculative fiction and the roles female characters can play in it.

The story centres around the young (presumably virginal) woman Emily and her 'bosom friend' Charlotte and their resistance to patriarchal family structures. This resistance is crystallized by the appearance of a fascinating male vampire. Emily and Charlotte share the boarding school in the East, the train compartment on their way home to the West Coast, and the bed in the house of Emily's father. Although the two women are not directly related, Emily acts as Charlotte's elder sister. The choice of names connects the two to the Brontës and underscores the sororal character of their relationship.[7] Emily is to be married to Will, a nondescript bourgeois. However, she is far from being a pale and passive future bride. Her superficial acquiescence in the engagement and in Will's tepid advances is punctuated by aggressive rejections:

> Will, seeing they were alone, attempted to take Emily's hand again.
> 'Leave me alone!' Emily said angrily. He stared.
> 'I said leave me alone!'
> And she gave him such a look of angry pride that, in fact, he did. (121)

The train ride at the beginning of the story, which takes them home across the continent, reveals underlying tensions and hostilities between the two 'sisters' which centre around Emily's engagement. The need to attach oneself to a husband-proprietor undermines and disrupts the two women's friendship. Charlotte expresses her desire for erotic encounters with 'savages' (presumably triggered by her reading of the then popular captivity narratives): '"I should like to be carried off," she proposes, 'but then I don't have an engagement to look forward to. A delicate affair."' (118) At the mention of her impending marriage, Emily turns away from her reading of 'Mr Emerson's poems.' Disconcerted, she accidentally pinches herself with Charlotte's binoculars, which in imitation of her friend she had intended to use for spotting some of the romantically eroticized 'savages':

> 'They hurt me,' she says without expression, and as Charlotte takes the glasses up quickly, Emily looks with curious sad passivity at the blood from her little wound, which has bled an incongruous, passionate drop on Mr. Emerson's cloth-bound poems. To her friend's surprise (and her own, too) she begins to cry, heavily, silently, and totally without reason. (118)

In this passage, which foreshadows Emily's later encounter with the vampire, two aspects of Romanticism which are apparently irreconcilable for women clash: the idea of total self-realization as an individual and the need to seek fulfilment as the complementary yet inferior half of a heterosexual pair. Thus, this early short story identifies a contradiction, which Russ's later characters, beginning with Alyx, will struggle to overcome.

Emily's blood is drawn by her subconscious or half-conscious rejection and fear of marriage and domesticity. It is the philosopher Emerson rather than one of the European writers of literary Romanticism, such as Blake, Wordsworth or Goethe, who is disfigured by the 'incongruous, passionate drop'. This choice is significant. The American Transcendentalist is, after all, the one who in his lectures and poems calls for 'self-reliance', and the development of an unalienated *American* sense of self. This romantic, full humanity may have appeared within reach for Emily in the all-female space of her school, but the train that brings the two young women across the continent also moves them away from the fantasies and unfocused desires created by their readings. Just as Charlotte's fantasized 'savages' never materialize to provide the two desirous women with passionate erotic encounters in the unmarred wilderness, Emerson's image of an unfragmented self remains a false promise. Her fiancé and her father at home smugly expect Emily to return unchanged by her education and to be self-effacing rather than self-reliant.

To the two women, the westward movement across the vast distances of the American continent is not an act of liberation and democratization, but confirms the loss of self-determination and the subjection to domesticity. Androcentric narrative conventions leave only two options open to the female protagonist: death or marriage (Lanser, *Fictions of Authority*, 27). To Emily, marriage means virtual death because it requires her to relinquish the dream of a self-reliant individuality, which her culture poses as prerequisite for an unalienated, fully human life.

Such polarities are repeated on many levels of the text. The tension between the supposedly generic, Transcendentalist ideal of self-possessed humanity and the alienating reality of the narrated world is only one example of the multiple dualities which are the prime motor of the narrative. Much of the force of the story, accordingly, stems from the ironic disjunctions between the various contradictory poles.

The text makes some of these disjunctions apparent by having the narrative voice implicitly reveal what the character's speech attempts to disguise:

> Charlotte (who slept in the same room as her friend) embraced her at bedtime ... and then Emily said to her dear, dear friend (without thinking):
> 'Sweet William.'
> Charlotte laughed.

'It's not a joke!'

'It's so funny.'

'I love Will dearly.' She wondered if God would strike her dead for a hypocrite. Charlotte was looking at her oddly, and smiling. (120)

In disclosing Emily's unspoken thoughts, the narrator here gives away Emily's double-think, and Charlotte's laughter acknowledges her complicity in this disjunction. Yet the ambiguity contained in adding 'sweet' to the name of her fiancé, though ironic, is indeed no joke for Emily. While explicitly commending William's agreeable character, she relates him to a common garden flower, metaphorically depriving him of the masculinity that will give him power over her in marriage.

However, many such ironic pairs of opposites in the story receive their very force from remaining disguised. Although the text makes a pretence of *hiding* the tensions between the two 'sisters', which contain both rivalry and eroticism, the stylized show of affection ('dear, dear friend') makes them even more obvious. Yet each of the women knows her (gender-) role and plays it expertly: 'Then in the hall that led to the pantry Sweet Will had taken her hand and she had dropped her eyes because you were supposed to and that was her style.' (120) While Charlotte and Emily cannot control the explicit content of their speech and actions, they are able to manipulate the subtext, using it as a secret code between themselves. While this strategy points to a lack of agency in the logic of materialist feminism, it shows that the text does not cast its women characters as passive victims under male control.

The narrator, in avoiding explicit comment and evaluation, also remains concealed. Approximating a dramatic performance, the narrative moves in eighteen carefully constructed scenes, set off from each other typographically through spaces. The flow of the narrative action easily groups them in three 'acts' of exactly six scenes each. This reveals another doubleness or ambiguity on the level of representation: suspending the choice between a dramatic performance and a narrative text, the short story implicitly destabilizes the concept of 'true essence' or unalienated self as referent and desired counterpart to the impersonation. The short story is a narrative of a well-structured performance. Emily and Charlotte accept their gender-role much like actresses would take on a role in a theatre play, with the exception that their performance is continuous and dropping the role not an easy option. The original 'self' in this setup cannot be localized.

It is Emily's desire for this shifting, unrepresentable and highly eroticized sense of self which conjures up the vampire, rather than the other way around, although this aspect of the story also remains ambiguous. The reference to Emerson in conjunction with her blood supports such a reading. Although she cannot name her desires, which are as much intellectual as they are sexual, she knows full well what she *doesn't* want: marriage as the proper continuation of her role in the narrative. In the logic of binary thinking, which patriarchal stories forcefully suggest for their female characters, the rejection of the 'proper' role leaves only one option for Emily: the 'improper' role, the role of the 'fallen lady,' which, as I will show below, also relates her to the original woman, Eve.

The obligatory male partner for her role as the bad woman is Martin Guevara, the vampire. She meets him at one of her father's garden-parties:

> 'I can't move,' she says miserably.
> 'Try.' She takes a step towards him. 'See; you can.'
> 'But I wanted to *go away!*' (122, italics in original)

Since she only has two options—becoming a domesticated middle-class wife or being regarded as an evil slut—escaping the one inextricably confines her to the other. Guevara visits her at night and sinks his teeth into her unblemished virginal neck, an event which remains untold and is represented merely through its effects (blood stains), leaving the visualization of the deed to the reader's imagination. Although the act itself is obscured, the story makes no effort to hide the sexual character of the bloodsucking:

> 'You've killed me.'
> 'I've loved.'
> 'Love!'
> 'Say "taken" then, if you insist.'
> 'I do! I do!' she cried bitterly. (128)

Being a traditional vampire, Guevara can by definition only *rape* her as a completely passive victim, but he reminds Emily that it was she who first called him up: 'we like souls that come to us; these visits to the bedrooms of unconscious citizens are rather like frequenting a public brothel' (127). In this analogy to prostitution, Guevara also makes the parallel to heterosexual intercourse apparent.

However, no discourse is ever purely and entirely 'patriarchal', much less the aggregate of texts that makes up the complex system of signification called culture. It is in the spaces where texts and discourses become inconsistent that oppositional writers have been able to place their subversive creations. The vampire in 'My Dear Emily' mocks and parodies the self-contradictory narrative of male sexuality, which demands of *him* full physical control over the woman's body and requires *her* to derive pleasure from submission to these acts of violence. The normative pleasure derived from either control or relinquishing control in the discourse of twentieth-century popular science is solely based on the biology of the participants.

> Emily's eyes are fixed and her throat contracts; he forces her head between her knees... . 'We're a passion!' Smiling triumphantly, he puts his hands on each side of her head, flattening the pretty curls, digging his fingers into the hair, in a grip Emily can no more break than she could a vice ... 'we're desire made pure, desire walking the Earth'... He throws his arms around her, pressing her head to his chest and nearly suffocating her, ruining her elaborate coiffure and crushing the lace at her throat. (126f)

In the vice of Guevara's insurmountable physical superiority, the woman's body represents her absolute inability to act. The moment when Guevara pushes her head between her knees figuratively condenses the degrading reality of Emily's remoteness from 'self-reliance', or agency. It is important to note, however, that such acts of forced submission are not degrading in themselves. They are degrading because they supposedly represent the reality of the woman's existence. Emily's submission, however, displaces this connection to her social position as a woman just as Guevara's maleness loses significance since he does not use his penis to perform the penetration. Indeed, as I showed above, the vampire's existence in the text is controlled by Emily's own desires.

Thus, while it seems that her refusal to submit to domesticity has brought her even further away from her unnameable yet desired self-control, the text inserts another duality at this point of tension. While Emily at first appears to be as completely subjected to the will and whim of Guevara as she would have been to her prospective husband's, Guevara is not a human male. With no biological claim to the role he enacts, he is a dissembler, a con-artist, who, existing as he does outside the capitalist economy, can freely violate codes of bourgeois social interactions. The roles in this imaginary underside of capitalism, this world beyond life and death, are not as fixed as the analogy to heterosexual rape may suggest. Sarah Lefanu observes in a different context:

> The image of the vampire represents transgression, the breaking of social codes, a denial of death. It is interesting that so many women writers are attracted by this image for the vampire is traditionally a male figure, active over his female victims' passivity; a barely concealed symbol of phallic penetration. (Lefanu, 83)

Russ's text transforms the vampire figure by foregrounding the analogy to penetration. Emily is indeed raped, but this violent loss of virginity also ironically bestows power on her. Once penetrated by the phallic teeth, they become available to her as well. She turns into a vampire herself and overcomes her enforced passivity. Sarah Lefanu explains the fascination of women writers with vampirism and its implicit liberating potential: 'It is perhaps that identification with the vampire figure allows a claim to be made for a libertarian sexuality for women, a transgression—no longer the prerogative of men—from the constraints of social order' (83).

The identification with the vampire here is more profound than Lefanu's statement suggests: the woman, in becoming the vampire, gains far more than her sexual freedom; the loss of humanness also relieves her of her eternal lack and disrupts the Judaeo-Christian myth of creation. Here also lies one of the crucial differences to penile penetration: the displaced phallus ceases to be the prerogative of the male. As vampires, men and women become equals, and, more importantly, sexuality is thoroughly detached from reproduction. Unlike in the human male, then, the surface of the vampire's body does not mark a defining difference.

As Emily metamorphoses into a vampire, she is also relieved of her role as a delicately decorous young lady. Her diction changes accordingly: 'I have to stay in the damned bed the whole damned day ...' (129). What is more, she stops putting on a show of self-effacement and begins to act more like Russ's later characters, such as Jael, the fierce assassin from The Female Man (I will further explore the connections between these two characters in my discussion of Jael as a killer of men in Chapter Two). Crowds of people in the red-light district, rather than frightening her, rouse the newly hatched vampire's appetite:

What a field of ripe wheat! One of the barkers hoists her by the waist onto his platform.

    'Do you see this little lady? Do you see this—'

    'Let me go, God damn you!' she cries indignantly.

    'This angry little lady—' pushing her chin with one sun-burned hand to make her face the crowd. 'This—' But here Emily hurts him, slashing his palm with her teeth, quite pleased with herself ... (141f, italics in original)

She has come quite a way from her former self who, sitting in the train-compartment, 'look[ed] up from Mr. Emerson to stare Charlotte out of countenance, properly, morally, and matter-of-course young lady' (118).

Guevara himself represents another duality, positioned as he is in a highly contradictory and supremely ambiguous space. He is first introduced in his vulnerability, his sickness, his suffering—that is, in the light of day. At night, in the darkness, he is powerfully seductive as well as ruthlessly violent. In his relation to Emily, he enacts the role of perfect masculinity, yet his instrument of penetration is not unique to his sex: Emily most definitely does not lack teeth. He impersonates the role of a man and is therefore gendered masculine, but his biological sex is virtually irrelevant for his performance. As Emily becomes more like him, his shaky gender-identity becomes even more unstable.

Vis-à-vis Charlotte, old and new vampire are equals, almost rivals. Even if Guevara claims the prerogative of the 'elder' in Charlotte's dehumanizing 'deflowering', Emily is not excluded from the practice. Magnanimously, he offers her the second bite:

    'She'll be somebody's short work and I think I know whose.'

        Emily turns white again.

    'I'll send her around to you afterwards.' (126)

A few scenes further on in the text, the young vampire initiate does not pale at the thought of biting her friend and metaphorical sister any more than he does:

    [Reclining on the parlour sofa, Emily kneeling beside her:] 'Oh, sweetheart!' says Charlotte, reaching down and putting her arms around her friend.

        'You're well!' shouts Emily, sobbing over Charlotte's hand and thinking perhaps to bite her. But the Reverend's arms lift her up. (132)

Emily, in her changed state as a vampire, has transformed her 'feminine' role—at least partially. This transformation also shifts the role of masculinity in the text. Guevara not only impersonates a human male, he impersonates the romantic *ideal* of a male hero—violently sensual and irresistibly seductive. He plays the role of Milton's Satan in his romantic interpretation. However, even this impersonation is highly ambiguous: it is the woman, yearning for intellectual and sexual self-determination, who causes his appearance. Emily, like Milton's Eve, desires the forbidden fruit of knowledge and full humanity, but she does not end up as Adam's wife. She rejects Will as Adam and turns to Charlotte instead.

Intersecting 'My Dear Emily' with the classic feminist interpretation of Mary Shelley's *Frankenstein* in *The Madwoman in the Attic*, which was published almost twenty years after Russ's short story, highlights the political significance of such intertextualities for feminism. Gilbert and Gubar relate both Victor Frankenstein and his monster not only to Satan, but also to Adam and even to Eve: 'though Victor Frankenstein enacts the roles of Adam and Satan like a child trying on costumes, his single most self-defining act [the creation of the monster] transforms him definitely into Eve' (232). Gilbert and Gubar use metaphors of role-playing and play-acting to represent the relation of the characters in *Frankenstein* to the ones in Milton's *Paradise Lost*. Russ's short story, as I have shown, takes similar recourse to the theatrical on a structural level. Both *The Madwoman in the Attic* and 'My Dear Emily' use the concept of performance to detach the acts of their characters from their sexed bodies. Because 'he' is not fully human, the vampire in 'My Dear Emily', like Shelley's monster, can transgress traditional notions of gender. Both the monster in Gilbert and Gubar's interpretations and Guevara have the acting inscribed in their very being, since neither of the two has a legitimate claim to a biological essence as its imagined foundation.

The allusion to Frankenstein's monster in 'My Dear Emily' is more direct than the one to the romantic Satan-hero. The text introduces Guevara as he is waking up in the twilight, painfully, slowly, just as Frankenstein's monster wakes from 'his' pre-life state. Guevara's physical ugliness in the light of day is a further indication of his similarity to the monster. Yet Guevara is also closer to the attractive aspects of Satan than the monster can be. The vampire's brutal seductiveness, the emphasis on his evil yet attractive desires, and his ambiguous relation to Emily-Eve clearly link him to the glamorous Prince of Darkness. Thus, in the subtext, Guevara and Emily re-enact the myth of creation as interpreted in *Paradise Lost* filtered through the romantic imagination. Their existence is a life in death or beyond life and death. Neither paradise nor hell applies to them; Emily-Eve is not subjected to child-birth and does not have to defer to Adam, who remains in his self-defined capitalist utopia—the paradise of modern patriarchy.

The displaced myth in 'My Dear Emily' contains the possibility of change, even if it does not provide the protagonist with what she desires. Disrupting the patriarchal threesome Adam–Eve–Satan and its relation to the all-powerful Creator and Author of all things, the story supplies an alternative way out of 'the Garden of Eden'. Emily does not hope for the lost paradise before the fall. The fundamental structure of duality in the short story is her double-bind: she is left with a choice between two at first equally degrading alternatives. She can either marry Will or be raped by Guevara (who is on one level just Will's exact opposite). However, the multiple dualities and ambigui-ties in the narrative give her the option to stay un-dead, if not alive, with Charlotte. Neither woman attains agency within their society, but they both escape the dilemma of their lives in Victorian patriarchy. One is reminded of the classic quote from 'The Women Men Don't See' by James Tiptree, Jr. (Alice Sheldon): *'We survive in ones and twos in the chinks of your world-machine'* (334, italics in original). Charlotte and Emily occupy such a chink in the world-machine: a common coffin becomes their place of refuge.

Just as Mary Shelley's male protagonists can be read as 'imperson-ators', Russ in this early story uses a vampire to make gender-assign-ments unstable and to place a woman in the centre of the stage. In 'My Dear Emily', the rescue-figure is an ambiguous male imperson-ator and a rapist, an evil yet fascinating Byronic hero. He is at the same time all-powerful and extremely vulnerable. From this perspec-tive, Alyx in 'Bluestocking' also emerges as an impersonator, since she enacts the masculine role narrative convention had reserved for a male. Yet Alyx, though exceptional, is not an alien in her world. She exists within the socio-economic and symbolic system of her world and represents a fundamentally different kind of gender discontinu-ity. Guevara, in his suggested androgyny, *dis*places the male, while Alyx, whom the narrative constructs as human and female with a vengeance, kicks him out. This open confrontation marks the advent of another phase in feminism, in which women characters in fiction as well as in feminist theory and cultural criticism demand and claim agency instead of merely pointing to the lack of it.

What is significant in terms of agency about these various intertextualities between Milton, Blake and Shelley as manifested in Russ
and Gilbert/Gubar is their underlying concern with the authority of
women's narrative voice. Women writers, particularly before feminism became a significant cultural force, frequently tried to legitimize
their authorship by using male or ungendered (by default also male)
narrators and protagonists and/or by choosing male pseudonyms. On
the basis of my analysis above I would argue that 'My Dear Emily' can
be interpreted, in a similar way to *Frankenstein*, as a renegotiation of
men's original claim to sole authorship via their direct likeness to the
supreme Author. Russ's short story participates in the discourse that
is represented here through *The Madwoman in the Attic*, but 'My Dear
Emily' also anticipates a critique of basic political categories in this
discourse: 'woman' as a category is not simply a given and most definitely not constrained to victimhood.

The reference to Milton and *Frankenstein* points to another important concern in Russ's writing: authorship as agency. In the 1970s and
1980s, Russ's criticism contributed to the debate on women and
authorship. As Gilbert and Gubar show in their classic study, many of
nineteenth- and twentieth-century women writers exorcized or tried
to exorcize their 'anxieties of authorship' by creating revisionary cri-
tiques of Milton's *Paradise Lost*:

> The story that Milton ... most notably tells to women is of
> course the story of woman's secondness, her otherness, and
> how that otherness leads inexorably to her demonic anger, her
> sin, her fall, and her exclusion from that garden of the gods
> which is also, for her, the garden of poetry. Milton is for women
> what Harold Bloom (who might be paraphrasing Woolf) calls
> 'the great Inhibitor, the Sphinx who strangles even strong
> imaginations in their cradles.' (191)

These intertextual aspects of 'My Dear Emily' connect the story to
Russ's poignant criticism as voiced, for example, in *How to Suppress
Women's Writing* and such essays as 'Why Women Can't Write'. In
these critical texts, Russ examines the stumbling-blocks still in the
way of women who write in critical terms.

What Russ's criticism and fiction most conspicuously evoke as the
real inhibitor of female authorship is not Milton, however, but the
great Creator himself, God as reinforced and repeated by texts such as
Paradise Lost. Russ herself uses the image of God to represent the
many overdetermined forces that suppress women's liberatory imag-

ination. In the interview in *Quest* from which I quoted above, Russ humorously draws from an anthropomorphized image of God who would strike down dead any woman with the gall to express the 'truth' about women's oppression (42). God in this passage serves as the instrument of women's internalized silencing.

In this interview and elsewhere, Russ evokes the image of God to account for the complex processes which create the feelings of anxiety experienced by her as a female author. Gilbert and Gubar give voice to these anxieties, relating women's precarious position within 'patriarchal poetry' to the ways in which this literature insists on the God-like authority of the writer:

> ... literary women, readers and writers alike, have long been 'confused' and intimidated by the patriarchal etiology that defines a solitary Father God as the only creator of all things, fearing that such a cosmic Author might be the sole legitimate model for all earthly authors. (188, cf. also 7)

One of Russ's key themes in her fictional and critical work is women's struggle to rewrite this narrative of authorship. The prototypical writer of patriarchal ideology, according to this feminist critique, is the perfect image of God. His pen is a metaphorical penis whose ink continually inseminates the always virginal page. However, the women's movement since the 1970s, to which both Russ and Gilbert and Gubar have contributed, together with postmodernism's disrespect for the *autho*rity of the writer, has disrupted or troubled the image of the penile pen. Women authors have reshaped the accepted literary canon, just as female characters in fiction have displaced male authority and authorship and unhinged the essence of their own identity as women.

These metaphors of authorship, with which writers of both sexes in the European and Anglo-American tradition have continually re-created men's sole claim to the legitimate production of texts, hark back to the Judaeo-Christian myth of creation. This connection again emphasizes how central the myth of creation is to feminist analyses of authorship and agency in Western thinking. Adam (in his romantic interpretation) was created in the image of God, but he depends on Eve for procreation. The metaphor of authorship makes the male a perfect image of a God who fathers the universe without dependence on a womb. However, the analogy, powerful as it may be, is also strikingly vulnerable to radical feminist critique.

Concern with these issues is one of the themes which Russ continues to develop in her writing. Her short story 'Life in a Furniture Store' (1965) for the first time introduces a fictional author as a character in the narrative to explore the psychological ramifications of women's limited access to agency, authorship and narrative authority. Whereas 'Bluestocking' and 'My Dear Emily' focus on the agency of the female protagonist, 'Life in a Furniture Store' is primarily concerned with the agency of the female author. Since Russ has continually tackled the question of women's authorship from a critical perspective, I will also examine the ways in which the short story intersects with Russ's own critical work.

In, in, in, to where the worm lies in the middle ... : down the rabbit's hole with the author

When I became aware [in college] of my 'wrong' experience, I chose fantasy. Convinced that I had no real experience of life, since my own obviously wasn't part of Great Literature, I decided consciously that I'd write of things nobody knew anything about, dammit. So I wrote realism disguised as fantasy, that is, science fiction. (*How to Suppress Women's Writing*, 127)

'Life in a Furniture Store' first came out in *Epoch* in 1965; the story was later included in Russ's most recent collection of short stories and other short fiction, *The Hidden Side of the Moon* (1987). Like *The Zanzibar Cat*, *The Hidden Side of the Moon* contains a variety of quite different texts, ranging from Russ's first published short story 'Nor Custom Stale' (1959) to the hilarious satirical piece 'The Clichés from Outer Space' (1984). However, while the earlier collection brings together stories that are closely affiliated with genre writing (science fiction and/or fantasy), *The Hidden Side of the Moon* also includes texts that are more experimental in terms of transgressing genre boundaries, such as 'The View from this Window' (1970) or 'The Little Dirty Girl' (1982). Although 'Life in a Furniture Store' clearly employs science fictional elements and can also be read as a 'ghost story' (as I will argue below), the text discards most conventional narrative paraphernalia of genre writing. There is hardly any recognizable plot and the space that is being explored is entirely within one woman's mind.

'Life in a Furniture Store', in marked contrast to 'My Dear Emily' and the Alyx stories, appears to give up most causal and chronological relationships, relying on a few marginal narrative elements. The events that the narrator does relate are grouped with images, fragmented, dream-like recollections from childhood, revolving around the vague notion of a centre, which is not named. In the first paragraph, the narrator gives a 'summary' of the plot, eliding, however, the most significant events that precede her retreat to a furniture store:

> I didn't always use to live alone; I once worked for a scientific institute that made bevels or bezels (I forget which) and published a magazine, but shortly after that there was a small incident that led to my being fired, and then I got married, and then I got divorced, and eventually I went to live in a furniture store. (162)

The small modifier 'eventually' contains and conceals the main part of the plot, her visit at her friend Laura's place and her moving into the furniture store.

Furthermore, the text repeatedly disrupts the plot that it conjured up in the first paragraph. Oscillating between maintaining a causally linked narrative sequence and destroying the very idea of coherent sequence, the narrator establishes a fundamental indeterminacy which also involves herself as a character. In this text, the narrator, whom conventional genre fiction presents as possessing perfect memory, nonchalantly lapses into guessing where she lacks certainty: 'I once worked for a scientific institute that made bevels or bezels (I forget which)' (162); 'I believe she is dead now' (166); 'We went into the kitchen and sat under the European colanders, or casseroles, I forget which' (168). This added uncertainty heightens the sense that this teller refuses to hold on to complete control of the tale. Loss of control therefore becomes an essential ingredient of the text.

This feeling of uncertainty is the only factor that gives some semblance of coherence to the narrator's representation of her inner space: 'Every step is a step away from order' (172). Shut out from ordinary life, she finds herself in 'Limbo' (164), neither fully dead, nor truly alive: 'Life buried, making patterns' (164). The distinction between life and death itself slips away from her. When she loses her job, she cynically opts out of society: 'I was out of a job. And everybody knows what that means; that means my life is over' (163). Unable to cope with everyday interactions with others, the narrator seeks refuge in this inner coherence that marks her as psychotic. She completely withdraws to her own apartment and erratic memories of pre-adult life, memories which are saturated with her childhood reading experiences, particularly *Alice in Wonderland* and *Through the Looking Glass:*

> Beyond the curtains, out in the dark, theatrical night, prevented from entering by the glass that gleamed or the thin gauze of the screen that made all the street lights into crosses, out there where I forever read my first book, I saw myself shutting the door after my sweet sixteen birthday party. (171)

The protagonist-narrator retreats into her childhood memories, to her life before initiation to sexuality. After her 'sweet sixteen' birthday party, parting from ten happy couples, she is alone with a silent butler, which comes to represent her exclusion from 'happy' heterosexual coupledom.

The text uses the acts of writing and reading on several levels to restore the narrator's integrity. She copes with her exclusion from society by 'forever read[ing her] first book' (171), in which the protagonist, Alice, escapes into a dream-world, removed from reality and causal logic. 'Life in a Furniture Store' makes this reference to Alice explicit when the protagonist enters the house of her friend Laura: 'I knocked the knocker on the little red door (like Alice's)' (166). Like Alice, the narrator speaks to herself, and as she does so, relates her constant movement inward: 'In, in, in, to where the worm lies in the middle' (163). Like Alice, who falls down the rabbit's hole towards the centre of the earth (towards her own dream-world), the narrator draws away from 'reality', seeking her inner self. But, again like Alice, she never reaches this imagined 'centre'. The only action that remains and connects the narrator with the world outside herself is the production of the text, which is only completed in the act of reading.

Moreover, 'Life in a Furniture Store' offers a number of indications that the (nameless) narrator-protagonist is also a writer and may be the fictional author of the short story. Seemingly out of touch with the primary story line, she scrupulously lists the contents of her purse at the moment of speaking (writing?), putting particular emphasis on paper and pencil (166). She sees paper as the condensed image of her existence:

> I wore paper flowers. I paraded. Like the soiled slippers that ballet dancers wear bound around their hearts, a sort of Yellow Star, so I wore my distinction—but *I* danced! I paraded! I stood with my arms *so*, and stamped, and looked terrors. I had only to think a thing and it was done. (163–64, italics in original)

This passage may appear like the deluded ravings of a person on the brink of madness. Yet in the context of textual clues which point to the narrator's authorship, it captures the creative act of imagining events, like in dreaming or writing. The narrator makes a point of telling that she wears paper like a ballet dancer wears her shoes, as signs of her ability and her pain (from bleeding feet). She wears paper like Jews had to wear the yellow star in Nazi Germany, as a sign which condensed their existence and marked them for death. A few lines further down the narrator makes another reference to the pain of imagining, addressing the reader directly: 'Yet you enjoy my agony' (164, italics in original). The text here emphasizes the painful aspects of writing rather than its liberatory potential. The pain of writing is represented as prerequisite for the enjoyment of reading, like the bleeding feet of ballet dancers are inextricably connected with the rigor of her art and the enjoyment the audience feels from watching a well-rehearsed performance. The ballet dancer interprets music and choreography with her body, bearing the inevitable pain.

This intense engagement with authoring and active reading distinguishes Russ's work from most conventional science fiction. Russ does not write for quick consumption. Subtle hints will disclose whole new layers of (albeit shifting) meaning. Critics have emphasized the significance of the act of reading in Russ's work. Sarah Lefanu in her chapter on Russ underscores the primacy of the (female) reader in Russ's texts: 'Russ is passionately concerned about her readers; in all her work they feature variously as voyeur, eavesdropper, willing or unwilling confidante' (177). While I do not argue with this assessment, I would suggest that the act of *authoring* is as important as a concern of Russ's work as a writer. In her fiction, the two acts, reading and writing, correlate in significant ways. Thus, the agency of the author in Russ's text always also depends on the reader for validation. I will come back to this issue in Part Three in my discussion of Russ's novel *We Who Are About To* ... (1978), in which authoring becomes the sole connection of the dying narrator to life and human history in even more pronounced ways than in 'Life in a Furniture Store'.

This (unstable) conflation of fictional author and narrator in 'Life in a Furniture Store' breaks apart towards the end of the story, when the narrator-author metamorphoses into a ghost and leaves the realm of realism:

> The spirit that rides the blast caught me as I walked past a

shop-face brilliant as a cave; with a whirl of last year's leaves
and refuse it blew me around the corner and into a brick wall,
hurrying the clouds between the narrow brick defile: black
night-clouds, purple clouds suffused with rain, slate-colored
clouds blowing dully at the edge, all streaming down the sky.
(172–73)

As a ghost, the narrator comes to haunt the furniture store, continuing her perpetual inward movement. In the empty furniture store at
night, as completely isolated from human society as the narrator of *We
Who Are About To*, her only remaining action is remembering.

The same types of women writers who populate Russ's fictional
texts also concern her critical work. Using the image of the female
author, she exposes the strategies with which dominant discourses
have silenced women's writing and denied or spoiled their agency as
writers. Russ demands of women who write to fight the limitations
imposed upon their texts and on the female characters they create
and to find a language to express that which cannot be expressed in
the terms of patriarchal stories:

> ... middle-class women, although taught to value established
> forms, are in the same position as the working class: neither
> can use established forms to express what the forms were
> never intended to express (and may very well operate to con-
> ceal). (*How to Suppress Women's Writing*, 125)

Thus, according to Russ, the material conditions of the writer's life
require her to consciously use the established forms to represent
what within their dominant logic must be unrepresentable. It is precisely these interrelations and tensions between the material life of
the fictional author and her text that motivate the stories of authorship in Russ's oeuvre.

'Life in a Furniture Store', although it may appear like a story of failure for the female protagonist, affirms her narrative authority, thus
anticipating Russ's later work regarding women's authorship.
Whereas in 'Bluestocking' and even more strikingly in 'My Dear
Emily' the narrator functions merely as a hidden mediator of the narrative, 'Life in a Furniture Store' moves the narrator to the front as
sole protagonist. The telling itself emerges as the subject of the tale.
The short story manipulates the 'established forms' in a way that
seems closed to a critical text, but Russ's criticism defies these
boundaries. *How to Suppress Women's Writing* (1983), for example,

deliberately uses the persona of the author, the speaking subject who produces the text, to comment on the act of writing and to subvert the god-like presence of the author in traditional, 'objective' criticism:

> Minority art, vernacular art, is marginal art. Only on the margins does growth occur. [Which is] why I, who am a science-fiction writer and not a scholar, must wrestle in my not-very-abundant spare time with this ungainly monster. Because you, you critics, have not already done so (preferably a century ago). If you don't like my book, write your own. Please! (129–30)
> 'I've been trying to finish this monster for thirteen ms. pages and it won't. Clearly it's not finished. You finish it. (132)

Meta-textual comments by a fictional author such as these are characteristic of Russ's later work. For example, Joanna, one of the protagonists in Russ's novel *The Female Man* (1975) is such a fictional author. She flippantly addresses the reader and sends her text off to the world in the closing section: 'Live merrily, little daughter-book, even if I can't and we can't; recite yourself to all who listen; stay hopeful and wise' (213).

Such destabilizations of the author's authority in Russ's writing also affect the act of narration. Starting with 'Life in a Furniture Store' and the fairy-tale/horror story 'Come Closer', both first published in 1965, Russ's texts display an increasing uneasiness with narrative omniscience. Her writing moves from traditional 'third-person' narrative—the 'public' form of genre fiction—to more 'private' forms which borrow from autobiography, diary and letter. This move from 'public' to 'private' discourses is also accompanied by a 'sexing' of the narrative voice, a development which I will discuss in more detail in Part Two. Even in such texts as 'Bluestocking', in which the narrator is not a protagonist of her tale, she makes her (human rather than divine) metafictional presence felt:

> ... the girl [Edarra] swept up to the deck with her plate and glass. It isn't easy climbing a rope ladder with a glass (balanced on a plate) in one hand, but she did it without thinking, *which shows how accustomed she had become to the ship and how far this tale has advanced.* (21, my emphasis)

Russ's later, explicitly feminist texts further explore the ways in which the presence of a fictional author may be deployed for purposes of disruption as well as for establishing agency. *The Female Man*

(1975), Russ's most widely read novel, is a prime example for these experiments. Joanna as fictional author, like the narrator in 'Life in a Furniture Store', is also present in the fictional world as a ghost. She points out, 'don't think I know any of this by hearsay; I'm the spirit of the author and I know all things' (166), ironically disrupting literary conventions of narrative omniscience, particularly those of science fiction or genre fiction. Similarly, the narrator in the novel *The Two of Them* (1978) suddenly appears as fictional author: 'She didn't take him. She didn't do it. I made that part up' (175). The insistence on agency by these fictional authors is always ironical and disrupting, but simultaneously also deadly serious.

'Life in a Furniture Store' is significant for a feminist reading of Russ's work in yet another respect. In addition to its introduction of the female fictional author, this early short story also employs textual strategies which Russ later formulated as crucial ingredients of feminist writing. While the two fantasy pieces 'Bluestocking' and 'My Dear Emily' emphasize creating new plot patterns for female characters, this short story experiments with *disintegrating* plot and the act of narration. Russ's critical work, which she began publishing in the early 1970s, has a similar double agenda. Like her fiction, her criticism sets out by exploring women's agency on the level of plot ('images of women') and authorship. Her examination of the literary tradition, however, also leads her to a prescriptive political aesthetics, in which she calls for the creation of new, feminist modes of writing, integrating questions of plot development, representation and style.

Two of Russ's early essays appeared in Susan Koppelman's pioneering anthology of feminist criticism *Images of Women in Fiction: Feminist Perspectives* (1972), as 'What Can a Heroine Do? or Why Women Can't Write' and 'Images of Women in Science Fiction'. Both of these texts interrogate the existing literary tradition as to which images of women it makes available and what these women can *do* other than fall in love or go mad. These traditional plot-patterns, as Russ asserts in 'What Can a Heroine Do?',[8] 'are dramatic embodiments of what a culture believes to be true—or what it would like to be true—or what it is mortally afraid may be true' (81). Furthermore, Russ vividly demonstrates that simple role reversal will not do the trick: 'Reversing sexual roles in fiction may make good burlesque or good fantasy, but it is ludicrous in terms of serious literature. Culture is male. Our literary myths are for heroes, not heroines' (83).

Another contradiction, however, which Russ does not make explicit, emerges from her proposed solution to the dilemma of the self-consciously feminist writer. The conflict is between the desire to drop literary conventions altogether (which are, as she maintains with John Barth, exhausted anyway), and the utter impossibility of fully escaping the 'male myths' shaped by these conventions. What women experience as their lives is already co-opted and contained by the web of patriarchal stories available to them. Russ points out that 'we interpret our own experience in terms of [these myths]. Worse still, we actually perceive what happens to us in the mythic terms our culture provides' (90). On the other hand, she rightly maintains that while for a writer like, say, Hemingway (to take one of Russ's own favourite examples) working with existing traditions is a relatively simple and advantageous route, to a woman writer this route is not easily accessible—nor is it desirable, for that matter.

Identifying two ways out of the cul-de-sac of patriarchal narratives, Russ appears to end up in another. She says: 'There seem to me to be two alternatives open to the woman author who no longer cares about How She Fell in Love or How She went Mad. These are (1) lyricism, and (2) life' ('Why Women Can't Write', 87). This recipe leaves crucial questions unanswered. How can women shape new myths from their own experience, if what they perceive as 'their own' life is already determined by patriarchal myths? And, more importantly, how is 'lyricism' which 'exists without chronology or causation' (87) distinguishable from the patriarchal definitions of the 'woman's sphere' and of 'women's shapeless literature'?

Here the enabling, oppositional practices seem to prove as limiting as the established plot-patterns. If the web of patriarchal narratives were indeed perfect and all-encompassing, there would be no escape from this double-bind. As some of her own fictional texts such as 'Life in a Furniture Store' or 'Bluestocking' prove, however, these limiting narratives contain interstices and inconsistencies which writers from the 'margins' may use to displace the stories that exclude them. Russ's essay, even if it does not explicitly explore the possibility, works from the assumption that these interstices exist and that the impasse is therefore not definitive.

Russ's fictional practice shows that her writing strategies success-fully disrupt narrative conventions by deploying several, even contra-dictory, strategies at the same time. Read along with 'What Can a Heroine Do?', the short story 'Life in a Furniture Store' would seem to emerge clearly as an example of writing in Russ's lyric mode. Yet I would argue that it is precisely the narrative aspects of the story which make its 'lyricism' function as a destabilizing factor. The first paragraph determines a seemingly clear, linear chronology for the events that the text relates. Narrative convention works with the logic that a given event is causally related to the event that precedes it. So, for example, when the narrator says 'I was fired the next day', one is led to assume that the events preceding this statement are the cause of her being fired. This assumption is encouraged by the first 'summary' paragraph: 'shortly after there was a small incident that led to my being fired' (162). However, her narrative does not provide events that would justify firing an otherwise reliable employee. She has a fit of hysterical laughter when her (spineless) boss breaks his back after slipping on some paint on the office floor. She also comments on the fact that he will not be able to bear the shameful knowledge that she saw him fall. She asks him whether he is all right, although it is obvious that he is almost dying. All of these are perfectly predictable reactions in a state of confusion when one is confronted with the sudden presence of near death. Any or none of these responses could have led to her being fired. The text thus invokes narrative logic, just to make it slip. One central question emerging from the narrator's story, for example, remains unanswered: where did the paint come from which led to the accident in the first place?

By identifying these inconsistencies, the paradoxical work of trying to utilize the interstices of patriarchy receives clearer outlines. If 'Life in a Furniture Store' indeed introduces, as I think it does, the feminist textual strategies Russ makes explicit in 'What Can a Heroine Do?', then her categories 'life' and 'lyricism' do not work as alternatives but as simultaneous, interdependent practices. In the terms of my reading here, they may be referred to as plot creation and its simultaneous disruption.

Other aspects of Russ's textual practice function according to similar oppositional patterns. The fictional authors Russ's short stories and novels create do not simply replace the image of the masculine all-powerful author-creator with the great goddess in a dubious manoeuver of reversal. These authors, existing as they do in spaces of supreme instability and disjunction, do not and cannot emerge as producers of grand counter-narratives. Rather they are mischievous destabilizers, who disrupt the narrative thrust at the same time as they construct it. These disruptions, however, are not just metafictional games and intellectual mind-teasers, but emphatically *political* strategies in the development of a feminist literary tradition.

Although 'My Dear Emily' comes years before Russ's transition to explicit feminism, the short story rewrites Mary Shelley's *Frankenstein* in ways that are politically relevant for feminism. I selected this short story for discussion in this chapter because it partially conflates the agency of the protagonist with that of the fictional author. As in many of Russ's later stories, the text inscribes in the act of narration the 'anxieties of authorship' inextricably connected with marginalized authors. For women, this troublesome relationship to writing is strongly invested with romantic notions of authorship, which reconfigured the woman as the muse of the male narrator (Lanser, *Fictions of Authority*, 34). Even when the narrator is female, she is routinely associated as constructed by a male author.[9] The narrating voice in 'My Dear Emily', remaining as it does outside the text and therefore ungendered, risks becoming, by default, the voice of a man who constructs his female subject. 'Life in a Furniture Store', on the other hand, in transforming the character into a writer, disrupts this pervasive image of authorship. In making the women writers' anxieties an object of the story, such texts are able to (at least partially) transform the limiting discourses which produce the anxieties into enabling ones. Thus, rather than reading the various women writers who frequently appear in Russ's fiction as autobiographical representations of herself, I read them as crucial elements in a narrative strategy with which the texts (among other things) tackle the privilege of the phallic pen.

Giving the fictional author a strong woman's voice is one of the most pervasive strategies employed by Russ's texts in order to claim the power of creating oppositional images and stories. The next chapter discusses another such strategy, which works on the level of the characters in the narrated world. In the character typologies of science fiction, non-submissive women await a fate of death and/or defeat; the female monster, killed by Alyx, may be seen as remnant and ironical reference to this mechanism. Perhaps in response to these narratives, the killing of a male becomes central to most of the stories of agency that Russ creates.

CHAPTER TWO
Acts of Violence:
Representations of Androcide

Anything pursued to its logical end is revelation—*The Female Man* (191)

Materialist feminism operates with the assumption that sex constitutes the most basic social class distinction. The utopian goal, then, is to eradicate sex as a socially relevant category by way of a feminist revolution. Beginning with the stories around Alyx, Russ's fiction develops androcide as the focused representation of a revolutionary war. Taking the life of a member of the sex that has denied women the capacity to act opens new ground for female characters in the existing archive of comprehensible and permissible story lines.

I will, therefore, examine androcide in terms of its narrative function within the texts, shunning too ready conflation between the 'real' lives of women and the stories of characters in fiction. Thus, while I acknowledge the analogy between the stories people live and fictional narratives, I also want to point to this analogy's limitations. Presupposing structural similarities between the stories of female fictional characters and the stories cultures tell about women's lives does not suggest their complete identity. In my reading of Russ's fiction, androcide is therefore not the celebration of violence, not advocacy of mass murder, but a *narrative* device, which (partially) endows female characters with the ability to act independently. In Russ's texts, androcide as a narrative device represents women's claim to agency, destroying as it does established gender-specific narratives in the handed-down set of basic story lines available to (genre) fiction writers. Women, who are conventionally supposed to *give* life, especially to male offspring, transcend this demand of patriarchy by taking the life of a grown man. Women, who are conventionally expected to help the male hero, become the heroes of their own stories, destroying precisely those characters in the story which would bar their access to heroism.

In the course of her career as a writer, particularly in the phase that

I labelled 'explicitly feminist', Russ has continuously transformed and developed androcide as a means to give female characters power and credibility. I will discuss a number of such killings from various points in Russ's development. The sword-and-sorcery character Alyx, in the stories collected in *The Adventures of Alyx*, is a single, outstanding woman whose ability to control her actions marks her exceptionality. In *Picnic on Paradise* (1968), Russ's first novel which is also included in the collection, for example, Alyx kills an individual man as an immediate reaction to an offence committed by him. She has no explicit consciousness of the necessity to fight for women as a group. In contrast, Jael from *The Female Man* (1975) kills the man not primarily as an individual, but as a member of the sex class she hates. Finally, Irene, protagonist from *The Two of Them* (1978), acts on the basis of a more complex concept of oppression. She kills the man she loves.

The Adventures of Alyx: Take the Sword and Win

As the discussion of 'Bluestocking' (1967) above suggested, Alyx is an individual woman, whose exceptional strength and independence within a patriarchal culture rest on her special relation to an altered myth of creation. A collection of the short stories around Alyx (excluding only one) was first published under the title *Alyx* in 1976. In 1983, the collection was republished under the title *The Adventures of Alyx*. The one story excluded in both of these editions, 'A Game of Vlet' (1974), later found a space in *The Zanzibar Cat* (1983). Russ remarks in her introductory note to the story: '["A Game of Vlet" is] the last story I ever wrote about my character Alyx, the last, the last, the last, I'm sorry, readers who want more of her, but there just ain't no more' (256). Russ's comment on 'A Game of Vlet' demonstrates that the character Alyx clearly belongs to an earlier stage in feminism. What was revolutionary and breathtakingly new in 1967 seems out of place in the environment of the feminism of the mid-1970s, which had already fully articulated the need to appropriate agency through revolutionary acts.

The short story 'I Gave her Sack and Sherry' (1967)[1] shows a version of Alyx at seventeen when she was still living with her first husband, who treats her as a slave. Once she decides to leave him, the first thing she does is cut her long black hair, in a gesture of liberation reminiscent of the cutting of Edarra's hair in 'Bluestocking.' When he attempts to keep her from leaving, she kills him:

> Her hands dropped with a tumbled rush of hair, she moved slowly to one side, and when he took out from behind the door the length of braided hide he used to herd cattle, when he swung it high in the air and down in a snapping arc to where she—not where she was; where she had been—this extraordinary young woman had leapt half the distance between them and wrested the stock of the whip from him a foot from his hand. He was off balance and fell; with a vicious grimace she brought the stock down short and hard on the top of his head. She had all her wits about her as she stood over him. (33)

As in the killing of the men in 'Bluestocking', the death of her husband is represented as a reaction to a direct assault on her rather than as a symbolic act that would fundamentally change her life. The act of killing for Alyx simply confirms the independence she already has, making this independence an explicit part of her character. Having made her escape, Alyx joins a group of smugglers, presumably the same men who had visited her husband just before she left him. Prevailing over a physically stronger man reinforces her self-confidence, which allows her to confront all males, even the wild crew on the ship: 'they reminded her uncannily of her husband, of whom she was no longer afraid' (35). She is always ready to fight. If she can kill one, she can face them all.

Young Alyx uses Blackbeard, the ship's captain, as a sparring partner and learns to fight with swords. He, surprisingly gentle and emotional for the type of character he represents, gives her a nightgown, which she at first refuses: 'Tcha! It's a bargain, isn't it!' (37) Since she 'lost' her first man, the plot needs to find another for the heterosexual romance required of a story in which a woman is the protagonist. The story quite deliberately frustrates these expectations, at least partially. She gets her man, but on her own terms instead of on his:

> 'Woman, what man have you ever been with before?'
>   'Oh!' said she startled, 'my husband,' and backed off a little.
>   'And where is he?'
>   'Dead.' She could not help a grin.
>   'How?' She held up a fist. Blackbeard sighed heavily. (37–38)

Slowly, she begins to notice—and enjoy—Blackbeard's body. However, as soon as he tries to constrain her freedom to move, she is ready to take off again, leaving no doubt that she would not hesitate to kill him as well if he tried to stop her. As soon as he is sure enough of being in possession of 'his girl' to say, 'Look, I am going into town tonight, but you can't come' (39), he has already lost her. She moves on to Ourdh, where she will become the famous pick-lock and 'kill-quick for hire' of 'Bluestocking' and 'The Barbarian' (1968). These stories represent a female character who already *has* agency, as something she magically possesses as part of her being. This 'extraordinary' woman kills only to maintain her independence, not to create it. Although the killing marks a major transition in the plot, it is not the cause of this transition.

Alyx's singularity makes her story a speculative model rather than a fundamental reformulation of how 'real' women can narrate their lives. The text's detached narrative voice parallels this isolation of women as individuals, which Russ's later texts make a pronounced effort to overcome. Keeping the narrator outside the text as an anonymous speaking subject, the story risks erasing both the female author and (potentially) female readers as well. A 'male' voice insinuates itself, even if ironically, into the voice of the, ostensibly un-sexed, narrator who hides outside the tale. Representing the point of view of the husband who is being left by his wife, the narrator says: 'They insist, these women, on crying, on making demands, and on disagreeing about everything. They fight from one side of the room to the other' (32–33). Because this mode of narration conceals its origin, the speaking subject receives a male body by default, even if the author as a living, historical being is known (or believed) to be a woman. Thus, the following representation of Alyx's body is filtered through the insidious male gaze: 'He looked at the nightgown, at the train she held, at her arched neck (she had to look up to meet his gaze), at her free arm curve to her throat in a gesture of totally unconscious femininity' (37). The narrative discourse here undermines the power that Alyx exerts in the plot. I would argue that it is the impossibility of resisting the authority of the male voice in this type of narrative which motivates the use of a more personal voice, clearly connected to a woman, in most of Russ's later—explicitly feminist—texts. As the previous chapter demonstrated, Russ began to develop this theme as early as 1965 in her short story 'Life in a Furniture Store'. I will return to this question in more detail in Part Two, which explores women's relationship to each other on the basis of their (presumably) shared physical existence. From such a perspective, the bodies of women serve as the basis of their identity as an oppressed class.

In the third short story collected in *The Adventures of Alyx*, 'The Barbarian' (1968), Alyx faces not an ordinary man, but an all-powerful sorcerer who shares many of the characteristics of Martin Guevara, the vampire of 'My Dear Emily'. This 'fat man', who does not age, hires Alyx without informing her about the task he wants her to perform; she accepts because she enjoys the thrill. The quick-witted pick-lock puts her skills to his service and the two break into the governor's villa, where she learns that she is to kill the infant daughter of the governor, as well as her nurse. The baby, he tells her, will, when she grows up, become an evil queen: 'She will be the death of more than one child and more than one slave. In plain fact, she will be a horror to the world. This I know' (56). Alyx refuses to kill the child, but cuts the nurse's throat to keep her from screaming. The sorcerer disappears, but not before striking Alyx's husband (a new one) with a mysterious disease for her disobedience.

At this point Alyx turns her skills against the sorcerer. Locking her raving husband in the house, she goes out to hunt her mysterious employer, eventually locating him in a tower outside the city. As a true sorcerer's hideout, the tower is furnished with a magical protective device to keep off trespassers. The device is an invisible yet impenetrable wall that bars her way up the stairs and has similar symbolic significance to the infamous 'glass ceiling' in women's careers. After a number of frustrated attempts to get through, Alyx discovers the secret of the wall: it keeps out only living beings, so she brings herself as near death as possible and comes through, barely alive. She struggles with the man, who pompously claims to be the creator of the entire world, and prevails:

> 'Yes, but—no—wait!' for Alyx sprang to her feet and fetched from his stool the pillow on which he had been sitting, the purpose of which he did not at first seem to comprehend, but then his eyes went wide with horror, for she had got the pillow in order to smother him, and that is just what she did. (66)

Before she kills him, she tricks him into showing her how to turn off his machine, with which he claims to have created and controlled the world. Again, Alyx encounters an alternative, ironic myth of creation, one in which all being originates in the machine of an uncanny wizard. Undaunted, she debunks the myth:

> *Make the world? You hadn't the imagination. You didn't even make these machines; that shiny finish is for customers, not craftsmen, and controls that work by little pictures are for children. You are a child*

yourself, a child and a horror, and I would ten times rather be subject to your machinery than master of it. (67, italics in original)

The death of the evil pretender saves the life of her husband. As in the other Alyx stories, the protagonist moves as a dissembler and impersonator in a plot template that narrative convention tailor-made for male characters. From a linear progression of adventures, she emerges victorious against seemingly insurmountable odds. In these stories, men and women are not yet seen as antagonistic classes. When she comes home from her successful quest, her man awaits Alyx as his hero:

> She got home at dawn and, as her man lay asleep in bed, it seemed to her that he was made out of the light of the dawn that streamed through his fingers and his hair, irradiating him with gold. She kissed him and he opened his eyes.
> 'You've come home,' he said. (67)

Having performed the role of the hero who solves all problems that confront him (sic) with wit and skill rather than with physical force, she now acts as the prince, kissing sleeping beauty awake.

A comparison between Alyx's interactions with males and the relationship between Emily and the vampire in 'My Dear Emily' demonstrates the crucial importance of androcide for the agency of the female protagonist. The central factor here is the ability, that is the knowledge and skill, to kill a male opponent, not the killing itself. After her dental 'deflowering' by Guevara, Emily seeks him out in his hotel room, with the intention of destroying the vampire:

> 'Nobody knows I came,' she says rapidly. 'But I'm going to finish you off. I know how.' She hunts feverishly in her bag.
> 'I wouldn't,' he remarks quietly.
> 'Ah!' Hauling out her baby cross (silver), she confronts him with it like Joan of Arc. He is still mildly amused, still mildly surprised. (125)

Emily's ineffectual attempt to 'kill' Guevara also seals her ties to him and further emphasizes her inability to act as an independent agent. In contrast to Alyx, she lacks the knowledge of how to destroy the representative man who bars or threatens her agency. Ironically, he informs her of how he could be harmed: 'My dear, the significance is in the feeling, the faith, not the symbol. You use that the way you would use a hypodermic needle' (125). Ultimately, it is Emily's father and her ex-fiancé who destroy the vampire, at a time when he has ceased to be a threat to the woman.

In Russ's first novel, *Picnic on Paradise* (1968), androcide takes a slightly different turn. This novel or long short story (such genre categories slip easily in science fiction) first came out as an independent publication but was later included in *Alyx* and *The Adventures of Alyx*. While in the stories discussed above, Alyx kills to save her life or that of her husband, in *Picnic on Paradise* her killings are motivated by grief and revenge. This story propels Alyx from the sword-and-sorcery environment into the different context of science fiction. In this story, she is a murderer and pickpocket from ancient Greece, who escapes execution by a coincidental propulsion through time to an alien world in the distant future. Alyx is thus not only slightly alien within the context of science fiction, but also literally becomes a 'visitor' from a different time and place.

The Trans-Temporal Authority, which had accidentally set her off on this involuntary journey through time, quickly promotes her from her status as guinea pig and object of study to a position as a military agent. She becomes an important asset in the commercial war that is taking place on the planet Paradise, a winter tourist resort which is claimed by two adversaries who remain obscure. Her mission is to rescue a small party of rich tourists and take them to a safe military base. This task has to be carried out without the help of any of the available high-tech equipment, without vehicles, and without firearms since these devices would be detectable by the 'enemy'. Her unique profile—she is skilled in all kinds of ancient survival strategies, but completely ignorant of modern technology—makes her the perfect candidate for this rescue mission.

Isolated from the rest of humanity on this sterile planet devoid of warmth, the two cultures, as well as the two narrative conventions, science fiction and sword-and-sorcery, clash violently. The rich tourists epitomize complete alienation, the society in which they live seeming perfectly smooth, clean and spotless. The ice that covers the planet is an externalization of the chill emanating from this culture, which is capitalism carried to an extreme. The individual tourists are isolated from each other and from the image of a core self, even though they constantly talk about their psychological problems and group dynamics in scenes reminiscent of psychotherapeutic group sessions. Plastic surgery can fit them with the artificial bodies they want, but this merging with machinery lacks the liberatory edge that it will take on in Russ's later texts in characters such as Jael. Their culture completely represses the reality of death. When one of the fugitives does die, it is at first impossible for the survivors to comprehend her death as the irreversible end of life. The authorities regulate every aspect of people's lives, including reproduction, but nobody is concerned with what or who these authorities represent. They experience the ice of Paradise as beautiful because it corresponds to the sterility of their own society. Alyx's body, which shows the marks and deteriorations of a physically active life, symbolizes the contrast between the two societies. Her scars and other signs of ageing represent her mortality. As a petty criminal, she operated in the interstices of her culture, partially outside of and independent from the laws her society represents.

As in the other Alyx stories, Alyx here has agency before she kills. The narrative relates a number of instances prior to the killing in which Alyx demonstrates her ability to act against male characters. A young military officer on Paradise, three heads taller than Alyx, is the first to experience her unwillingness to comply with conventional rules of decorum for women:

> I'm sorry, ma'am, but I cannot believe you're the proper Trans-Temporal *Agent*; I think—' and he finished his thought on the floor, his head under one of his ankles and this slight young woman ... somehow holding him down in a position he could not get out of without hurting himself to excruciation. She let him go. (5, my emphasis)

Alyx does not hesitate to react with violent physical force. She never stops to think if what she is doing is socially acceptable behaviour. Gunnar, the man whom she will kill later in the story, is next in line to have to submit to her physical skill. When he tries to take control over the group, she again asserts herself with immediate physical action:

> Gunnar came up to her sympathetically and took hold of her hands. She twisted in his grasp, instinctively beginning a movement that would have ended in the pit of his stomach, but he grasped each of her wrists, saying 'No, no, you're not big enough,' and holding her indulgently away from him with his big, straight, steady arms. He had begun to laugh, saying 'I know this kind of thing too, you see!' when she turned in his grip, taking hold of his wrists in the double hold used by certain circus performers, and bearing down sharply on his arms

> ... she lifted herself up as if on a gate, swung under his guard
> and kicked him right under the arch of the ribs. (26)

In both of these instances, the text sets up a narrative situation in
which the female character would conventionally be forced to submit
to a male who is barring her access to agency by the force of his physical superiority. It is in situations like this that Alyx's story quite
deliberately slips from the 'masculine' plot template to insert a story
line omitted in conventional genre fiction. Here, Alyx demonstrates
her exceptionality. Alyx's—exceptional—reaction creates an alternative turn in the story; instead of yielding, she asserts herself and prevails.

Significantly, Alyx's agency, that is her ability to control the plot,
also rests on her emotional distance from male characters generally,
even from her lover. Alyx, who has never loved a man before, falls in
love with the 36-year-old adolescent boy who calls himself Machine
because this is how he experiences his existence. When their relationship becomes known in the group (they make love within earshot
of the others), an intense rivalry between Machine and Gunnar
breaks out, and Machine fiercely wants to protect what he ultimately
perceives as his property:

> 'I shall take you tonight,' said Machine between his teeth; 'I
> shall take you right before the eyes of that man!'
> She brought the point of her elbow up into his ribs hard
> enough to double him over ... (114)

Again Alyx reacts immediately, without hesitation. She does not let
male presumption diminish her ego even if she is emotionally
attached to the perpetrator. In all of these passages, Alyx matter-of-
factly does the opposite of what is expected of her and in so doing creates a conceptual space in which women prevail in (physical or
discursive) confrontations with male characters. Since Alyx's agency
is solidly grounded in her scarred and efficient body (with all six fingers functioning), her presence in the text also destabilizes the privileged symbolic relation of the male body to power.

These smaller victories set the stage for Alyx's ultimate destruction
of the male body: androcide. When Machine falls into a glacier chim-
ney, Gunnar is the only one around who could save his life with minor
risk to his, Gunnar's, own safety. But Gunnar chooses not to rescue his
rival. After Machine's death, Alyx is devastated and even though Gunnar plunges himself into convulsions of guilt, Alyx coolly kills him:

'Defend yourself,' said Alyx, and when he did not—for it did not seem to occur to him that this was possible—she slashed the fabric of his suit with her lefthand knife and with the right she drove Trans-Temp's synthetic steel up to the hilt between Gunnar's ribs. It did not kill him; he staggered back a few steps, holding his chest. She tripped him onto his back and then cut his suit open while the madman did not even move, all this in an instant, and when he tried to rise she slashed him through the belly and then—lest the others intrude—pulled back his head by the pale hair and cut his throat from ear to ear. She did not spring back from the blood but stood in it, her face strained in the same involuntary grimace as before, the cords standing out on her neck. (133)

She does not kill him to defend her life; she kills him out of anger and grief over the death of the only man she ever loved. The murder is individual retaliation; Alyx has no sense of a common cause for women. The doctrines of patriarchy pre-date even the society of the sword-and-sorcery version of ancient Greece, where *Picnic on Paradise* places Alyx's home.

Her ability to defy the death-mills of indoctrination is inexplicable in materialist terms. Alyx has the same independence of mind and un-selfconscious ability to act as Janet from the all-female utopian society on Whileaway ('When It Changed', *The Female Man*), but without a social system that would provide the material conditions for her existence. The Mediterranean murderer and pickpocket is an isolated incident of an exceptional woman, while the Whileawayan is the product of her genderless community of strong, independent individuals. However, as Russ points out in 'Towards an Aesthetic of Science Fiction' (1975), characters in science fiction are never purely individual (113). Alyx is also a type, and her story is a potential model for female characters in genre fiction and beyond. Female protagonists who become killers of men in Russ's later work, such as Jael from *The Female Man* or Irene from *The Two of Them*, reverse the relationship between their own agency and the act of killing. While Alyx's agency is a precondition for her androcidal actions, these actions become the foundation of (partial) agency for Jael and Irene.

The Female Man: The hateful hero with the broken heart

In 1969, when 'feminism ... hit the university',[2] Russ wrote her first self-consciously and explicitly feminist short story, 'When It Changed', which she placed in Harlan Ellison's *Again, Dangerous Visions* (1972). The story, which won the prestigious Nebula Award in 1972, introduced the radical feminist vision of a class- and gender-less society, Whileaway. As an all-female utopian society, Whileaway harks back to earlier feminist books such as Charlotte Perkins Gilman's *Herland* (serialized in 1915). 'When It Changed' also shows intertextual connections to contemporary genre writing. The story was, according to Russ, in part a reaction to Ursula Le Guin's *The Left Hand of Darkness*, published in 1969:

> ... how can one call a hermaphrodite 'he,' as Miss LeGuin does? I tried (in my head) changing all the masculine pronouns to feminine ones, and marveled at the difference ... Weeks later the Daemon suddenly whispered 'Katy drives like a maniac,' and I found myself on Whileaway on a country road at night.[3]

Russ's version of a 'gender-less' society acknowledges the obstacles language and narrative conventions place in the way of such utopian visions. There are no men on Whileaway. Originally a Terran colony, Whileaway in 'When It Changed' lost contact with Earth at some point in the past. About 600 years before the narrated events, a plague swept away half the population—all the males. The remaining colonists, all women, created a thriving, rational and, above all, egalitarian society:

> 'Whileaway was lucky,' I said. 'We had a big initial gene pool, we had been chosen for extreme intelligence, we had a high technology and a large remaining population in which every adult was two-or-three-experts in one. The soil is good. The climate is blessedly easy. There are thirty millions of us now. Things are beginning to snowball in industry—do you understand?—give us seventy years and we'll have more than one real city, more than a few industrial centres, full-time machinists, give us seventy years and not everyone will have to spend three quarters of a lifetime on the farm.' (14)[4]

However, as functional and just as this utopian society may be, its existence is also highly precarious. The narrator in the passage quoted above is speaking to a representative from Earth, a male, who has just landed on Whileaway with an (all-male) delegation that wants to reclaim the colony. Another man from the Terran recolonization crew admits that the utopia is an accomplished and successful experiment, but then postulates: 'Whileaway is still missing something' (18). To the dismay of the Whileawayans, who miss nothing 'except that life isn't endless' (18), he goes on: 'There is only half a species here. Men must come back to Whileaway' (18). The story centres around the demise of the all-female utopia, which is defenceless against Terrans who command the more effective intergalactic weaponry. Again, the lack of agency, this time of the all-women society as a whole rather than of individual women, is emphasized through an ineffectual attempt to kill the male opponent:

> Katy [the narrator's wife] said in a brittle voice, 'You damned fool, don't you know when we've been insulted?' and swung up the rifle to shoot him through the screen, but I got to her before she could fire and knocked the rifle out of aim; it burned a hole through the porch floor. (19)

The man survives and the women-only utopia is doomed. Men (which in Terran logic ostensibly includes women as well) will return and, if necessary, they will use force. In a resigned note at the end, the narrator remembers the original name of the colony, which captures its only temporary existence: 'For-A-While' (21, italics in original).

As the examples from 'My Dear Emily' and 'When It Changed' demonstrate, ineffectual attempts to kill a man in Russ's fiction mark and confirm women's failure to attain agency as individuals or as a group. A deliberate and effectual killing, then, makes all the difference in the narrative. Russ's novel *The Female Man* (1975) retains the original idea of Whileaway as an all-female utopia, but the novel takes a more radical and more assertive stance which rests in part on a narrative of androcide. *The Female Man* is Russ's most important book— if only because it has received the most critical attention by far. It is doubtlessly Russ's most explicitly feminist novel and employs more complex narrative strategies than both of her two earlier novels, *Picnic on Paradise* (1968) and *And Chaos Died* (1970).

Russ began working on the project in spring of 1970 and finished it towards the end of 1971, but it took her almost four years to place it with a publisher. Russ herself attributes this delay partly to a misjudgement on the part of her agent, who tried to sell the book in hardcover (letter to the author, 21 Sept. 1995). However, the difficulties in finding a publisher may also relate to the book's explicit feminist politics and concomitant sophisticated narrative strategies.

In the early 1970s, women as authors, narrators and characters were only beginning to claim significant space within science fiction. This is particularly true of feminist women. Alice Sheldon still wrote under her pen-name James Tiptree, Jr., and people still believed she was a man. Ursula Le Guin's visions could be considered feminist, but the (mainly) male protagonists and (more or less) conventional narrative style of her early work (e.g. *The Left Hand of Darkness,* 1969) fit more easily into the generally masculinist science fiction environment. By 1975, the whole field of science fiction had changed. More feminists had made inroads into science fiction, and women writers had received important science fiction awards. That year also saw the publication of the *Khatru 3 & 4 Symposium: Women in Science Fiction*, in which writers like Joanna Russ, James Tiptree (still not 'revealed' as a woman), Ursula Le Guin, Suzy McKee Charnas, Vonda McIntyre and Samuel Delany discussed women's precarious situation within science fiction.

One could identify a number of other reasons why *The Female Man*, which is now regarded as probably the most outstanding feminist science fiction novel of the decade, was not published until four years after it was finished. However, there is no doubt that the book caused a great deal of confusion and irritation in science fiction circles, both when it first came out in 1975 and when it was republished by The Women's Press ten years later. Interestingly, most negative reviews cloak their undercurrent of homophobia and anti-feminism—the novel is the first of Russ's texts with explicit lesbian love scenes—in vague and self-righteous assaults on the book's transgressive narrative techniques. A reviewer in *The Magazine of Fantasy and Science Fiction*, for example, remarked in 1975:

> *The Female Man* is advertised as a science fiction novel, but it is not one. It is not a story. It is not an action. There is no narrative thread. Instead, one might more fairly call *The Female Man* a meditation or an *exercise in self-revelation* that uses some of the devices of science fiction... . Nothing is visualized, nothing happens. If there is a conclusion to be drawn from the book, it is *that the author feels that men are not altogether human, but that women without men are or might be.* (Rev. of *The Female Man*, 51, my emphasis)

In the context of this review, which uncritically conflates one of the

protagonists with the author herself, the phrase 'exercise in self-rev-
elation' most likely refers to the lesbian sexuality which this protagonist embraces (among other things) at the end of the novel. Such
evaluations that equate narrative complexity with bad writing in an
obscured critique of the novel's radical feminist politics resurfaced
after The Women's Press edition came out in 1985. For example,
Laura Marcus maintains in the *Times Literary Supplement*:

> Joanna Russ has learned all that a radical feminist science fic-
> tion writer should know about the genre; but this does not pre-
> vent *The Female Man* from being very nearly unreadable. Her
> prose is a singular affair, marked by a simplicity of diction and
> a remarkable obfuscation of temporality, context, place,
> addresser, addressee, and, ultimately, the point. (1070)

Similarly, the *Library Journal*, assuming the voice of liberal feminist
reason, insists, in 1988, that *The Female Man* 'marked Russ's transition from a writer of sensitive, skillful, feminist sf such as *Picnic on
Paradise*, 1968, and *And Chaos Died*, 1970, to the polemicist for feminist
perspectives' (Rev. of *The Female Man*, 30). From these reviews one
might conclude that *The Female Man* is not 'skilful' and 'sensitive'
because it is too radically feminist. It is not a novel because it has no
'action' and no 'narrative thread.' It is 'unreadable' because it does
not show its 'point'. Contradicting all of these claims on a number of
levels, my readings of *The Female Man* in this and the following chapters analyse the ways in which the novel skilfully explodes the very
narrative conventions in which these reviewers ground their criticism.

The Female Man significantly transforms Whileaway. Transferred to
the novel from the short story, the exclusively female society is no
longer an isolated colony like it is in 'When It Changed', but interacts
with women from other societies represented in the text. In the novel,
Whileaway is only one of four narrative worlds and thus has a different function altogether as the home of one of the four protagonists
whose story interlaces with the stories of the other, non-utopian
women. This section focuses on one of these non-utopian protagonists, Jael, whose name relates her to a biblical man-killer in Judges
4 and 5.[5]

There is indeed plenty of action in the *The Female Man*, only not of
the kind one might expect in a science fiction text. Russ's Jael represents violent feminist rage at women's oppression within patriarchy.
While Alyx does not think beyond retaliation, Jael uses her hatred

and vindictiveness as an instrument in a violent resolution of the sex-antagonism and the reappropriation of her sense of self. In Jael's world, which is in the future but exists on an alternative time continuum, women and men are engaged in a cold war against each other; the contradiction between the sex classes has been externalized. The two sexes live separated from each other on two different continents with an ocean between them. Women have created a nation of their own, 'Womanland', on a continent which could (if it were in our time continuum) be identified as North America, while men have moved to the area that in 1969 was still the Soviet Union. Their nation is—appropriately—renamed 'Manland'. Charlotte Perkins Gilman's 'Herland' echoes through these names, but there is no indication that a harmonious reintegration of both sexes in one culture is a possibility.

In contrast to Alyx, who merely acts without reflecting upon it, Jael is conscious of the process of gaining agency—and therefore self-respect—through androcide:

> Murder is my one way out.
> For every drop of blood shed there is restitution made; with every truthful reflection in the eyes of a dying man I get back a little of my soul. (*The Female Man*, 195)

On a diplomatic mission in Manland, Jael negotiates with a male representative, Boss, who tries to convince her that what women really want is to reunite with men. Brandishing his penis, he performs a satire of heterosexual 'seduction' clichés. He only nominally addresses her in his ritual soliloquy:

> You're a woman, aren't you? This is the crown of your life. This is what God made you for. I'm going to fuck you. I'm going to screw you until you can't stand up. You want it. You want to be mastered... All you women, you're all women, you're sirens, you're beautiful, you're waiting for me, waiting for a man, waiting for me to stick it in, waiting for me, me, me. (181)

This scene also underscores one crucial difference from Russ's earlier work. While, for example, Guevara's mocking performance of heterosexual intercourse refers to the same sexual politics within patriarchy as Boss's soliloquy, Boss makes these politics explicit. The character of Guevara requires an active, feminist reading to identify its subversive implications; Boss's ravings constitute a scathing caricature of normative masculine behaviour from a clearly feminist perspective, which (as the reviewer's reactions demonstrate) must be painfully obvious even from the perspective of an anti-feminist reader. While 'My Dear Emily' works with strategies of disguise and dissemblance, *The Female Man* leaves no doubt about its politics.

The killing of Boss is not represented as the spontaneous, erratic action of a helpless victim. To the contrary, it is a carefully planned, deliberate act which is contextualized as part of a revolutionary war. Jael, who has turned her body into a killing-machine through plastic surgery and metal implants, does not execute Boss immediately; she lets him ramble on along his never-changing line of argumentation about how women need men to 'do' them since they 'don't have nothing to do it with' (168). Her apparent patience at this point is merely a prelude to the great killing frenzy about to break out. Jael knows how she will react to a situation like this; her anger is not an *immediate* reaction to the pathetic pseudo-come-on of a man who poses no direct threat to her. Her anger is much larger and more thorough than a direct reaction to the ramblings of a single would-be rapist.

Boss's killing becomes highly symbolic, his death denaturalizing the defeats and (virtual) deaths of women at the hands of male hero-conquerors in science fiction. In her essay '*Amor Vincit Foeminam*: The Battle of the Sexes in Science Fiction' (1980), Russ analyses anti-feminist science fiction novels and short stories that depict strong women and all-female societies. In these stories, the women are brought down by such male heroes, whose sole claim to domination is their biology:

> So 'natural' is male victory that most of the stories cannot offer a plausible explanation of how the women could have rebelled in the first place... The conflict is resolved—either for all women or for an exemplary woman—by some form of phallic display, and the men's victory (which is identical with the women's defeat) is not a military or political event but a quasi-religious conversion of the women. (43)[6]

In Russ's story of Jael, the phallic display does not turn the woman into victim of biology, driven to worship the penis. On the contrary, Jael thoroughly debunks this logic. 'Rosy assassin' that she is, she relishes the act of slaughtering the man instead of submitting to the supposed pleasures of penile penetration:

> I could have drilled him between the eyes, but if I do that, I all but leave my signature on him; it's freakier and funnier to make it look as if a wolf did it. Better to think his Puli went

mad and attacked him. I raked him gaily on the neck and chin and when he embraced me in rage, sank my claws into his back. You have to build up the fingers surgically so they'll take the strain. A certain squeamishness prevents me from using my teeth in front of witnesses—the best way to silence an enemy is to bite out his larynx. Forgive me! I dug the hardened cuticle into his neck but he sprang away; he tried to kick but I wasn't there (I told you they rely too much on their strength); he got hold of my arm but I broke the hold and spun him off, adding with my nifty, weighted shoon another bruise on his limping kidneys. Ha ha! He fell on me (you don't feel injuries, in my state) and I reached around and scored him under the ear, letting him spray urgently into the rug ... (182)

When she has completed the killing, the text depicts the relief of tension as cathartic: 'Jael. Clean and satisfied from head to foot. Boss is pumping his life out into the carpet' (182).

Jael here reverses and distorts the act of heterosexual intercourse, orgasm being analogous with death. She relates her rage to the man's sexual arousal: 'Boss was muttering something angry about his erection, so, angry enough for two, I produced *my own*—by this I mean that the grafted muscles on my fingers and hands pulled back the loose skin ...' (181, my emphasis). Under this loose skin, Jael has artificial claws, with which she proceeds to penetrate Boss's body to kill him. The killing here is more than just the taking of life, it is a celebration of Jael's physical power, an atrocious violation of the male body. The passage mimics and thus exposes the violation of women's bodies in patriarchal narratives. As men have stabbed women with their penises, Jael stabs the representative man with her claws, letting him spray blood instead of seminal fluid. Boss pumps out his own life instead of pumping new life into the female reproductive organs, which in this process had become the site of her oppression. The male character's death enables the power of the female character in the narrative.[7]

This analogy to sexual acts works because it is normative patriarchal sexuality which most effectively helps to bar women from agency. In '*Amor Vincit Foeminam*,' Joanna Russ quotes a passage from Edmund Cooper's *Gender Genocide*, which came out in 1972—after *The Female Man* was finished, but before its publication. The parallels between Cooper's rendition of heterosexual intercourse and Jael's killing scene are nevertheless striking (italics mine):

No woman—particularly an *exterminator*—who is conscious and uninjured can be raped... The revulsion and feeling of sickness just sort of died. And the weight on top of me seemed to be—well, interesting. And *when he pinioned my arms and bit my throat and dug his fingers into my breast, it all hurt like hell but it aroused me*... So I let him enter... I tell you, I never knew what a climax was until that red-haired animal squirted his semen into my womb. (50)

Since it is highly unlikely that either writer knew the work of the other when they worked on their respective scenes, both must have drawn from a well-established convention in (genre) literature, which points to a deeply ingrained plot pattern of patriarchal discourses in general. What is particularly insidious about Cooper's text is that it is ostensibly narrated by the defeated woman herself, who thus sanctions her own subjugation as natural.

In such defences of patriarchy, male biology justifies the dominance of men as a class. Science fiction texts that use androcentric plot templates uncritically have accordingly produced stories that culminate in women's failure when they dare to assume a position of power. In *The Female Man,* Russ relies on existing genre conventions, but transforms them into stories in which women are able to de-throne the male genital: when Boss displays his penis, Jael does not submit but gloriously prevails.

Man-slaughter for Jael as a character is her way of forcing men to recognize her own responsibility for her actions:

I am the force that is ripping out your guts; I, I, I, the hatred twisting your arm, I, I, I, the fury who has just put a bullet into your side. It is I who cause this pain, not you. It is I who am doing it to you, not you. It is I who will be alive tomorrow, not you. Do you know? Can you guess? Are you catching on? It is I, who you will not admit exists. (*The Female Man,* 195, italics in original)

Jael constructs herself as force and fury personified, as the female redeemer, who, turning herself into a killing-machine, sacrifices herself for the sake of all women. Mercilessly destroying the male body, she transfers women's physical and psychological pain to him. Only when he recognizes her as an agent, expressing this recognition with a 'truthful reflection in [his] eyes' (*The Female Man* ,195), can she recognize herself. In the very act of becoming independent, she looks for recognition from a man, reaffirming her dependence. This dependence, however, has been transformed: it is she, now, who is the master, not he. The former slave, through revolution, has negated her relation to power. Marilyn Hacker notes that 'Jael lives for The Man in just as consuming a way as Jeannine does' (74), but this does not fully capture Jael's predicament: while Jael is deeply entrenched in the gender antagonism, she does not live for 'the man', she lives against, and in spite of 'him'. Androcide has two sides for Jael: her assertion of agency is invariably tied to the reaffirmation of the categorical dependency. Her impasse points to the need to develop strategies which move beyond straightforward opposition.

Russ's later characters share a number of attributes with the indomitable early creation Alyx, but there are significant differences which parallel transitions in Russ's feminism. Jael is a character who merges science fictional devices with fantasy. She is a high-tech feminist vampire who kills to suck the blood out of patriarchy. Although she fights for women collectively, her technologized body, very much like Alyx's, also marks her as an exception. As in the stories around Alyx, her body disrupts the connection between female anatomy and lack of agency. However, while Alyx is born with the physical advantage that makes her exceptional, Jael creates this advantage, which gives her access to agency, herself. Furthermore, Jael kills the man out of principle rather than as reaction to one of his acts. The androcide narrated in the text is not unique, but one of many similar killings which together constitute Jael's violent oppositional strategy. Similarly, the protagonist Irene Waskiewicz in Russ's novel *The Two of Them*, which first came out in 1978, is also reminiscent of Alyx,[8] particularly of the Alyx of *Picnic on Paradise*. Yet Irene's narrative transforms her from an extraordinary woman, who fights for her own independence, to an ordinary woman, who takes on patriarchy *as* one woman among others rather than *for* women as singular and sole heroine of the narrative.

The Two of Them: To hell with the universe!

The Two of Them combines strands from Russ's earlier work, integrating their contradictions to a new vision of feminist oppositional politics within science fiction. Although this novel uses simpler narrative techniques than *The Female Man* and at first seems to remain well within the boundaries of science fiction, with some fantasy elements for flavour, the reverberations of earlier themes in the text highlight the development of Russ as a writer. I have already mentioned Irene's affinities to the early feminist character Alyx. *The Two of Them* also takes up the idea of parallel universes from *The Female Man*: in *The Two of Them*, the two interstellar spies, Irene and Ernst Neumann are sent on a mission to the planet Ka'abah, a colony which has adopted a social structure that uses stereotypical elements from Islamic cultures and exaggerates patriarchy to an extreme. On this mission, Irene is in charge for the first time and not Ernst, her partner, lover, teacher and mentor. Irene and Ernst come from alternate worlds, the headquarters of their employers are located on yet another alternate world, and Ka'abah also exists in another possible universe.

Irene's home world is, like Joanna's, similar to the Earth of the fictional author. Ernst was instrumental in Irene's escape from American suburbia, which had been in the process of stifling her ambition. In a number of flash-backs, the narrator relates Irene's rescue, presenting her as an apparently independent young woman, who knows exactly what she wants and does not want. Irene is 16 in 1953 (*The Two of Them*, 29) when Ernst Neumann walks into her home as a mysterious stranger. He visits Irene's mother, for reasons which remain obscure. Irene senses that Ernst is different from the males she knows, specifically from her boyfriend David, who comes to embody all the elements in her environment which coalesce to force her into a subdued existence in the footsteps of her mother. The stranger seems to recognize her as an equal. Boldly seizing the opportunity, she uses him to escape from her home, which she knew would restrict her severely as soon as she entered what her society considers to be sexual maturity. However, her enthusiasm is already mixed with an element of doubt: 'What if David and Goliath turned out to be the same?' (*The Two of Them*, 55)

Ernst is an agent of the Trans-Temporal Authority, an 'interstellar espionage organization' (Russ, 'Recent Feminist Utopias', 80), and helps Irene get the kind of training she needs to become an agent herself. The relative freedom and independence she manages to achieve are nevertheless deceptive. Even though she is nominally in charge of their mission on Ka'abah, she still has to defer to her former teacher when it comes to more far-reaching decisions. The encounter with patriarchy in a 'pure' form on Ka'abah serves as a catalyst, revealing the superficial nature of her supposed equality. Irene can act and she carries the title 'agent', but she does not have *agency* because it is Ernst who validates her actions. She has no connection to the authority that orchestrates their missions, and she does not know the larger project which her job serves. She works as a wage-labourer without knowledge of the products of her activity.

Events and interactions with the people of the alien culture on Ka'abah gradually disclose to Irene the alienated nature of her work and her essential dependence on Ernst. Since Ernst acts as a quasi-father and teacher, this process of emancipation is the liberation from both the father *and* the male lover, the breaking free from what the text represents as the patriarchal fetters that constrict Irene's mind. Ernst is the epitome of the understanding male partner, who respects his female lover and appreciates her knowledge and skill. In the beginning of the book, the two are distinguished by age, not by gender. However, when Irene becomes active on her own account, outside the regulations of the male-dominated authority, Ernst's behaviour takes a surprising turn.

The 12-year-old daughter of their host on Ka'abah, Zubeydeh, wants to become a poet, a profession closed to women in this society. Since the planet's surface is uninhabitable, the life of the colony takes place underground, where women are locked in secluded women's quarters. Being confronted with a girl who goes through some of the same ordeals that tortured her own early adolescence, Irene becomes aware of her own subtle oppression. She discloses her doubts to Ernst about the Trans-Temporal Authority as well as her determination to rescue Zubeydeh, but he is unsympathetic. Irene, however, already plans to go even further than rescuing one poetic little girl: her project becomes dissolving patriarchy itself, not only on Ka'abah but also in her own world, to make agency possible not only for herself, but for all women. She asks Ernst: 'What about the unpoetic ones? What about their cousins and their sisters and their aunts?' (135) Margaret Fuller, who has herself come down in history as an isolated, exceptional woman, is supposed to have said: 'I accept the universe!'—Irene goes beyond that and is ready to reject it:

> 'Well, my dearest dear,' [Ernst] continues in the same deliberately lightened tone, 'we can't save them all, can we? Think! All the rebels, all the refugees? No planet would hold them all. The universe itself wouldn't hold them.'
>
> She says promptly, 'Then to hell with the universe!' (135)

When Irene insists on taking Zubeydeh with her and proposes to reveal their employer's hidden agenda by breaking into the computer files, Ernst secretly has her privileges as an agent of the Trans-

Temporal Authority cancelled. Instantly, Irene, who has always been part of 'the gang', one of the boys, is suddenly completely isolated. In spite of this isolation, she manages to fool the computer system and orders a shuttle for herself and Zubeydeh. When Ernst tries to stop her, she fights. Again, as in Jael's case, the struggle is intensely physical and curiously analogous to copulation:

> To you—
>   To an observer—
>   —they would look like dancers, half the time on their heads, arms and legs flying. Both of them seem to have forgotten why they're fighting or what they're trying to do. (161)

The struggle has lost its original focus. The object is not primarily the rescue of Zubeydeh, but something quite different. Ultimately, the object of the fight is control over Irene's actions. Will she act for herself or will Ernst continue to mediate her actions? Since neither of the two has a decisive advantage over the other, the physical confrontation seems endless—until Irene stops the one-on-one confrontation and brings in a deadly weapon:

> In such a contest of strength and skill it's always significant who wins and who loses. It's crucial that the man is stronger than the woman or the woman stronger than the man. Ernst's age weakens him; there's not much to choose between a woman of thirty and a man of fifty. Her endurance is greater than his, but nonetheless he's stronger and his muscle hurts her. She's coming out of a thirty years' trance, a lifetime's hypnosis. She used to think it mattered who won and who lost, who was shamed and who was not. She forgot what she had up her sleeve.
>   Sick of the contest of strength and skill, she shoots him. (162)

This passage lifts the 'contest of strength and skill' between Irene and Ernst onto a generic plane. The two individuals represent 'woman' and 'man' in general, the gender antagonism which according to a materialist feminist analysis can only be resolved by violent action—revolution—on the part of the oppressed. Making the death-struggle analogous to sexual intercourse, the text lets the act of liberation directly refer to the act that instituted the oppression and that seems to confirm it every time a man (in a patriarchal culture) sticks his erect penis, charged with cultural meaning and significance, into a woman. Unlike Jael, Irene does not wait for the dying man's recognition. It is not anger that drives her to kill the man, but plain necessity, not hatred of the man, but love of self.

The conventions of formula genre fiction in this case would have dictated conciliatory behaviour on Irene's part. Yet the text creates a story that violates society's idea of female/feminine behaviour and creates a counter-story which displaces male dominance and patriarchal plot conventions:

> This is not a comedy; Zubeydeh will never come across it in the library. A comedy is where Ernst would marry Irene in the end … Ernst (thinks Irene) was kind and gentle, he was a truly good man; nonetheless he was going to return her to Center (for her own good), stick her in a desk job (if they had one), or maybe just send her home. (164-65)

As in *The Adventures of Alyx* and *The Female Man*, androcide is directly linked to agency. However, while both Alyx and Jael are represented as in possession of agency *before* they kill the man, Irene's transformation takes place in the act of killing itself. Irene has the body of an ordinary woman. Since agency in her story is not tied to her body, but to the acts she performs, the concept loses its stability. In order to maintain her agency, Irene has to continue performing subversive acts and she is in perpetual danger of lapsing back to a state of enforced passivity. The revolutionary act of killing her lover is only the first of many more every-day confrontations which she faces at the end of the novel.

Furthermore, the concept of oppression challenged by androcide in *The Two of Them* is far more complex than in the other two novels. Alyx's and Jael's motives for killing fit within the frameworks of conventional narrative logic, even if they subtly reverse and/or subvert gender-roles. The men killed by Alyx and Jael clearly represent and epitomize the idea of the oppressing class in the patriarchal power structure. Both Gunnar and Boss are patronizing and misogynist to an extreme, both commit an offence against the protagonist which seems to justify retribution on the part of the victim: Gunnar refuses to save Machine's life, and Boss attempts to rape Jael both verbally and literally. Although both texts additionally stress these perpetrators' status as victims of the gender system—their actions are represented as typical, not individual—they seem to 'deserve' punishment within the logic of poetic justice. Not so Ernst. Ernst is represented as gentle, understanding and open for discussion—exceptionally so for a male character: 'Ernst is one of the few men [Irene]'s ever met who likes women. Most men don't' (*The Two of Them* ,144). Not only is he the quintessentially 'good, liberal man', he also supports Irene's professional career.

Therein, however, also lies one of the problems. As her teacher and male partner, he has direct access to the authorities and thus power over her on a professional level beyond their emotional relationship, which becomes apparent to her only when she chooses to transgress the rules of that authority:

> She thinks, *But I have no such power.* She has never had the numbers of Ernst's I.D.'s, not even when she was his Conscience. Yet he must have a record of hers and must have gotten it from Trans Temp at Center, months ago at the very least. Keeping them all the time. Holding her identities in the palm of his hand. Trans Temp guards against the different one, the unstable one, the female one ... (146, italics in original)

'Holding her identities in the palm of his hand', Ernst controls Irene's existence, since the privileges attached to the numbers of her identity cards give her access to the computer and are therefore prerequisite for her ability to act in a meaningful, that is unmediated and independent way (in the logic of materialist feminism). The control she had thought she had over her actions is revealed to be a mirage created by Ernst's behaviour and rhetoric. As long as she played by the rules of the male game, Ernst's superior position remained below the surface and Irene could maintain her imaginary status as an equal partner, without conscious awareness of the fundamental class difference between them. However, as soon as Irene decides to break into Trans Temp's files and to begin to sabotage Ka'abah (i.e. patriarchy), Ernst removes his support, ostensibly to keep her out of further trouble. He acts as he feels he must. Killing Ernst, Irene severs her affiliation with dependency and transforms the story of her life. Instead of a quasi-agent for an abstract Trans-Temporal Authority she becomes an agent for herself—with other women.

Because Ernst displays the best egalitarian behaviour one can hope for in a male character in genre fiction, his murder is the most shocking and effective of the three, although it is executed with the least gore and violence. Marilyn Holt admits that '[i]nitially [she] felt a wrongness' ('No Docile Daughters', 98) when Irene killed the man, but comes to the conclusion: 'I realized that this was a reversal of the literary tradition which allows a helpmate woman who shirks her duties towards her man to be killed by that man' (98). However, Ernst's swift death not only destroys the reader's expectations about plot development, it also shatters the illusion that this is finally a feminist novel about an egalitarian society which is able to accommodate both biological males and females in the double binary system of sex and gender. Like materialist feminist theory, the text exposes the fundamental structures of subordination and oppression within patriarchy that make reconciliation impossible even with exceptionally sympathetic males. For the oppression functions not on an individual but on a structural level—woman cannot get away without murder, even of the man she is emotionally attached to.

The stories of Alyx, Jael and Irene illustrate the ways in which the narrative function of androcide develops in Russ's writing. The Agency of both Alyx and Jael is relatively stable, anchored as it is in the women's own bodies. However, while Alyx's ability to kill is naturalized by her culture's myth of creation, the story of Jael celebrates the artificial origin of her man-killing body. *The Two of Them,* then, detaches the female protagonist from such stories of exceptionality and makes the agency she claims through androcide perpetually precarious. Irene's story, which is a story of separation from men in favour of a primary link to women, also points to the possibility of simply *ignoring* men instead of killing them. In Part Two, I will focus on the ways in which Irene's relationship to Zubeydeh maintains and recreates a different kind of agency. In the 1980s, Russ's critically feminist phase, in which lesbian sexuality and gender discontinuities become more pronounced themes in her work, androcide all but disappears as a narrative device.

These transformations in Russ's work also influence the ways in which the texts use figurative language to expand the discourses and permissible narratives about women. The most significant recurrent trope in relation to androcide in Russ's texts is the ambiguous and troublesome image of the cat, which is emblematic of the power women acquire in the act of killing a member of the antagonistic class.

The Cat As a Metaphor: Positively Not a Pussycat!

... not everything with claws and teeth is a Pussycat. On the contrary! (*The Female Man*, 188)

Cats in Russ's fiction appear in various guises, utilizing and subvert-

ing the traditional connection between stereotypical characteristics of
women and cats. Edarra in 'Bluestocking', for instance, compares the
independence of her rescuer to that of a cat:

> You remind me of a cat we once had, a very fierce, black, female
> cat who was a *very* good mother,' (she choked and continued
> hurriedly) 'she was a ripping fighter, too, and we just couldn't
> keep her in the house whenever she—uh—'
> 'Yes?' said Alyx.
> 'Wanted to get out,' said Edarra feebly. She giggled. 'And she
> always came back pr—I mean—'
> 'Yes?'
> 'She was a popular cat.' (27–28)

Edarra here combines contradictory characteristics that Western cultures attribute to the image of domestic cats. The cat, like Alyx, is sexually active, a warrior and a mother who does not rely on a male
whose semen impregnates her. However, cultural memories also have
other versions of cats in store, which emphasize passivity and recep-
tive sexuality.

Like the vampire, the cat is thus marked with a fundamental ambiguity which makes it a momentous image in feminist texts. In her
influential collection *Sisterhood is Powerful* (1970), which crucially
helped shape the leftist women's movement in the 1970s, Robin Morgan included a quote from Eldridge Cleaver which brings this ambiguity to the point and reveals the predicament of women active in the
New Left and the Civil Rights movements. According to Morgan,
Cleaver said in 1968: 'Women? I guess they ought to exercise Pussy
Power' (36). 'Pussy' is a term used either to refer to a domestic cat or
to the female genital organs, both of which meanings are alluded to
in Cleaver's statement. Loaded with scornful irony, it creates an image
of the woman as a purring pet cat whose only access to power lies in
her role as the object of men's sexual desires. 'Pussy Power' in this
context therefore means no power at all.

Many of Russ's texts deploy precisely this double (or multiple)
innuendo of the cat image to destabilize fixed patriarchal stories
about women. The texts take up the conventional trope of the woman
as a cat, shifting its tenor so as to thoroughly transform it from an
image of powerlessness into one of power. In this process, the concept of power itself is transformed. This power, or agency, is continuously provisional, never fixed to one person or group.

The contradictory images of the cat in patriarchal discourses are exemplified by the conflict between the professional killer Jael and the idealist 'Arcadians' in Womanland:

> They thought I [Jael] was Ultimate Evil. They let me know it. They are the kind who want to win the men over by Love. There's a game called Pussycat that's great fun for the player; it goes like this: Meeow, I'm dead (lying on your back, all four paws engagingly held in the air, playing helpless) ... (186)

To Jael, the idealist Womanlanders are innocuous and helpless, exposed to attack like a cat who expects to be petted. Jael herself, on the other hand, transforms herself into a cat who shows (and uses) her claws instead of meeowing trustfully for the owner:

> It took me years to throw off the last of my Pussy-fetters, to stop being (however brutalized) vestigially Pussy-cat-ified, but at last I did and now I am the rosy, wholesome, single-minded assassin you see before you today. (187)

Jael as a narrator also use the cat image in representing her moment of greatest power, in the act of killing the man. She celebrates the execution and lets the man die slowly, playing the same deadly game with him as a cat would with a mouse. She has even externalized this metaphor via plastic surgery and has fitted her body with a cat's killing instruments: 'I do not have Cancer on my fingers but Claws, talons like a cat's but bigger, a little more dull than wood brads but good for tearing. And my teeth are a sham over metal' (*The Female Man*, 181).

This image transformation is made possible by and points to the self-contradictory character of the cat metaphor as used by patriarchal discourse, of which Cleaver's statement is just one example. As innocuous as the domestic cat may seem to the owner, to a small rodent it is a dangerous predator. A materialist feminist analysis may therefore detect a third, undesired element in the 'pussy' of Cleaver's metaphor: the male class's fear of its oppressed antagonist. Russ's texts surface this element, exposing it to multiple subversive readings—a move which makes a power potential for women *within* patriarchal narratives about them accessible.

Moreover, the cat analogy emphasizes the point that the women murder by necessity, not whim. To a cat, killing its prey is a matter of survival, its existence depending on its ability to carry out the deed ruthlessly. Jael is very much aware of her identification with the cat and the potentially liberating other images available to women:

At heart I must be gentle, for I never even thought of the pray-
ing mantis or the female wasp; but I guess I am just loyal to my
own phylum. One might as well dream of being an oak tree.
Chestnut tree, great rooted hermaphrodite. (136)

The Female Man uses the cat metaphor in its relation to power most
explicitly, but the cat makes its ambiguous appearance throughout
Russ's fiction. The ways in which the texts deploy cat images correspond to the different function androcide has in these texts as a liberatory act. Alyx, in *Picnic on Paradise*, right after she has wiped out
Gunnar, wipes his blood off her white suit 'carefully and automati-
cally like a cat' (134). Gunnar, who is physically a giant compared
with the slight Mediterranean murderer, is by implication dwarfed to
the size of a cat's prey. The text here plays with the way in which
physical size is generally used as a metaphor for potency. However,
the instruments of death are not part of Alyx's own body as in Jael's
case. Alyx kills the man matter-of-factly with *two* knives and there is
no reference to sexuality in the killing scene. This difference demonstrates a development in Russ's writing which I have already indicated. In contrast to Russ's later work, *Picnic on Paradise* emphasizes
the liberation of the individual woman. Russ's first novel does not
conceptualize sex as a social class but as a biological given. *Picnic on
Paradise* does not yet incorporate the crucial role of reproduction and
sexuality as sites of women's oppression, which explains the absence
of sexuality in the act of liberation.

In *The Two of Them*, on the other hand, the cat is completely absent
from the scene of killing itself, but it surfaces in one character's
dream: Zubeydeh's mother Zumurrud, who is perpetually medicated
to fit into the restrictive patterns of behaviour deemed appropriate for
women on Ka'abah, in a dream imagines herself as a cat:

> ... a cat in a cat garden with cat servants, a free cat rummaging
> in garbage with cat allies, a heartless cat who had walked
> along a fence made of real wood in the Outside in some kind of
> loving mist and had sung in earsplitting shrieks. (99)

Zumurrud's desire for emotional and mental independence as well as
her need to articulate her pain, transferring it to others via their audi-
tory organs, is synthesized in this dream-image. However, when
Zumurrud wakes up from this presumably drug-induced dream and
Irene enthusiastically offers her the opportunity to leave Ka'abah, she
declines, again retreating into her dream world:

Zumurrud slips back into her cat dream, in which cat friends tell her admiringly that she's a stubborn cat, all right, in which the walls of the sleeping room melt into the illimitable vistas of Outside, and—for she is a dangerous cat—she goes off to have cat adventures, to bear famous kittens and seduce handsome toms, but all somehow in a key that doesn't matter, in a way that doesn't really count, for she's also alone, and what really matters are the trees and the plains, the endless forests, the rivers she follows for miles, all this mixed up with a lot of explanation and self-justification, mixed up, in fact, with endless talking, and with the sensation of walking, walking forever, never stopping, pulling a little harness with bells on it like Yasemeen's, like a cat she saw once in a picture in her childhood, a cat in a shop who pulled a little rotisserie, or like Dunya.

Zumurrud turns in her sleep and sighs, sunk forever in her beautiful, troublesome, unsatisfying dreams. (103)

Zumurrud feels that leaving Ka'abah for her is impossible because Ka'abah is etched into her own mind, which makes her unable and unwilling to openly revolt against the naturalization of her inferiority and subordination as woman. Only in her dreams can she slip into the role of a cat who has a satisfying sex life and freely roams the wilderness—alone. Zumurrud's cat is also a highly ambiguous creature. It is both a free, wild creature of the forest and a domestic, harnessed pet that enjoys the safety of a loving human home. This cat is both completely free and totally confined, which relates her to the theme of madness in *The Two of Them*, which I will discuss in Part Two. Because Zumurrud cannot make this tension productive for a liberatory narrative of her own, she remains caught in her dreams.

Russ's stories thrive on tensions and paradoxes such as the ones posed by the cat metaphor. Each of her texts further develops and hones such strategies of feminist cultural change. As my discussion of androcide showed, her work shifts its political emphasis from violent revolution to the love of women as foundation for its stories of liberation. As Russ's first larger explicitly feminist project, *The Female Man* in many ways enacts these transitions. The novel's four protagonists individually and collectively struggle for the power to define their own stories. Three of these characters act out a (disrupted) dialectic which moves the narrative from a materialist sex-class antagonism to a postmodernist disintegration of such stable identities, without, however, invalidating any of the stages in the 'dialectic'. In spite of what reviewers have said, my reading of Jael's murderous deeds made evident that *The Female Man* not only has at least one powerful *point*, but also plenty of *action*. Chapter Three will identify a strong *narrative thread* in the novel which intersects with materialist feminist analyses of social structures and change.

CHAPTER THREE

The Revolutionary Act: A Dialectic of Sex/Gender in *The Female Man*

The Female Man partially shares the radical materialist feminist premise that positions women as a sex-class in a dual system of oppression formed by patriarchy and capitalism. To demonstrate precisely how the novel uses and departs from this premise, I will put it in dialogue with the materialist feminist classic, *The Dialectic of Sex* (1970) by Shulamith Firestone. Firestone was one of the first 'second-wave' feminists to utilize Marxist concepts for the interpretation of patriarchal power structures, taking sexual difference as the most fundamental category of social division. This view of sex-class as a natural category has been subject to severe attacks by feminists, since it is based on the assumption that the unequal power distribution in the biological family is inherent, but Firestone envisioned a social system that goes beyond the limitations she thought biology imposed upon women. In *The Dialectic of Sex*, the sexed human body determines the most basic power structures in human society, structures which predate all human socio-economic systems. According to Firestone, women's childbearing functions necessitate the original division of labour and establish the biological family as basic unit of reproduction. Since women as a class are oppressed because of their reproductive function in society, she greets the advent of new technologies capable of interfering with a destiny predetermined by biology:

> So just as to assure elimination of economic classes requires the revolt of the underclass (the proletariat) and, in a temporary dictatorship, their seizure of the means of *production*, so to assure the elimination of sexual classes requires the revolt of the underclass (women) and the seizure of control of *reproduction*: not only the full restoration to women of ownership of their own bodies, but also their (temporary) seizure of control of human fertility—the new population biology as well as all

the social institutions of child-bearing and child-rearing. (19, italics in original)

Within this logic, technology, particularly artificial reproduction as a tool in the hands of a feminist revolution, severs the (supposedly) transhistorical tie that fixes women in a state of oppression and liberates both the child and the mother from domination by the father.

Such a sex-class antagonism which is grounded in women's reproductive function also shapes the dynamics of interactions between males and females in many of Russ's texts. Female characters in her work frequently secure their agency by appropriating control over reproduction. For example, women of the non-patriarchal human colony in *And Chaos Died* (1970) use their mental powers to effect parthenogenesis, and the genderless society on Whileaway in 'When it Changed' and *The Female Man* has found a way to merge ova. Within the narrative worlds these texts create, this strategic move renders the dominant sex-class's prime claim to power in modern Western patriarchies superfluous in economic terms. Thus, the first step in the dialectical process of liberation in both Firestone and Russ is to access history by claiming agency in the reproductive process. Furthermore, in her explicitly feminist texts, Russ puts special emphasis on eliminating gender distinctions by letting her female protagonists claim as their own qualities stereotypically assigned to (white) men in western patriarchal societies.

The Female Man both uses and subverts the dialectical antagonism between men and women which is constitutive of patriarchal societies. One level of this complex novel delineates the historical progression from the alienated woman via the feminist revolution to the woman conscious of herself and able to act. However, the novel makes this historical progression ambiguous: each successive stage is in the future, but not the future of the former stage. *The Female Man* thus acknowledges the symbolic power of dialectical thinking but challenges its fixed linearity. The three steps in this progression mimic the classic concepts of thesis, antithesis, and synthesis but place disjunctions between them. Time for each of the represented possible universes in *The Female Man* is linear, but the novel does not establish *necessary* causalities between events. The worlds are linked by a disrupted and disruptive chronology.

Staging these disjunctive dialectical transformations, the text creates four worlds which exist on parallel time lines in chronological order, but not in direct succession. Using a common trope in science fiction, the novel explains the existence of an infinite number of possible universes—which may differ only slightly from one another—with minute historical and material variations that each create a new possible universe:

> Sometimes you bend down to tie your shoe, and then you either tie your shoe or you don't; you either straighten up instantly or maybe you don't. Every choice begets at least two worlds of possibility, that is, one in which you do and one in which you don't; or very likely many more, one in which you do quickly, one in which you do slowly, one in which you don't but hesitate, one in which you hesitate and frown, one in which you hesitate and sneeze, and so on ... Every displacement of every molecule, every change in orbit of every electron, every quantum of light that strikes here and not there—each of these must have its alternative. (6)

Even though the four parallel universes represented in *The Female Man* do not exist on one time continuum, they are close enough to share a similar history. All of the worlds have in their present or in their past a patriarchal society that shapes the existence of each of the protagonists. Jeannine's world is a stark patriarchy, Jael's world is in the process of violently overcoming the oppressive system, and Janet's world, Whileaway, has eliminated males. On one level of the narrative, these three women stand for the three phases in the dialectic path. This dialectic starts out with a patriarchal society, the narrative world associated with Jeannine. A revolutionary war against the oppressive sex-class on Jael's world negates this patriarchy, and the dictatorship of women's sex-class supersedes it with the 'gender-less' utopia Whileaway.

However, the novel also contains factors which challenge such a linear reading. For the purpose of my analysis, I have separated different narrative strands and spaces of intersection with materialist feminism. Yet the dialectic in Russ's text is far from faithfully repeating the unambiguous, linear progression suggested by Karl Marx's and Shulamith Firestone's theories. Although *The Female Man* uses the concept of a linear, progressive history, it also subverts this concept: versions of Jael and Janet may be in Jeannine's and Jael's futures, but the text establishes no direct historical connection between the three worlds. The fourth world, then, the world of the fourth protagonist Joanna, acquires a special status outside this dialectic as 'basic' narrative world. It is a world very similar to the

United States in 1969, the place and time in which the author Joanna Russ produced the text for a contemporary audience. Joanna as fictional author is not only outside the dialectical path, the dialectic also takes place within her, creating an assemblage of stories that make up the narrative of her self. I will discuss the complex mutual interactions and connections between Joanna's world and the other three in Part Three.

Beauty Asleep: Jeannine, the Self-less

The starting point for the dialectic of sex in *The Female Man* is Jeannine's universe. It is a place in which World War II never happened and America in 1969 still has not recovered from the Great Depression. Jeannine in this narrative world epitomizes the emerging awareness of oppression, which, however, she cannot yet frame in a narrative of liberation. Jeannine is represented as having no existence of her own because she has neither agency nor conscious awareness of her oppression. Therefore, in order to take part in human existence within her culture, she needs to make herself available to become the property of someone who can act. In the process, she must suffer complete negation of self: 'There is some barrier between Jeannine and real life which can be removed only by a man or by marriage' (120). Yet Jeannine's oppressive universe is not a thing of the past. The time is 1969 and her world is painfully close to the basic narrative world of Joanna, the starting point and end point of the novel's analysis of the fictional author's self.

From this perspective, Jeannine's inability to tell her own story becomes her defining characteristic in the novel. Jeannine's disregard for her prospective husband Cal, a character who criticism has all but ignored in the past,[1] highlights this inability. Cal's alienated existence is directly equivalent to Jeannine's separation from what would be her self. Unable to kiss her awake to a satisfying sexual and social existence, Cal fails to perform his role as the prince whom Jeannine desires. Conversely, Jeannine does not act the role of the demure princess for him. He calls her the 'vanishing woman' (4), which also links Jeannine to Janet because he is quoting the words from a newspaper headline that refers to Janet, the Whileawayan protagonist. Jeannine, wondering whether she should break up with Cal because there is 'something wrong with him', says in a conversation with Joanna:

> He doesn't take me any place. I know he doesn't make much
> money, but you would think he would try, wouldn't you? All he
> wants is to sit around and look at me and then when we get in
> bed, he doesn't do anything for the longest time; that just can't
> be right. All he does is pet and he says he likes it like that. He
> says it's like floating. Then when he does *it*, you know, some-
> times he cries. I never heard of a man doing that. (84)

Jeannine, who does not see how her own life is circumscribed by
patriarchal discourses, transfers the disgust she feels for her own failure to perform the proper feminine role to Cal. He is as weak as she
is; he suffers from the constricting effects of the same binarism, but
from the perspective of the 'master' class. He is endowed with the
penis, but cannot adequately perform the act that would confirm his
power. The limp genital therefore just confirms his failure. Like Jeannine, he desires to escape to the theatre, where, as an actor, he can
perform the roles that life denies him. The role the actor plays on the
stage does not intrude into his or her story of self. Jeannine observes:

> Sometimes—*sometimes*—he likes to get *dressed up*. He gets into
> the drapes like a sarong and puts on all my necklaces around
> his neck, and stands there with the curtain rod for a spear. He
> wants to be an actor, you know. (85, italics in original)

On his imaginary theatre-stage, Cal can transcend the masculine role
that his position in the cultural narratives casts him for. With the help
of domestic implements and 'feminine' devices of beautification, he
endows himself with the paraphernalia of both femininity and power.
His pathetic attempt to act out a role of power independent of his
anatomy appears like a faint echo of the vampire Martin Guevara in
'My Dear Emily'.' However, Cal's performance falls flat, emphasizing
his failure rather than offering a valid alternative.

   Jeannine's derision does not give her a voice in her narrative world.
Mouthing the words her culture prompts, she remains ultimately
speechless. Jeannine is the only one of the four protagonists who
never acts as a narrator in her own right: her speech acts remain on
the level of dialogue and free indirect speech, both controlled by
another speaking subject. This inability to retell her own story on a
level beyond the confines of a narrative told by another connects
Jeannine to Emily in 'My Dear Emily'—both cannot articulate a story
of liberation since they do not perceive the crucial gaps and inconsistencies in patriarchal discourse. Thus, her own speech acts repeat the

stories that frame her in a narrative of inferiority, and Cal, who might be her ally against this narrative, emerges as a failure in her tale.

What distinguishes Jeannine from other, apparently more 'successful' women in her world is a vague awareness of a desire for something that she cannot name: 'That's my trouble, too. My knowledge was taken away from me' (124). As a result, she turns her destructive energies against herself. The older she gets, the more intense becomes the pressure put on her by society to fulfil her 'feminine' role, marry and immediately activate her maternal instincts. At 29, considered an old maid, she yields to the pressures of her culture and decides to marry Cal, whom she neither loves nor respects. But she pays dearly for recognition by the community: she loses the chance to overcome the self-alienation. What she cannot name remains beyond her grasp: 'Fleeing from the unspeakableness of her own wishes—for what happens when you find out you want something that doesn't exist?—Jeannine lands in the lap of the possible' (125). The narrative of romance and marriage in Jeannine's and Cal's culture positions both in a double bind which forces them to repeat the narratives that produce their predicament: 'Somewhere is the One. The solution. Fulfillment. Fulfilled women. Filled full. My Prince. Come. Come away, Death. She stumbles into her Mommy's shoes, little girl playing house' (125). The patriarchal family as an institution serves as the disciplinary centre which conditions Jeannine to objectify herself and to enter a marriage that confirms her status as a commodity.

In 'My Dear Emily', the unnameable desires of the protagonist conjured up the male vampire Guevara, who routinely rapes his victim, transforming her from material life to an unreal imaginary space of un-death. Cal, on the other hand, as a human male whose sex endows him with a power over Jeannine that he cannot wield, must fall short as fulfilment of her displaced desires. Instead, her contradictory and unfocused wishes call up an entirely different 'vampire', Jael, the woman of one of the possible futures, the unyielding antagonist of the male sex-class.

Jael, 'The Woman Who Has No Brand Name'

Jael, in contrast to Jeannine, is fully absorbed in her selfishness and obsessed with striving to acquire knowledge of self. While Jeannine stands for the inability to name her oppression, Jael gives it a name and therefore a possible solution. Thus, Jeannine can only raise complaints against an individual man in her immediate life, but Jael raises a revolution against what she identifies as the whole system of oppression. Jael thus exemplifies the significance of naming and names in Russ's texts: her biblical namesake in Judges 4 and 5 becomes active in a war by killing the leader of the opposing army. In Jael's world, which represents the second stage in the dialectic, the archetypal antagonism between men and women has escalated to a physical, though still 'cold' war. Jael says about this confrontation that it is the 'only war that makes any sense if you except the relations between children and adults, which you must do because children grow up' (164).

Naming the problem, Jael can frame it in a narrative that is (at least partially) under her own control. Jael presses for a real military confrontation between Manland and Womanland to destroy the antagonist, yet her motives for waging this war are also deeply personal. When she was younger her life very much resembled that of Jeannine:

> I knew it was not wrong to be a girl because Mommy said so; cunts were all right if they were neutralized, one by one, by being hooked on to a man, but this orthodox arrangement only partly redeems them and every biological possessor of one knows in her bones that radical inferiority which is only another name for Original Sin. (187)

This passage, narrated by Jael herself, names specific aspects of the culture in which she grew up. In this act of naming, she identifies the sources of her suffering as a child and young adult. This reference to her youth connects her to Jeannine: structurally, Jael's story is also the story of Jeannine's life. Generalizing her own story as universal for all women, Jael legitimizes her acting as a representative of her sex-class.

In her brief analysis of patriarchal oppression, which I quoted above, Jael superimposes her own, ironizing voice over the social knowledge imparted to her by her mother. Her angry irony puts a distance between the naturalized 'body knowledge' of her mother, which enforced the girl's feelings of inferiority, and her own, verbalized knowledge of the oppressive structures. The woman's external mark of sexual difference, her visible lack, turns into the 'possession' of 'cunt'. Thus, she exposes the external sign of an inferiority that the culture's myth of creation has naturalized and inscribed on the body's internal, structural frame, her 'bones'. In framing this process of naturalization in a narrative that exposes its oppressive effects, Jael can direct her destructive energies against what she perceives as the source of her oppression. Unlike Jeannine, she has a name for her desire. She commits herself to a story of liberation, in which she found a place as revolutionary force. Jael's materialist feminist story is effective because it allows her to negate denigrating patriarchal discourses about herself and because it gives her a clear position in the historical process. This story allows Jael to say about herself: 'I come and go as I please. I do only what I want. I have wrestled myself through to an independence of mind that has ended by bringing all of you here today. In short, I am a grown woman' (187). Jael has become active. She has become active not only for her own redemption as an individual, but also for the redemption of all women as universal sex-class and their collective selves: 'Mommy never shouted, "I hate your bloody guts!" She controlled herself to avoid a scene. That was her job. I've been doing it for her ever since' (194).

Jael devotes all her energy to the war against the 'Manlanders', who to her embody the abstract structures of oppression named by her analysis. Devoting the better part of their energies to the re-creation of patriarchy, the men confirm Jael's evaluation. However, their nostalgic attempts to restore their former power are doomed to fail. Womanland has superior technology and superior knowledge, but most importantly, women are in control of reproduction: 'Manlanders have no children. Manlanders buy infants from the Womanlanders and bring them up in batches, save for the rich few who can order children made from their very own semen ...' (167).

As in Firestone's utopian vision, the Womanlanders in *The Female Man* have become the ones who propel history by appropriating the means of reproduction. However, there is also a crucial difference between the feminist revolution proposed in *The Dialectic of Sex* and its equivalent in *The Female Man*, that is Jael's struggle. While Firestone wants to eliminate sex as socially relevant category, Jael wants to eliminate men. In Jael's revolution, the physical destruction of the Manlanders equals the resolution of the antagonism. Entrenched in the anger which makes her such an effective warrior for women, Jael lacks the speculative vision to imagine a society without fixed sex distinctions. Her function in the text is similar to that of androcide. As a point of convergence, she also represents and embodies the pain and anger of the primary narrator, Joanna. Russ herself explains how she conceptualized Jael:

> I thought of Jael as almost a medieval personification of Anger—something you might find in stone on a cathedral, like the gargoyles. She originally had bat's wings but I realized I couldn't justify that in sf terms and took them out. The echo of 'angel' in the 'devil' is quite intentional, if it is still there. (Letter to the author, 9 March 1995)

The biblical reference here to the double role of Jael as personification of good as well as evil is significant as well as fitting. Jael as allegory of Anger is produced by what is wrong with the Judaeo-Christian patriarchy. In her function as allegory she gives a concrete, physical shape to the diffused, self-destructive feelings of inferiority that stifle Jeannine. At the same time, she is also a rounded character in the novel, who has the life history of a human woman.

Jael's devotion in her actions to dialectical thinking make her a singular individual even in her own home country. Her focused anger and radically materialist politics isolate her from her fellow-Womanlanders who are unwavering idealists. Jael remarks: 'There is a pretense on my own side that we are too refined to care, too compassionate for revenge—this is bullshit, I tell the idealists' (184). These women, who live underground in 'sentimental Arcadian communes' (186), deny the material threat of Manland and live in an imaginary space free of conflict. It is a utopia which resists and denies the dialectic and contrasts sharply with the other, materialist utopian creation in *The Female Man*, Whileaway, which Jael casts in her own future. Jael scornfully says about these idealists: 'They are the kind who want to win the men over by Love' (186).

Since her fellow-Womanlanders turn out to be unreliable allies in her war, Jael explores other time-continuums or possible universes to seek out other versions of herself. She plans to meet Jeannine, Joanna and Janet: 'It came to me several months ago that I might find my other selves out there in the great, gray might-have-been, so I undertook—for reasons partly personal and partly political ... to get hold of the three of you' (160). Planning to install military bases on the worlds of her other incarnations, Jael intends to lead the revolutionary war to its logical conclusion, the annihilation of Manland. This is also where Jael's and Jeannine's stories reconnect. Jael wins the support of Jeannine, who tells her without hesitation: 'You can bring in all the soldiers you want. You can take the whole place over; I wish you would' (211). Jeannine, the self-less, becomes Jael's accomplice in her life-struggle for self-acceptance.

However, Jael also pays a price for the success of her narrative. In order to do her job, she has to become thoroughly brutalized, cynical, devoid of sympathetic emotions. She cannot relate to others on a basis other than hatred and scorn. Jael can externalize her anger because she can frame it in a positive story of liberation (the materialist dialectic), but she cannot name herself as a type: 'Who am I? I know who I am, but what's my brand name?' (19) Within patriarchal language, there is no name for her. In Womanland, she is isolated from other women of her kind. It is interesting to note that she seeks to create a category for herself in the language of capitalist economics: 'brand name' ironically emphasizes her commodification. She is the product of the very system of oppression that she fights, capitalist patriarchy, and she casts her liberation in the terms that deprecate her as a woman.

Ultimately, Jael's concept of society beyond the gender-war does not include herself, so she cannot progress beyond the revolution. This impossibility to live the utopia that she fights for has its equivalent in the novel. Just as Jeannine's inability to speak for herself excluded her from taking her place in the novel as a narrator, Jael is the only one of the non-utopian protagonists who never visits Whileaway. Jeannine and Joanna travel there without her. Jael, whose existence is necessary for Whileaway, cannot move beyond her hatred and rage. She is barred from enjoying the results of her struggle since the accomplishment of her goal would also destroy the basis of her identity. Shulamith Firestone defines the objectives of materialist feminism as follows:

> just as the end goal of socialist revolution was not only the elimination of the economic class *privilege* but of the economic class *distinction* itself, so the end goal of feminist revolution must be ... not just the elimination of male *privilege* but of the sex *distinction* itself: genital differences between human beings would no longer matter culturally... For unless revolution uproots the basic social organization, the biological family— the vinculum through which the psychology of power can always be smuggled—the tapeworm of exploitation will never be annihilated. We shall need a sexual revolution much larger than—inclusive of—a socialist one to truly eradicate all class systems. (8, italics in original)

Jael exemplifies the fundamental dilemma of all revolutions: only focused hatred and fierce anger will instigate the necessary radical outburst of violence directed against the oppressors. Thus, a feminist revolutionary needs a deeply etched sense of 'Us' and 'Them', that is a clear sense of identity and otherness. However, it is exactly this extreme polarization that ultimately makes eliminating the social and symbolic distinction between the 'oppressors' and the 'oppressed' impossible.

Reading *The Female Man* in relation with materialist feminist dialectical thinking thus underscores Jael's crucial function in the novel. Yet critics have frequently diminished Jael's role in the text. Richard Law in 'Joanna Russ and the "Literature of Exhaustion"' for instance declares that Jael 'embodies the age-old yearning for nemesis' (153). But in the context of materialist feminism, vengeance is not what her struggles are primarily about: Jael goes through intense agonies to fight for her right to exist as an agent in society, not merely for petty feelings of personal revenge. Similarly, Law misreads Russ's fierce humour as mere playfulness, and her manipulations of patriarchal genre conventions as formal experiments: '*The Female Man* is a madcap *tour de force* with droll devices that transform the fictional mode' (154). Law, although superficially sympathetic, thus trivializes the text as well as Jael's struggle, and fails to recognize that both are deadly serious. Jael kills men not for revenge, but to assert her existence: 'Murder is my one way out' (195).

Similarly, some critics have suggested that Jael's world represents a dystopian, 'false' future, similar to the one in Marge Piercy's *Woman on the Edge of Time* (e.g. Bartkowski 61). Nancy A. Walker in *Feminist Alternatives* (1993) also relates Jael's world to Piercy's dystopia:

> *The Female Man* also presents utopian and dystopian alternatives, and Russ, like Piercy, proposes that present actions create future probabilities, but she does so in a far more complex manner by insisting on parallelism and relativity instead of direct historical progression. (179)

I agree that *The Female Man*, in employing the science-fictional topos of parallel universes, contains the *possibility* of a dystopian future, but I would argue that this possibility is never articulated in the novel. The universe of Jael differs radically from Piercy's dystopia and does not represent a 'false', dystopian future. The historical progression, while it is not *direct*, is nevertheless suggested—as possibility—by the time-frame in which the protagonists are placed, even if the chronology is disrupted. Even though the four universes are not identical, they are close enough to share crucial characteristics, which makes it very likely that one version of Jeannine precedes Jael, and some kind of altered Janet follows her on her own time-continuum. The parallel universes allow the text to inscribe in the stories the liberatory narratives of radical materialist feminism, while at the same time disrupting them with alternative, even contradictory stories. From the point of view of the dialectic, Jael's world is not a dystopia (dystopia for whom?) but rather a necessary step on the way to utopia. Janet's world, Whileaway, then, represents the final stage in this dialectic (which is only one of many stories told by the text) and the end point of the (partial) resolution of the sex antagonism in *The Female Man*.

Janet, the 'Saviour' from the Paradise Built on Corpses

If Jeannine—in the logic of the materialist feminist dialectic—stands for the total negation of self and Jael for total obsession with self, then Janet represents the utopian image of the self in balance with society. On Whileaway, the deadly antagonism is resolved. Whileaway is a just, 'genderless' society and consequently decentralized and anarchistic. However, Russ does not construct Whileaway as a harmonious solution to all the problems in the other worlds. In spite of its status as utopia, Whileaway is also a world in its own right which is neither completely egalitarian nor free of conflict. Russ escapes the essentialist femin*in*ist[2] pitfall and does not create a sugar-coated romanticized vision that merely extrapolates from current stereotypes about femininity. Conflict and aggression are not absent from Whileaway, nor is violence. Whileawayans work, sweat, fight duels and scorn romantic love because it is possessive. They copulate passionately and love their families (which are quite different from patriarchal families). Furthermore, Whileaway is (possibly) the result of a war that is in stark contradiction to its present peaceful social system. Attacking Janet's blissful oblivion, Jael reveals her version of the death of all men in Whileaway's past, and confronts her with the brutal, ruthless massacres of the revolutionary war that, according to Jael, made the Whileawayan paradise possible:

> Whileaway's plague is a big lie. Your ancestors lied about it. It is I who gave you your 'plague,' my dear, about which you can now pietize and moralize to your heart's content; I, I, I, I am the plague, Janet Evason. I and the war I fought built your world for you, I and those like me, we gave you a thousand

years of peace and love and the Whileawayan flowers nourish themselves on the bones of the men we have slain. (*The Female Man*, 211)

Since she is the one whose life is spent in anger, Jael is more than aware that a radical transformation of society is not effected by chance or natural causation, but by human effort (Moylan, 72), while Janet can be oblivious to social struggle. The Whileawayan is naively unaware of the significance of agency because she does not lack it.

However, the text does not authorize one version of Whileaway's history over the other. Jael's voice speaks of war, while Janet insists on the plague. The text remains open to a multiplicity of other, even contradictory, readings. For example, Manlanders (or the Whileawayan equivalent) could conceivably have killed themselves in a foolish attempt to eradicate a version of Jael, wearing a suit infested with deadly viruses. (This reading would also explain why the 'plague' killed only males, sparing the women.) Thus, the contradiction inherent in revolutions exemplified by Jael remains unresolved— it does not need to be resolved. The ambiguity subverts the logic of dialectic historical progression. It is this indeterminacy which lets the text move on beyond Jael's crucial yet limiting anger.

Similarly, Whileaway, although it represents the endpoint of the materialist dialectic in the text, is not entirely free of social structures. It is organized by age, which is an inherently dynamic category. As Jael points out, the opposition of child versus adult does not have to be resolved, because it resolves itself when the children grow up (164). Everyone on Whileaway moves through different stages in life that have different functions: childhood, youth, adulthood, motherhood and old age. Everyone—at a certain point in her lifetime—has equal access to reproduction, which is why reproduction on Whileaway has lost its economic significance. Power on Whileaway is thus based on age, which resists binary coding. As the Whileawayan individual grows older, she develops informal networks of associations, becomes part of a family, and learns to form links to computers with increasing sophistication. The more thoroughly she can merge, the more power she has. The women on Whileaway move from powerless ('low class') occupations to increasingly powerful and creative ('high class') occupations. Thus, Whileaway conflates the complexly interrelated power structures of racist, patriarchal capitalism in a single basis for stratification, age, which, since it resists the deadly binary, also resists the dialectic. Whileaway must therefore find its own utopia, one which is not fully articulated in the novel. The text only represents the search for utopian visions, of which Janet's journey may be a part. A Whileawayan utopia is unrepresentable in the terms of the primary narrator, whose consciousness defines the limits of the novel's speculative scope.

From the perspective of the non-utopian visitors to Whileaway, Janet Evason 'knows who she is', that is she has access to a life story in which she is an active protagonist. She has consciousness of self, and fulfils her responsibilities towards the community. Very much in contrast to both Jeannine and Jael, her story gives her a strong ego that enables her to form mature relationships with others. Even though she knows she has a lower IQ than most women on Whileaway, and that 'they can spare [her]' (22) for trips to the other worlds, this does not hurt her self-confidence. Within the logic of her narrative, her value resides in her own being. To shape her story of self, Janet does not need the support or the reassurance of others because she defines her existence through her own actions. While Jael only reacts, Janet acts, which means she has achieved the objective of this feminist dialectic: agency. Paradoxically, this concept must be meaningless to Janet herself because she must be unaware of an existence without agency.

Janet's oblivion therefore also demonstrates that for this kind of feminist revolution it is not enough to eliminate the dominant class; a culture without a sexual difference that puts one sex at a symbolic and social advantage needs to undo the very categories that made its existence possible. *The Female Man* operates with the premise that a utopian society, to avoid stasis, must rewrite its history, that is the narratives of which it is a creation. Thus, while the materialist dialectic is the prerequisite for Whileaway, the dialectic ceases to be functional there. The utopian society is both based upon patriarchy and imagined as beyond it, expressing the need for such a utopian space and the ultimate impossibility of reaching this space. Janet represents a (provisional) image of an elsewhere, of a space beyond patriarchy whose dynamic does not rest on the resolution of contradictions but on negotiating tensions between them.

The materialist feminist analysis of patriarchal capitalism, as exemplified by Shulamith Firestone's text, rests on a relatively monolithic concept of culture. In breaking the linear causality of the dialectic, *The Female Man* partially gives up all-encompassing theories about 'women' and their 'oppression' in 'patriarchy'. This move away from grand explanations and liberatory narratives, however, is already implicit in early, supposedly 'reductive', materialist feminism. Even if Firestone herself does not make this deconstructive edge of her theory explicit, she already makes the integrity of the 'natural', 'original' body vulnerable by embracing advanced technologies to free women of their ties to biology. If the body can be shaped according to cultural definitions and ideological needs, the distinctions between bodily reality and discourse about it begin to become leaky. Cybernetic technologies, biotechnologies and a humanistic concept of 'nature' are unstable and explosive together, the combination invariably culminating in the destruction of 'nature's' claim to original wholeness and innocence. Thus, the narrative elements in *The Female Man* which destabilize the dialectic just articulate what is already an integral part of the materialist feminist cultural critique.

More recent feminist theory, reflecting upon its situatedness in the historical context of postmodern culture in transnational corporate capitalism, has foregrounded this instability. Such theories have also called into question the concept of individual agency and with it the category of 'the subject' who acts. Judith Butler in *Gender Trouble*, for example, interrogates the very basis on which earlier feminists had demanded agency, the category 'woman', delineating the limits of liberatory identity politics: 'Gender ought not to be construed as a stable identity or locus of agency from which various acts follow; rather, gender is an identity tenuously constituted in time, instituted in an exterior space through a *stylized repetition of acts*' (140, italics in original). While earlier feminists had relied on the idea that agency constitutes identity and subjectivity, and thus existence, Butler defines human acts as performative, resulting in multiple, fluid, non-fixed identities. Although Russ does not explicitly acknowledge her feminist agenda before 'When It Changed' and *The Female Man*, even her early texts clearly participate in these developments in late twentieth century feminism. Emily of 'My Dear Emily', the nameless narrator of 'Life in a Furniture Store', and Alyx anticipate and are prerequisite for Russ's later characters whose stories are more explicitly critical of these three texts' implicit humanist premises. Part Three, 'Indeterminacy', will pick up this thread, to further analyse the ways in which Russ's texts undermine the notion of agency within a singular liberatory narrative.

Very early in her development as a writer, Russ's texts also show a concern with what Sandra Gilbert and Susan Gubar have called 'anxiety of authorship'.[3] Russ's critique of the literary tradition is centrally concerned with women's agency as authors and as characters. In her critical work, Russ has extensively analysed the 'anxieties of authorship' as well as the non-existence of women protagonists in established literary plot-patterns. The attention many of her texts pay to the acts of authoring and reading corresponds to their concern with the materiality of women's lives. Creating an imprint of the author and the reader in the text, Russ connects their bodies in their economic and material existence as (mostly white, middle-class American) women. Although her later texts, particularly in the late 1970s and the 1980s shift the focus of attention to a critique of this simple political stance, Russ remains a materialist. In spite of these shifts of emphasis, her texts always operate in the space of tension between the unattainable materiality of (middle-class American) women's lives and its textual formation.

Thus, Russ began the process of moving away from affirming patriarchal plot templates well before Alyx entered the stage. Alyx confronts patriarchy as a hero in her own right, while earlier female protagonists, unable to attain full agency, use strategies of deception and displacement, withdrawing to an imaginary or inner space. At the end of the 1960s, when feminism became an explicit component of Russ's fiction, there is a distinct shift in the function and foundation of agency in her texts. In her work before explicit feminism, the emphasis is on the individual woman. In the Alyx stories, for example, agency is an integral part of an individual's being and not directly related to other women. Alyx's acts are a *result* of her agency rather than its foundation. Her relationship to the lives of women as a group is that of a model. In Russ's explicitly feminist texts, on the other hand, the agency of the individual is inextricably tied to women as a social class. Agency becomes based on acts rather than on inherent characteristics of an individual. Consequently, the focus shifts from the exceptional woman who serves as an ultimately unattainable model to the 'ordinary' women whose acts establish partial agency. The beginning of this period in Russ's career as a writer is marked by the short story 'When It Changed' (1969), which for the first time connects the struggle for agency with lesbian sexuality and emotional relationships among women. The significance of such woman-centred relationships in Russ's writing represents the second thread in my exploration of her work. Transcending the anger and hatred directed against their antagonistic class, women characters in Russ's fiction also create emotional and erotic ties to women and by ignoring men gain access to a narrative which promises them ownership over their own bodies and control over their sexuality.

PART TWO
Sexuality

Eros, weaver of tales—Sappho

The repossession by women of our bodies will bring far more essential change to human society than the seizing of the means of production by workers. The female body has been both territory and machine, virgin wilderness to be exploited and assembly-line turning out life. We need to imagine a world in which every woman is the presiding genius of her own body – Adrienne Rich (*Of Woman Born*, 285)

Introduction to Part Two

Kristeva's delineation of Western feminism uses the trope of a circle for the concept of time which inspires her second feminist moment. This circularity corresponds to a focus on the female body as a site where feminist politics ground their liberatory narratives. The purpose of Part Two is to analyse the ways in which Russ's fiction participates in such liberatory narratives. As Part One has shown, Russ's fictional texts intersect on many levels with her own critical work as well as with other contemporaneous materialist feminist discourses on agency. My analysis of these intersections foregrounded how Russ narrativizes the issue of agency in her fiction and how her texts destabilize agency at the same time as they appropriate it for women. Similar intersections exist between Russ's work and feminist discourses on sexual difference. At these crossroads, the female body, sexuality and the act of storytelling coalesce and become the basis for an analysis of power whose ultimate aim is not to establish equality, but to confirm difference and to celebrate women's bonds to other women.[1] Thus approaching Russ's oeuvre from the thematic angle of 'sexuality' further underscores how agency remains an unstable concept in her writing. Russ's texts do not attempt to resolve the fundamental contradiction between the explicitly anti-essentialist claim for equal agency on one hand, and the ultimately essentialist demand for an autonomous, genuinely *female* sexuality.

Since radical materialist feminism explained and demanded agency in Marxist terms, I explored the function of agency in Russ's novels by intersecting these texts with Marxist dialectics, showing similarities and significant departures. Part Two shifts the focus onto psychoanalysis as an exploration of how oppressive power structures work in Western patriarchal cultures. These two systems of analysis have become useful for feminism not in spite of their origin in patriarchal discourse but because of it. The pre-feminist version of Marxism was gender-blind, and psychoanalysis regarded female sexuality as the mirror image/negation of the male norm. However, if one reads Marx and Freud and their followers as descriptions not of 'reality' but of patriarchal *constructions* of reality, and if one turns the tools of both systems against patriarchy, they become powerful resources for criticism. Toril Moi, in her critical analysis of Freud's *Dora*, his case history of a young, 'hysterical' woman, succinctly reiterates this feminist paradox:

> The attack upon phallocentrism must come from within, since there can be no 'outside,' no space where true femininity, untainted by patriarchy, can be kept intact for us to discover. We can only destroy the mythical and mystifying constructions of patriarchy by using its own weapons. We have no others. (Moi, 'Representation of Patriarchy' 398)

Therefore, I will work with central concepts of psychoanalysis as they were appropriated by feminist theory. I will not, however, attempt a psychoanalytical reading of Russ's work. This would be quite a different project. The following readings mark and analyse spaces of intersection between Russ's fiction and feminist discourses on sexuality, which always either use or argue against psychoanalysis.

While the women's movement and feminism have always been concerned with sexuality, in the 1970s and early 1980s 'self-possession' of the female body moved to the centre of feminist politics. In 1969, when feminism was just gathering force throughout the campuses of the United States, a small group of women got together at a Boston women's conference to discuss 'women and their bodies' (Boston Women's Health Book Collective, 11). The project that emerged from this gathering met with immense success. By 1973, the first edition of *Our Bodies, Ourselves: A Book by and for Women* was published commercially, inaugurating the fight against limiting medical discourses about women: 'We are our bodies. Our book celebrates this simple fact. Sexual feelings and responses are a central expression of our emotional, spiritual, physical selves. Sexual feelings involve our whole bodies' (39). Much more radical and thorough in her analysis than these very pragmatic attempts to change women's relationship to their bodies, Mary Daly elaborated a feminist critique of the American medical establishment in her landmark study of misogyny, gynocide and violence against women *Gyn/Ecology* (1978). Gynaecology, she argues, was created to counteract the first wave of feminism in the nineteenthth century: 'For of course the purpose and *intent* of gynecology was/is not healing in a deep sense but violent enforcement of the sexual caste system' (227, italics in original). Daly exposes the medical discourses on women as well as the practices of genital surgery (clitoridectomy, for example, was introduced as a 'cure' for female masturbation) and psychotherapy as cynical means to maintain women's subordination and to separate them from their 'original' femaleness: 'This man-made femininity, the normal state of femininitude, grows and swallows up the remnants of naturally wild femaleness by its supernatural/unnatural "life" (undeadness)' (231). In 1981, Andrea Dworkin published *Pornography: Men Possessing Women*. The previous year had seen the publication of 'Compulsory Heterosexuality and Lesbian Existence' by Adrienne Rich. These texts, as well as a host of others, although radically different in their approaches (Adrienne Rich, for instance, joined the pro-free-speech feminists who opposed Dworkin's stance on pornography), are primarily concerned with the issue of female sexuality and how it has been grossly misrepresented by patriarchal discourses. Thus, feminists of the second moment rally around the call for claiming their bodies and their sexualities as their own. These feminists furthermore express—and live—the need to separate sex from reproduction. The focus in radical feminisms in the United States shifted from the need to fight men as the oppressive gender class, to the possibility of ignoring them altogether.

As feminism was going through these transformations in the 1970s, separatist utopian visions proliferated in feminist speculative fiction. Suzy McKee Charnas imagined a parthenogenetic all-female society in *Motherlines*, which came out in 1978 as a sequel to the dystopian *Walk to the End of the World* (1974). Another classic feminist utopia was envisioned by Sally Miller Gearhart in *The Wanderground* (1979). Joanna Russ, with 'When It Changed' (1969) and *The Female Man* (1975), was among the first to revive (and transform) the separatist utopia, which had been a major factor in earlier feminist writing such as Mary E. Bradley Lane's *Mizorah: A Prophecy* (1880–81) or Charlotte Perkins Gilman's *Herland* (1915)[2]. One aspect crucially distinguishes the 'second-wave' utopias from earlier texts, that is the way in which sexual relations among women become central for these utopian visions' political momentum.

Even this cursory sketch of discourses on female sexuality and the body as sites of oppression as well as liberation—although it is far from being in any way comprehensive—reveals fundamental oppositions to the feminist concepts explored in Part One. Russ's texts to different degrees intersect with separatist and essentialist discourses even when they put their dominant force into destroying biological determinism. These tensions and contradictions are, as I have shown, in part already implicit in the materialist analysis of reproduction as foundation of patriarchal sex-class. However, many of Russ's texts move contradiction to the front, exploring the powerful connections between women's bodies at the same time as they attempt to eradicate sex-class distinctions. Janet, from the utopian society of Whileaway in *The Female Man*, exemplifies this strategy: she is not-a-woman, that is without gender in a genderless society, but at the same time also emphatically female in a women-only utopian version of the future.

Yet Russ's fiction is not a homogeneous body of texts. Interacting with the developments that transformed the concept of agency in her work, the role and conceptualization of sexuality and the female body change as well. In Part One I delineated a progression from the individual, exceptional woman in the stories around Alyx to the woman who acts as part of her sex-class in the later texts. In terms of sexuality, the shifts in paradigm are even more fundamental. I agree with Samuel Delany, who notes in his essay 'Orders of Chaos' that '*The Female Man* mounts a radical critique, on every level, of the social, aesthetic, and sexual assumptions of *And Chaos Died*, just as *The Two of Them* mounts an equally radical critique of *The Female Man*' (116). In spite of all the other developments, sexuality is the one category that distinguishes Russ's earlier short stories and novels (for example, *Picnic on Paradise*, *And Chaos Died*) from her later work. Her most recent fiction, particularly *Extra(Ordinary) People* (1984), shows another such transition, deconstructing as it does both agency and sex as stable foundational categories of feminist politics.

As in Part One, my readings of Russ's texts vis-à-vis the radical separatist feminist moment set in at the beginning, the word. In this feminist moment, one of the central themes in the critique of patriarchal sexual politics is the inability of women to speak in a language which does not erase them as female subjects of their speech. Another radical feminist goal is to show how patriarchy blocks relationships among women and how such relationships can be productive in feminist stories of liberation. Russ has used and transformed such liberatory stories which link female characters to other women and lets them reconstitute and claim motherhood, daughterhood and female sexuality.

CHAPTER FOUR

Author-izing the Female: Women Loving Women Loving Women

> I stopped loving men ('It's just too difficult') and in a burst of inspiration, dreamed up the absolutely novel idea of loving women—Russ ('Not For Years But For Decades', 28)

Women as a group have been denied a public voice and access to discursive authority. The ways in which women have submitted to and written against their confinement to 'private' discourses (for example, the epistolary mode) has been explored by feminist literary scholarship. The feminist narratologist Susan Sniader Lanser in *Fictions of Authority: Women Writers and Narrative Voice* goes back to the mid-18th century, when both the novel and modern gender identity emerged simultaneously:

> Certainly taboos against women's public writing, along with the practice by which novels were presented as the 'true' histories of their narrating protagonists, discouraged the presence of the author's name on a novel's title page. In this way, just when, according to Foucault, individual authorship is becoming the ground of textual validity, the dominant female identity in eighteenth-century fiction becomes not the author's but the character's. (33)

Thus, even though women were serious competitors in the economics of narrative production from the eighteenth century onwards, literary histories consistently erased their contributions. Women writers as a class were separated from the androcentric literary canon and separated from each other by making every woman writer an exception to the rule that 'women can't write'. 'Essentialist' feminist discourses confront patriarchy's definition of the woman as the 'eternal' non-writer by constructing a *female* literary tradition on the basis of a shared biology (which had also been the basis of the exclusion). Russ participates in this discourse in her essay collection *How to Suppress Women's Writing*, but also throughout her fictional work. Reconstructing women as authors and characters of fiction is a significant factor in the sexual politics particularly of Russ's explicitly feminist texts. Rewriting images of the woman as author and as character, Russ tackles the 'anxieties of authorship', which Part One discussed from the angle of agency, also from the perspective of sex.

Mother-lines: Linking 'Female' Literature

The power of the word and the pleasures of the female body are intimately related. (Marks, 287)

From the point of view of the need to shape a female literary tradition, the implicit references to Charlotte and Emily Brontë and to *Franken-stein* in Russ's short story 'My Dear Emily', which I discussed in Part One, take on additional significance. For these references create a subtext of female authorship. Such implicit or explicit links to literary women are pervasive throughout Russ's work. The dedication of *The Two of Them* (1978) to Suzette Haden Elgin, whose short story 'For the Sake of Grace' served as a basis for Russ's novel, is a case in point.

One of Russ's short stories that explores the female experience of writing on a number of levels is 'Sword Blades and Poppy Seed', which first appeared in 1983 in the anthology *Heroic Visions* edited by Jessica Amanda Salmonson.[1] The short story conjures up the ghost of George Sand through Amy Lowell's poem 'Sword Blades and Poppy Seed' *and* through Ellen Moers's pioneering delineation of a female literary tradition, *Literary Women* (1976). Thus, the text creates a web of interrelations among female writers, including the ghostly narrator, George Sand herself: 'Where do we writers get our crazy ideas?' (23). The narrator makes clear that the phrase 'we writers' refers to women only, namely Lowell and Sand, but also Mary Godwin Shelley, Harriet Beecher Stowe, Charlotte, Emily and (possibly) Anne Brontë, Jane Austen, Emily Dickinson, George Eliot, Gertrude Stein, Virginia Woolf, Willa Cather, Zora Neale Hurston and Colette. All of these writers have received attention and respect even in androcentric literary canons, but they appear isolated as 'exceptional' women (usually towards the end of chapters on the great men of the particular period). Basing her assessment primarily on Elaine Marks's and Shari Benstock's work on female modernists, Susan

Lanser notes in *Fictions of Authority*: 'despite extraordinary, innovative achievements, writers such as Gertrude Stein, Colette, Djuna Barnes, Zora Neale Hurston, and Richardson were dismissed for decades as precious, irrelevant, and eccentric' (107). Lanser speculates that Virginia Woolf, who is missing from this list, escaped the sweeping derogation of modernist women writers because of her 'carefully distanced narrative devices' (107) which distinguish her from other female modernist writers. Yet it is precisely this (partial) appreciation which singles her out as an exceptional, isolated incident, corroborating instead of debunking the patriarchal maxim that 'women can't write'.

All-female utopian societies imagine an existence for women 'outside' such male-dominated spaces. The lineage of literary women in 'Sword Blades and Poppy Seed' creates a separatist utopian vision that explodes the all-male spaces of literary histories. Unlike the connections of solidarity among women as an economic class, a political concept which relies on men as the antagonistic force, women writers here link on the basis of their female body, seen as a stable transhistorical entity. They do not turn against men with ripping hatred like Jael, but towards each other, with love. Writing along similar lines, Sarah Lefanu concludes her reading of 'Sword Blades and Poppy Seed' with a statement that also embraces the historical author of the short story in the lineage of women writers: 'Joanna Russ situates herself within a tradition of women writing and struggling to write, or living and struggling to live' (198). In pointing to these 'essentialist' reverberations in such adamantly anti-essentialist writers as I take both Russ and Lefanu to be, I do not mean to suggest failure. Quite to the contrary, such partial affiliations with discourses which celebrate the liberatory potential of the female body-community to my mind are a necessary component of any feminist politics in the second half of the twentieth century. For there is no indication that the body has ceased to be the site of women's oppression and suffering, and patriarchal discourses all over the world still define women through their bodies as the other.

However, while 'Sword Blades and Poppy Seed' does set up the female body as basis for bonding among women, the story, as with most of Russ's texts, plays with sex and gender uncertainties as well. The narrator George Sand relates a fictional incident that goes back to when she was still alive, 27 years old and struggling with her novel *Indiana*. Returning from a theatre performance in men's clothing, she meets an old man who leads her to his store, where he sells, as he informs her, 'Sword blades and poppy seed ... Dreams and visions there, over here, edged weapons. Both for your trade ...' (25). He gives writers their 'crazy ideas' and they, in turn, pay with a lifetime of work. The man relates to her 'as one man to another' (24), which to her is 'no surprise', presumably because she can successfully pass as a male. Sex and gender of the old man, the *'Marchand des Mots'*, however, are unfixed as well: 'So there in the firelight the old man—or was it an old woman?—handed to me the measure of poppy seed that was mine ...' (27). He (or she) gives to Madame Aurore Dudevant a name that is neither French nor 'feminine': her disguising 'masculine' pseudonym George Sand.

This reading of the short story also puts intertextual relations in some of the earlier texts by Russ in a different light. The implicit comment on *Frankenstein*, which I located in 'My Dear Emily', is made explicit in 'Sword Blades and Poppy Seed'. The old man (or woman) refers to Mary Shelley, who received radium in the mythical store as follows: 'the young English girl who lost her baby and brought women's life-giving back into my trade with the myth of a monster that has made the world tremble' (27). The fictional incident takes place in the early eighteenth century, yet both characters, old man (woman) and narrator, speak with a late 1970s consciousness. The narrator's text thus participates in the feminist discourse which enabled books like Moers's *Literary Women* or Gilbert and Gubar's *Madwoman in the Attic*.

As in 'Life in the Furniture Store', the narrator is cast as an author and as a ghost. George Sand, however, is not alone, but linked to other women writers. Unlike the narrator of 'Life in the Furniture Store', she has a name as well as a voice which speaks with authority and self-confidence. She presents herself as in control of the discourse of the novel-writer as well as that of the literary critic:

> And the other wall! The prospect here was as flat, hard, and glittering as the first was capacious and rough, an expanse of steel that testified (or so I thought, for to tell the truth I was as fascinated and amused as Madame Lowell's poetic *persona* was frightened—or was to pretend to be—some ninety years later) to humanity's dual passion for cutting things to pieces and then putting them into containers afterwards. ('Sword Blades and Poppy Seed', 25)

Speaking as a ghost from a space beyond her own life-span, the narrator George Sand is able to endow the voice of the narrator-protagonist with the kind of authority only a narrator not involved in the tale could otherwise command. In reference to the female body that she once was, she can speak as a woman, which a so-called 'omniscient' narrator, who has no body in the text, never could. As Lanser demonstrates in her analysis of narrative voice from the eighteenth century to the present, *Fictions of Authority*, the voice of the 'omniscient' narrator is by default masculine in gender, the privileged origin of this voice being a male author.

In speaking as a woman, the narrator in 'Sword Blades and Poppy Seed' is able to gather authority from other women writers. She refers to Amy Lowell to legitimize her (ironic) tale of female creativity: 'In the main, however, events went much as the poet has described (you would do well to read Madame Lowell's account, which she called 'Sword Blades and Poppy Seed' in her volume of the same title)' (24). 'Life in a Furniture Store', on the other hand, represents such female solidarity as a painful absence. The narrator of 'Life in a Furniture Store' makes an effort to relate to her lesbian friend Laura, but fails to make the connection and is even unable to find words to express her resistance. Her only connection to life is the precarious one to the actual reader, while George Sand, although dead, lives on in the imagination of many women, including the fictional author of the short story who places the epitaph from Ellen Moers's *Literary Women* before the text: 'For this was something new, something distinctive of modernity itself, that the written word in its most memorable form ... became increasingly and steadily the work of women' (23).

In her first book of non-fiction, *How to Suppress Women's Writing* (1983), Joanna Russ delineates a number of strategies that women can use to author-ize their work. The most empowering of these strategies, according to Russ, is consciously feminist linkages to other women:

> Nowadays the statement ['women can't write'] sometimes meets with ... a drastic shift in perspective which can only occur in the context of explicit feminism, after considerable open anger, and with the backing of feminist solidarity. This is a response I can call woman-centeredness. (107–08)

Like the narrator in 'Sword Blades and Poppy Seed', authors who can rely on 'feminist solidarity', that is women relating to women, can move beyond 'anxieties of authorship' and create tales of women's lives without preoccupation with the struggle against men. The most effective response to 'women can't write', then, is to ignore the statement as well as the one who makes it. As Russ phrases this response (characteristic of radical separatist discourses of the 1970s and early '80s): '... What? from a group of turned-away, preoccupied female backs' (109).

Thus, while 'My Dear Emily' and 'Life in a Furniture Store' embrace structures of inequality and identify strategies of authorization, they stop short of positively asserting alternatives. 'Sword Blades and Poppy Seeds', published twenty years later, creates such alternative visions of female authorship. Entering a literary women-only space, George Sand as narrator appropriates an authority not based on dominance but on cooperation. However, the gender discontinuities instituted by the text also disavow the female body-community at the same time as it is being established. The affiliation with radical separatist feminism remains provisional.

Most Women Do Not Creep by Daylight: Intertextual Fabrics in *The Two of Them*

> This is another of those uncomfortable books which Russ regularly produces, her analysis of the sex-gender system increasingly complex, subtle, and disturbing (Kathleen Spencer on *The Two of Them* in 'Rescuing the Female Child', 178)

> Authors do not make their plots up out of thin air (Russ, *To Write Like a Woman*, 80)

Referring to women in literature or history most often means referring to narratives about women, which are by necessity embedded in the dominant discourses of a culture. The specific function of woman-based intertextuality in feminist writing is therefore to manipulate these narratives, liberating women's voices muted in the texts which tell their stories. Russ's work makes extensive and ingenious use of this technique. This is not to say, of course, that there are no other intertextualities in her work that involve texts by or about men. Russ draws from a rich knowledge of world literature as well as of genre fiction and children's literature. Her texts juxtapose Shakespeare and William Blake with H.P. Lovecraft, Sir Arthur Conan Doyle, Lewis Carroll, Fritz Leiber, Hemingway and the Bible (to name just some of the most prominent examples). However, the linkages to female characters and writers occupy a privileged position in Russ's intertextualities. The connections to women, particularly in her work after 1969 (when 'When It Changed' came out), are both systematic and systematically *marked* as such. Acknowledging Suzette Haden Elgin's short story as the basis for her own work also links the historical author Joanna Russ to the newly developing recognized tradition of female science fiction writers. The previous section discussed such references to women authors, whom the text also identified by name and whose stories were transferred from stories of isolation to those of community. The political implications of naming women characters and authors reach beyond the text itself to embrace the material(ized) bodies of female readers and writers. In this section, I will discuss the ways in which such references function in Russ's fictional work, taking as an example one of her later novels, *The Two of Them* (1978), which I introduced in Part One. Creating webs of interrelations among women, the novel recovers the inherent power in characters such as Shahrazad of *The Arabian Nights,* or Irene Adler, the only woman Sherlock Holmes grudgingly comes to respect. These interrelations ground women's power to create meaning through storytelling in their bodies rather than in their struggle as a socioeconomic class.

Feminist discourse in the 1970s and early '80s consciously attempted to disconnect from male-defined narratives revealing the way in which access to power and normative heterosexuality dovetail. Recovering and establishing connections with women both in history and in women's lives served as a primary strategy of resistance. In the essay 'Compulsory Heterosexuality and Lesbian Existence' (1980), Adrienne Rich critiqued a number of feminist texts on the basis of their unacknowledged heterosexual bias. This bias, according to Rich, prevents feminism from recognizing compulsory heterosexuality as one of the most powerful forces in the overdetermined oppression of women:

> [H]eterosexuality, like motherhood [i.e. women's role in reproduction], needs to be recognized and studied as a political institution—even, or especially, by those individuals who feel they are, in their personal experience, the precursors of a new social relation between the sexes. (657)

Far from proselytizing for 'compulsory Lesbianism', Rich demands from feminism an awareness of the powerful impetus the women's movement can derive from asserting membership in their sex-category by consciously associating with women. Rich differentiates two basic aspects of relating to women:

> *Lesbian existence* suggests both the fact of the historical pres-
> ence of Lesbians and our continuing creation of the meaning of
> that existence. I mean the term *Lesbian continuum* to include a
> range—through each woman's life and throughout history—of
> woman-identified experience; not simply the fact that a
> woman has had or consciously desired genital sexual experi-
> ence with another woman. (648)

I find Rich's terms useful for a discussion of Russ's novels because
they include the lesbian experience without at the same time necessarily excluding women who sleep with men. The 'lesbian continuum' allows women who identify and act as 'heterosexuals' to share
the subversive potential of lesbianism and posits a vision of a society
which transcends categories of 'sexual orientation'.

The Two of Them activates such a critique of patriarchal heterosexual relations, grounding it in an emphatically feminist intertextuality.
The novel assembles a variety of literary women in/as text to make a
radical feminist politics in a fictional narrative. As I said above, the
book is dedicated to Suzette Haden Elgin, the author of the short
story 'For the Sake of Grace' (1969), which Russ used, as she says in
her dedication, 'as a springboard to a very different story of [her]
own'. Such references and borrowings are common practice in science fiction, but Joanna Russ in her work specifically and systematically refers to *female* characters and authors who were originally
defined by androcentric literature or literary historiography. In these
explicit allusions to images of women in patriarchal discourses, particularly discourses within or about literary production, the name of
the woman is of crucial significance, as my reading of 'Sword Blades
and Poppy Seed' demonstrated. The name identifies the woman both
as unique individual and as member of the female body-community.

Thelma Shinn in her comparative essay 'Worlds of Words and
Swords: Suzette Haden Elgin and Joanna Russ at Work' (1985)
appeals to the need for what she calls 'sisterhood' among women,
arguing that in this respect Elgin 'has a convert in Joanna Russ'
(209). Shinn suggests that Russ's women protagonists before *The Two
of Them*, particularly the individualist hero Alyx, are isolated from
other women as strong, exceptional individuals: 'Only in *The Two of
Them* does she [Russ] expand this framework to demand the sisterhood of women, although her awareness of this sisterhood begins to
emerge as early as *Picnic on Paradise*' (207). In the light of the developments delineated in Part One on agency, I would challenge these

claims as well as the usefulness of the term 'sisterhood' in discussing Russ's participation in essentialist discourses. Instead, I would contend that the community and lineage of women created by *The Two of Them*, while they are based on the female body, resist such universalizing visions at the same time as they evoke them. The reference to community and lineage is as disrupted and disruptive as the use of the materialist dialectic in *The Female Man*. Using the family metaphor 'sisterhood' to refer to all humans with a female body—as empowering as it still seemed in 1985 when Shinn's essay came out—conflates differences among women and imposes precisely the kind of definitional closure that Russ's texts abandon.

If one compares 'For the Sake of Grace' with Russ's novel, the latter emerges as conscious of the need to connect to women as a basis for political action, but Russ's connections are always provisional, never fixed. While Elgin's text, read in conjunction with *The Two of Them*, projects a static image of patriarchy and emphasizes individual struggle, Russ's novel faces the awesome complexity and overdeterminedness of the patriarchal symbolic order. In comparing the two texts, I do not want to pass a value-judgement and find one of them lacking. What I do want to do is explore the ways in which Russ rewrites and transforms the original story by Elgin, which, if Thelma Shinn is right in claiming that it embraces 'sisterhood' as central concept, positions itself within American liberal-essentialist feminist discourses.

Jacinth in Elgin's 'For the Sake of Grace' is an extremely exceptional individual, who is able to accomplish the impossible and dedicates her accomplishment to one other woman, her less fortunate aunt Grace. She escapes the 'normal' fate of women (either absolute confinement to domesticity or to madness in isolation) through an achievement that is clearly unattainable to less gifted individuals. Her position in the story is analogous to Virginia Woolf's in the narrative of modernism as told by traditional literary historiography that I referred to above: her existence is ultimately not a signal for hope, but further underpins the inadequacy that her culture identifies with women as a group. The two female protagonists in *The Two of Them*, to the contrary, come to discard their status as extraordinary individuals and cooperate in a rescue operation which ultimately aims at the 'rescue' of *all* women from patriarchy.

The unidentified narrator in 'For the Sake of Grace' tells the story of 12-year-old Jacinth primarily from the perspective of her father, the Khadilh ban-harihn. The setting is an extremely misogynist patriarchy on a planet which is at least a nine-months' interstellar journey from Earth. Women are excluded from all the professions and confined to women's quarters, where they exist only to be beautiful and to produce offspring. The highest and most prestigious of the professions is that of the poet. Since poetry is a religious office, regulations for practitioners differ from those for the other professions:

> The law provides that any woman may challenge and claim her right to compete in the Poetry Examinations [the passing of which secures the right to enter the university programme for Poetry], provided she is twelve years of age and a citizen of this planet. If she is not accepted, however, the penalty for having challenged and failed is solitary confinement for life, in the household of her family. (218)

The Kadilh's sister Grace, who entered the examinations at age thirty, suffered the fate dictated by law and exists in the madness of complete isolation. Against seemingly insurmountable odds (there have been only three women poets in nearly ten thousand years of the culture's existence), Jacinth not only passes the examination, she is awarded the rank of the seventh—the highest—level. Before the authorities isolate her from all contact with her family and other women because she is a female poet, they grant Jacinth one more visit. She uses this last opportunity of communicating with her family to dedicate her accomplishment (which subjects her to an isolation virtually as complete as her aunt's) to the woman who failed: 'You will send someone at once to inform my Aunt Grace that I have been appointed to the Seventh Level of the Profession of Poetry ...' (230).

Although *The Two of Them* takes over both setting and central characters from 'For the Sake of Grace', the novel creates a fundamentally different story. The 12-year-old would-be poet Zubeydeh, unlike Jacinth, does not enter the secured status of a professional poet within her culture, but leaves her home planet to open up the *possibility* of becoming a writer in an alien culture. Leaving the culture of her origin allows Zubeydeh to participate in a project which aims to collect 'women and little girls from the far corners of the Universe' (168). Zubeydeh in Russ's novel thus becomes part of a (coalitional) community of women from which Jacinth in 'For the Sake of Grace' must remain excluded. The community of women in Elgin's short story is one of anonymous victims, a community based on shared oppression. Conversely, Irene and Zubeydeh in *The Two of Them* move beyond the oppression to become agents of change. The web of acknowledged or unacknowledged allusions to images of women in patriarchal discourses extends the community beyond the text to the bodies of male-defined female characters.

One of the problematic issues which the text only touches upon marginally is the cultural imperialism implicit in Irene's rescue of Zubeydeh. The tacit assumption of the text is that Zubeydeh is old enough to decide whether she wants to leave or change her own culture from within. Zubeydeh's mother Zumurrud chooses to stay behind. It is important to point out that Ka'abah, for all its superficial similarities, is not an Arab culture.[2] Its existence spans only three generations (compared to more than ten thousand years in Elgin's story). Its exaggerated fakeness and rigidity point to totalitarian fantasies of complete control over women which are closer to the ones expressed in Margaret Atwood's *The Handmaid's Tale* (1985) than to any real society. Furthermore, Ka'abah has been excommunicated by the intergalactic version of Islam represented in the text (*The Two of Them*, 3).

Another intertext within genre fiction which Russ wove into the narrative of *The Two of Them* recalls one of the major icons of popular genre writing in the nineteenth century: Sherlock Holmes.[3] The protagonist of *The Two of Them*, Irene, identifies with Sherlock Holmes's opponent in Sir Arthur Conan Doyle's short story 'A Scandal in Bohemia' (1891). The basis for this identification is the woman's exceptionality, which Irene initially also claims for herself. In her teens, as a response to the denigrating position of 'ordinary' women in her own culture, Irene decides to become 'one of the boys'. Partially disinheriting her body, she becomes not-a-woman and from this borderline position is later able to enter the space of men, represented by the all-powerful Trans-Temporal Authority. Young Irene gives this aspect of her fragmented personality the name of the exceptional woman in Sir Arthur Conan Doyle's stories about the famous misogynist Holmes: 'Waskiewicz was given her at birth, but ... she saved herself in adolescence by thinking of herself as Irenee [sic] Adler, *the* woman' (5). The variant spelling points to the different pronunciation of the name in American and British English (*The Two of Them*, 3). Irene Adler from 'A Scandal in Bohemia' is the only woman who Sherlock Holmes respects as having reasoning powers (almost) as formidable as his own. To Sherlock Holmes and to the narrator Dr Watson, Irene Adler is the ideal woman, endowed as she is with both a beautiful body and a keen intellect (which 'saves' her from her body).

The woman Irene Adler represents an idea which Western patriarchal societies have perpetuated since the Enlightenment, namely that
true (that is 'masculine') intellect will succeed even in a female body.
This image of the 'masculine' mind in the female body re-enforces the
naturalized inferiority of women and re-inscribes both patriarchal
gender relations and compulsory heterosexuality. Irene Adler in
Conan Doyle's story erases all other women, excluding them from the
possibility of attaining agency in this text: 'To Sherlock Holmes she is
always *the* woman. I have seldom heard him mention her under any
other name. In his eyes she eclipses and predominates the whole of
her sex' (206). Sherlock Holmes's client, Wilhelm Gottsreich Sigis-
mond von Ormstein, Grand Duke of Cassel-Falstein, and hereditary
King of Bohemia, identifies her as a dissembler, as a man who occupies the body of a woman, thus setting her, but only her, free to think
and act independently of the limitations her body would ordinarily
impose on her: 'You do not know her, but she has a soul of steel. She
has the face of the most beautiful of women, and the mind of the most
resolute of men' (217).

The woman is thus both the perfect woman and not a woman at all.
Miss Irene Adler's mind does not conform to her body—yet she can
become a positive protagonist precisely because of her body. Her
beautiful body opens the possibility of romance, without which narrative convention would force her into the role of a monstrous female
foe. She is able to beat Holmes at his own game because he underes-
timates her powers of reasoning.

However, Holmes is right in assuming that she will cease to be a
threat as soon as she becomes the possession of a legal spouse in the
plot of romance which she cannot escape. Following Irene's pre-
sumed suitor across town, Holmes accidentally—and ironically—
becomes best man in their hurried marriage ceremony. He observes
correctly (in the logic of the narrative): 'This marriage rather simplifies matters' (226). Matrimony neutralizes Irene Adler's extraordinary
powers of reasoning, and she 'reverts' to her 'original' state, determined and circumscribed by her body. Holmes's plan to trick her into
exposing the location of a hidden photograph (which Holmes is hired
to secure from her) is now certain to succeed, even though it is based
on a sequence of generalizations which sound rather simple-minded
for a great 'scientific' reasoner: 'Women are naturally secretive, and
they like to do their own secreting' (226–27). Holmes continues in the
same vein:

When a woman thinks that her house is on fire, her instinct is at once to rush to the thing which she values most. It is a perfectly overpowering impulse, and I have more than once taken advantage of it … A married woman grabs at her baby; an unmarried one reaches for her jewel-box. (230)

In a situation of crisis, the woman's body ('instinct', 'overpowering impulse') will make sure she behaves in calculable patterns. As he expected, Irene Adler at the fake cry of 'fire' reaches for the desired photograph, exposing its secret hiding place. Yet her 'masculine' mind also recognizes Holmes's deception, and she is able to flee the country with her husband and the photograph. Her victory, however, is ultimately ineffectual—because she is married.

In her essay 'What Can a Heroine Do?' Russ analysed this dilemma of female protagonists: 'For the heroine the conflict between success and sexuality is itself the issue, and the duality is absolute' (84). The King of Bohemia can rest assured that Irene will not expose the incriminating photograph to raise a public scandal that would ruin his monarchal-matrimonial career plans—because she is already safely attached to a male. Sherlock Holmes ironically receives his fee in the form of a photograph which shows *the* woman, *Miss* Irene Adler, on whose image he can now continue to fix his gaze—without fear. Appropriating the female character Irene from an androcentric narrative for herself, Irene Waskiewizc moves the angle of vision from the original narrator in 'A Scandal in Bohemia' to *the* woman, rescuing her from her place as other. Reading the patriarchal text against the grain, Irene thus becomes the voice of the woman who is silenced in Conan Doyle's text.

Initially, Ernst Neumann seems to indeed recognize her as Irenee Adler, whose exceptionality allows her to transgress the limiting boundaries of her female body. When he, the 'earnest new man' (*The Two of Them*, 5), addresses her as 'I-REE-nee', using the British—Holmes's—pronunciation of her name, she infers that he does represent *the* New Man, who will not impose on her the confining stories of the past. Therefore, Irene at 16 decides to leave her middle-class American home for a life of adventures with him. However, as Part One demonstrated, the New Man proves to differ only superficially from the 'old men' from Irene's patriarchal past. Like Irene Adler, whose name in German refers her to a powerful bird of prey, she does act, but without consequence because her primary attachment to a male limits her range of action to precisely the scope of this relationship.

However, *The Two of Them* connects Irene with a number of other female characters and these connections ultimately break up the single identity that fixes her to Ernst in a heterosexual constellation in which she can only lose, no matter how exceptional she may be. Irenee Adler is the name of one only of Irene's multiple personalities in the text, which, similar to *The Female Man*, subvert the notion of the stable, singular identity suggested by revolutionary acts of power against men as well as by identity politics solely based on the female body.[4] Irene as (unmarried) Irenee Adler is a possible self uninhibited by patriarchal concepts of femininity. As Irenee Adler she can become an interstellar spy. Yet Irene is also Maria Sklodowska Curie, Mikolaj Kopernik and Lady Lovelace, each name representing a different self within the woman who received the single name 'Irene' at birth. Irene plays a deliberately confusing game with 'female' as well as 'male' identities, displacing them from their 'original' culture as well. As an impersonator, Irene is able to appropriate for herself the ability to fight physically, to reason scientifically and to enjoy sex actively without the burden of romance: 'Let's fuck' (8).

The power of these identifications, however, remains precarious as long as Irene is emotionally and sexually tied to Ernst. The text represents the moment when Irene trusts Ernst enough to let him know about her powerful other self, Irenee Adler, as the moment when this self loses its 'virginity' as well. Once caught up in an emotional relationship with a man, Irenee's skills and abilities become ineffectual:

> In the dark [16-year-old Irene] decided to tell [Ernst] about Irenee Adler *The* Woman, and so she did, in a dry, self-mocking, grown-up voice that scared her and made her bones ache; here is the little girl (said the voice), here is the trap, here is the little girl in the trap. (*The Two of Them*, 52)

Her reveling in pleasurable erotic activities with Ernst's body leads her to enter the trap unawares, a trap which the narrator's (feminist) voice in this passage recognizes. The knowledge of Irene Adler's story allows Ernst to harness the power of his lover's alter ego. Naming them, he also gains control over Irene's other personas, Sklodowska, Kopernik and Lady Lovelace. When he appropriates their names, the different selves of Irene begin to serve him instead of her. Like Holmes, who comes to own a photograph of the singular Irene Adler, he is able to subject her to his own definitions. Therefore, when Irene kills Ernst, she not only rescues Zubeydeh, but also Irene(e) Adler, Marie Sklodowska Curie, Mikolaj Kopernik and Lady Lovelace.

Irene's involvement in anti-essentialist discourses demonstrates once more that the text does not rely on confronting one master narrative with another monolithic counter-story.

The killing of Ernst is meaningful on yet another level, since it refers to and reverses the story of King Shahrayar and Shahrazad from *The Arabian Nights*. The beginning section of *The Two of Them* includes a long quote from a Ka'aban book, a phoney imitation of stories from *The Arabian Nights*, which Irene, infuriated by its blatant racism and sexism, reads to Ernst. Irene explicitly compares the Ka'aban version with the original: 'She says, "*The Arabian Nights* is genuine. It wasn't published last week"' (3). The society of Ka'abah is an exaggerated and simplified version of the one represented in *The Arabian Nights*, a use of the text which corresponds to traditional Western readings. Husain Haddawy in the introduction to his new translation (1990) observes: 'From Galland to Burton, translators, scholars, and readers shared the belief that the *Nights* depicted a true picture of Arab life and culture at the time of the tales and, for some strange reason, at their own time' (xxi). The artificial culture created by the inhabitants of Ka'abah mimics such interpretations. The narrator in *The Two of Them* calls Ka'aban society 'mock-Arabian' (11), but it also effectively mocks all patriarchal societies' claims to genuineness and authenticity, exposing the interest and constructedness of their respective myths of origin.

Irene's and Shahrazad's stories share characteristics which are crucially relevant in terms of how Russ's texts link women's writing with the way in which they position themselves in relation to compulsory heterosexuality. Shahrazad is forced to continually tell stories to save her life from a tyrannical husband, an ardent woman-hater, who is intending to kill her the morning after he had 'satisfied himself with her' (16). In putting her own life at stake by choosing to become King Shahrayar's wife, she also saves the lives of other women whom he would have slept with and killed the next day. As the King controls the life of the storyteller, Ernst controls Irene's life—in spite of their supposedly equal relationship. Irene, in killing Ernst, activates the disjunctive analogy to Shahrazad and creates an effective story, but for her own life and other women instead of for a tyrant's languid pleasure.

A further trait which Shahrazad shares with Irene Adler, the young Irene in *The Two of Them*, is that she possesses extraordinary gifts that distinguish her from other women:

> The older daughter, Shahrazad, had read the books of litera-
> ture, philosophy, and medicine. She knew poetry by heart, had
> studied historical reports, and was acquainted with the say-
> ings of men and the maxims of sages and kings. She was intel-
> ligent, knowledgeable, wise, and refined. (*The Arabian Nights*,
> 11)

At this point of intersection, 'For the Sake of Grace', *The Two of Them*,
and *The Arabian Nights* meet. Shahrazad tells stories for her life and
Jacinth takes the mortal risk of competing in the poetry examination.
Zubeydeh, although she is more like an ordinary 12-year-old, risks
going with Irene to be able to tell her own stories. To all of them, writing, or storytelling, is a matter of survival. In this respect, the narrator of *The Two of Them* has a special position. Although this narrator is
never identified as female, s/he most definitely speaks with a feminist
voice.

Furthermore, Zubeydeh in *The Two of Them*, in contrast to Jacinth in
'For the Sake of Grace', has a voice of her own, even if this voice is
controlled by the narrator. She wants to become a famous writer, but
on Ka'abah the position of a poet enjoys an elevated social status and
is only open to males, as is any kind of productive activity. The young
girl, however, has been able to create a story of her own life in which
the rule that women cannot write magically does not apply to her.
This story preserves a space within herself that allows her to believe
in her own ability to become a published poet although she has fully
absorbed the gender stereotypes of Ka'abah:

> 'I will be a poet! I won't give in!' ... 'Daddy doesn't want me to
> be a poet, but that's only because he's afraid I'll fail. He doesn't
> understand, but I'll convince him. I know it's not good for
> women to be poets, but I'm different.' (*The Two of Them*, 84)

Since women cannot be writers (a dogma which stands in blatant
contradiction to the source of Ka'aban culture, the tales told by
Shahrazad), Zubeydeh can only conceive of herself as something
other than a woman. Like Irene, she has to construct herself as an
exception to enter the world of activity—even if only in her imagination—without fundamentally questioning the precepts of her culture.
But in joining forces with the older woman, Zubeydeh can also take
part in abandoning that imaginary safe space for the struggle that
aims to transform rather than escape the social and symbolic forces
that silence them. Although this struggle deprives both women of the

security and stability that accompanied their silencing, the novel represents it as ultimately infinitely more rewarding.

In this respect, there is a distinct difference between *The Two of Them* and the stories around Alyx. While Alyx is clearly an exceptional woman, the image of a role-model that demonstrates women's potential, Zubeydeh and Irene exemplify the limitations of such exceptionalism. The narrator in Russ's short novel *On Strike Against God* (1980) brings this shift to a different agenda to the point, changing Woodrow Wilson's famous First World War slogan to a battle cry for the liberation of women's agency from the exile of exceptionality: 'Make the world safe for mediocrity' (81). This example demonstrates the dangers always also involved in using such patriarchal patterns: the feminist text necessarily risks reinscribing the very hegemonic discourses that it is intending to destroy. It is my point in this chapter that, by connecting a number of different patriarchal story patterns about women, *The Two of Them* and many of Russ's other texts are able to create provisional authorizations of female writers and characters. These authorizations do reinscribe the principle of power, appropriating it for women as members of the female body-community, but this power is fragmented, decentralized and temporary. This strategy again points to a skewed reversal of another significant American cultural narrative: out of the one, many.

The representation of Zubeydeh's aunt Dunya in the text follows a slightly different pattern of resistance. Dunya also exists and functions in a web of deliberate intertextualities, but her story combines feminist intertexts with the patriarchal canon. As with all major characters in the novel, she is primarily modelled on a protagonist in Elgin's short story, Grace. As in 'For the Sake of Grace', the mad aunt represents the women who were killed because they could not tell stories in *The Arabian Nights*. Again, in Russ's text, using the name to identify the woman is significant. The text explicitly refers Dunya to Shahrazad's sister (Dinarzad in Haddawy's translation): 'It is nothing living but only the memory of another voice, the voice of Dunyazad, Shahrazad's sister, that mad, dead, haunted woman who could not tell stories, who could not save herself' (*The Two of Them*, 181). Woven into the story of Dunya in *The Two of Them* is a feminist reinterpretation of the 'madwoman'. This empowering reinterpretation intersects with feminist critical discourses of which *The Madwoman in the Attic* is an example. However, there is yet another possible intertextual level to the sound of Dunya's name which relates her to the modernist writer and lesbian icon Djuna Barnes, creating a lineage of women's resistance to their silencing. These feminist twists to Dunya's story of confinement and insanity give her a dignity and self-control that Grace as unambiguous victim must lack.

One of the ways in which the novel exercises this reinterpretation of women's madness is in representing Dunya, the rebel who has gone insane in her confinement, through the eyes of Irene and Zubeydeh at the moment when the girl begins to become rebellious herself. As long as Zubeydeh was considered biologically not a woman but a child, she was allowed some freedom to 'scribble'. However, when she enters puberty, the apparatus of oppression closes in on her. Her mother, who has to be medicated to remain an obedient wife, is the one to confront her with the ghastly fate of a woman who insists on wanting to write on Ka'abah: Zubeydeh's aunt Dunya, who has been locked up in an unfurnished cave with only rudimentary sanitary facilities. Mortified to see that her aunt has been reduced to a dehumanized 'heap of clothes', Zubeydeh takes Irene, who has become her confidante, to Dunya's prison cell:

> The little girl is crying, 'Daddy did it! Daddy did it!'
>
> At first Irene can see nothing. The walls beyond are bare rock; there is an undecorated, naked bulb in the ceiling and someone has left a few crumpled pieces of paper on the floor and what look like smears of food. There is an odd smudge along the wall, some sixteen inches off the floor, as if furniture had been moved there repeatedly over the years and had scraped or in some fashion partially smoothed the rock...
>
> Then the heap of clothes begins to stir. It fits itself into the smudge on the wall—so that's how, Irene thinks—and moves slowly along the floor. From time to time the woman whom one can't even see inside the rags becomes still, not stopping in any human attitude but ceasing the way a snail might do upon encountering an obstacle. Then the heap shivers a bit and for a few moments rocks back and forth, a movement in which Irene sees a faint echo of Zubeydeh's extravagant grief. And again the slow creeping along the wall. (*The Two of Them*, 81–2)

Zubeydeh and Irene observe the incarcerated woman from the outside, perceiving her as non-human. However, the episode is a direct and controlled allusion to Charlotte Perkins Gilman's 'The Yellow Wall-Paper' (1892). The subtext thus created simultaneously shows the perspective of the 'it', the 'heap of clothes', the woman.

'The Yellow Wall-Paper' performs a similar reversal in perspective by giving the 'madwoman' control over the text as narrator. Her husband, who is a physician, confines her to her room ostensibly to cure her of a 'nervous condition'. Part of this 'rest cure' requires that the patient is not allowed to do *anything*, a restriction which especially refers to writing. The narrator manages to keep a diary of her confinement in spite of her husband's and her sister-in-law's attempts to prevent it. Condemned to inaction, she watches the wallpaper, whose pattern, colour and smell begin to occupy her mind completely. At once terrified and fascinated, she sees a woman—herself—caught in the pattern, shaking it in the attempt to break free: 'And she is all the time trying to climb through. But nobody could climb through that pattern—it strangles so ...' (810). Gradually, she escapes to the only place available to her, her own mind, severing all connections to the outside world. Having pulled off most of the wallpaper, she is determined to stay in the room: 'here I can creep smoothly on the floor, and my shoulder just fits in that long smooch around the wall, so I cannot lose my way' (812). Aunt Dunya has, like the narrator in 'The Yellow Wall-Paper', also found refuge in what from the outside perspective looks like 'madness': complete isolation from a society that deprives her of an existence. The allusion to Gilman's story makes Dunya, the woman who has no voice, a potential narrator. The woman in 'The Yellow Wall-Paper' is confined to her room, but she is the one whose voice is heard.

At her visit to the cave of the mad aunt, Zubeydeh is for the first time forced to see what adulthood has in store for her, and it is her mother—a victim herself—who comes to enforce the 'law of the father'. Zumurrud says, speaking to her daughter and Irene:

> 'I took my daughter to see her because I want her to know what happens to women who go mad in our family.' ...
>
> 'Your Aunt Dunya wanted to be a poet.'
>
> She adds, 'We kept taking her papers away from her. They weren't good for her. And then we knew we had done the right thing because she went mad.' (*The Two of Them*, 83–4)

Zubeydeh, however, still clings on to the idea that she is a poetic genius and will be able to become a writer in spite of her father. Confidently, she submits her poems to his judgement, but to her dismay he rejects them: 'Alas, my daughter, you have no talent. Your poems are worthless. They are no good at all' (93). What makes this rejection especially painful is that it comes from Zubeydeh's own father.

This personal policing of gender boundaries by someone the girl loves marks another crucial difference to 'For the Sake of Grace'. In Elgin's story, the 'law of the father' is static, fixed by an impersonal authority, out of reach for Jacinth's real father. The characters in the short story live according to rigidly enforced laws, which do not change, while *The Two of Them* shows the constant re-creation of the law by the agents who live in it. Zubeydeh's father, as well as the girl herself, is part of the process of reinscription.

Yet Zubeydeh finds a way to disrupt this process of cultural reproduction. The traumatic experience that destroys her hope creates another, more powerful vision. Only when Zubeydeh sees her father tear her writings into pieces does she realize that no matter how good she might become as a poet, he will never accept her writing because she is of the wrong sex:

> She starts to cry. Everyone is against her. No one, neither mother nor father, is willing to admit the truth. She starts to cry more hysterically then for it seems to her that she will wake tomorrow in the cell with Dunya, fouled by the madwoman's excrement, daubed with her food, with a mad, whispering voice in her ears saying horrible poetry until Zubeydeh's own brain begins to turn, until she gets dizzy, until she too goes mad, and then there will be no poetry, no marriage, no friends, no happiness, no sanity, but only madness forever and ever. (93–94)

This eye-opening experience leads her to decide to come with Irene to a world which, though it is also patriarchal, provides gaps for women to exist in. However, Zubeydeh carries her culture's stories about sexual difference with her. So the escape can never be completed. On the spaceship away from Ka'abah, she meets a six-year-old orphaned boy she wants to take with her, and Irene observes: 'Zubeydeh knows he's a good boy. Zubeydeh is willing to give poetry readings for him, to scrub floors for him, to work for him and sacrifice for him' (168). Zubeydeh's rescue from Ka'abah demonstrates that each liberating action also has its limitations, but each step expands the gaps in the strangling patterns of patriarchal discourse.

Thus, *The Two of Them* complexly interweaves multiple layers of relationships among women across texts and within its own narrative. Zubeydeh's moment of insight is paralleled by Irene's breaking free from her lover. The moment when Irene realizes that Ernst is not what she took him to be, she connects the supposedly egalitarian

Trans-Temporal Authority with the constrictive patriarchy of Ka'abah:

> Trans Temp guards against the different one, the unstable one, the female one, the Wife-stealer! She remembers 'Alee peering in horror through his beard: *Where are your children?* Center must have been asking the same question, asking it for years, expecting that any moment she would revert and turn back into Rose. (146–47)

Rose is the name of Irene's mother, who stands for the women who are not extraordinary, the women who remain within the discursive limits of their bodies without taking possession of them. In the horror of 'Alee's face Irene recognizes the potential power of 'reverting' to the female body. Just as there is no way for Ernst to escape the limits of his own body to become the earnest new man he aspires to be, a man who 'loves and respects women', the individual solution is ultimately closed to Irene as well. They share the opposing ends of one fate dictated by the patriarchal narratives that define their bodies as binary opposites. In killing him, she takes her fate in her own hands and embraces her own being as female, turning towards other women for validation instead of turning against men. The end of the novel has brought her '*Back to Square One*' (176). She is now a thoroughly ordinary woman, 'a thirty-year-old divorcée with a child to support' (176), on her way to Albuquerque. Irene has shed her adolescent dream of escaping her body and now wholeheartedly embraces the community of women. Again, she gives a name to this newly developed aspect of her personality. Her adult name is Irene *Rose* Waskiewicz (177). By rescuing the female child, she also becomes her own mother's daughter. Yet this reconciliation with the mother does not happen on the basis of identification. Irene does not repeat the story of Rose but constructs her own from the fragments of other women's stories. Her mother had validated her femaleness through attachment to a male and thus made Irene's existence possible. Irene connects to her mother directly, as a woman, using her body—defined by patriarchy as limiting—as the basis for her liberatory politics.

Towards the end of the narrative, Irene thus finds herself thoroughly 'outside' the 'system', a seemingly powerless nobody. But the text has also placed her inside multiple (inter)textual webs which connect her to other women. In the end, Irene dreams a hopeful message of possible change which reiterates and brings together these connections to a female lineage and a reassuring albeit fragmented

sense of body-community. This dream, a somewhat Blakeian apoca-
lyptic vision, creates an extraordinary image of a vast vulva that contains the dead bones of the slain women but also a faint inkling of
hope:

> In her dream Zubeydeh is a grown woman and in her Ka'abite
> dress sits on a rocky promontory, a little above Irene, brooding
> behind her veil like the Spirit of the Abyss; Zubeydeh is wait-
> ing for something to happen. Far below the two of them Irene
> can see a desert valley and an old, dry watercourse where a
> river ran ages ago; the rock walls of the valley rise not into the
> sky but into a half-lit, interior greyness like the roof of a vast
> cavern; Irene knows that they are in the centermost vacancy of
> someone's mind, that they have found their way at last into the
> most secret place of Ka'abah. Farther out towards the surface
> there may be tumultuous winds, fiery conflagrations, and rains
> of blood, but here all is still, and in the gray, colorless half-light
> Irene can see that the floor of the valley below is thickly cov-
> ered with bones. (179–80)

The valley, the abyss, the roof of a vast cavern in this passage may be
read as the enormously amplified echo of Zubeydeh's grown body, yet
the text does not flatly tie the woman back down to earth. The image
contains an ambiguity which keeps it open to a multitude of readings.
The dead valley, a vast mirror image of Zubeydeh's living vulva, also
links her to her aunt Dunya: 'It is so dry, so still, so movelessly gray
that Irene knows at once whose soul it is—it is Aunt Dunya's soul ...'
(180). The eroticism that is suppressed between Irene and
Zubeydeh—represented in the dream through the physical distance
between them—is implicit in the imagery.

The same image, however, whose visual forms can be read as a
vulva is simultaneously also shaped like the mad woman's head from
the inside. The desert valley from this perspective corresponds to the
groove in the brain inside the dome of Dunya's skull. Irene's dream
thus in a physiological image conflates what patriarchal narratives
have separated for women like Irene Adler, her brains and her sex. On
the other hand, the image of the cavern—oscillating between two
vital parts of the female anatomy—also *separates* what patriarchal discourses have linked in a continuous manoeuvre of naturalization,
namely the reproductive function of the woman's body and the supposed inferiority of her mental abilities. According to this patriarchal
logic, women cannot write because they have a vagina rather than a

protruding organ. Correspondingly, this narrative tells woman that because her economic function is grounded in her womb, she cannot become a nuclear physicist.

Ultimately Irene reaches a point where she sees that the power to act she thought she had was only vicarious power mediated through her lover. In this final section, she reaches for the unnameable. The imagery of the passage suggests that the text locates this unnameable liberating something in the mad woman's mind as well as in her body, precisely where Ka'aban patriarchy locates its most secret and most terrible fear:

> For the first time, something will be created out of nothing. There is not a drop of water, not a blade of grass, not a single word.
> But they [the bones of the dead women] move.
> And they rise. (181)

Irene's dream uses one of the stock tropes of horror fiction, the rise of the living dead, for an image of hope for the female body-community. The title of the book, *The Two of Them*, which in the beginning seems to refer to Ernst and Irene, by the end has shifted to the intimate relationship between the two women. Thus, it is not the physical removal that rescues Zubeydeh and simultaneously also Irene, but her actively accepting the lesbian continuum. The two women break with their loyalty to patriarchal structures, which are predicated upon isolating women from other women.

The Two of Them thus interweaves the stories of two female protagonists, Irene and Zubeydeh, who both start out insisting on their individuality and uniqueness but through their interactions come to appreciate the political potential of recognizing commonalties. It is, in other words, precisely the interactions between fundamental (cultural) differences which instigate the creation of the body-community across cultural and age boundaries. *The Two of Them*, in similar ways to *The Female Man*, thus enters highly contested and contradictory discursive grounds. The contradiction is between the desire to identify individual women as exceptional, that is distinct from other women, and the political need to build a community of ordinary women which levels out distinctions among them. Both novels negotiate these irresolvable contradictions through conjuring up the ghosts of women from patriarchal literature. Russ thus derives oppositional force from acknowledging a lineage of exceptional women, but her texts simultaneously also question discourses of exceptionality.

Beauty Awake: Re-reading the Male-defined Female
(*The Female Man* and *On Strike Against God*)

> The insistence that authors make up their own plots is a recent
> development in literature; Milton certainly did not do it ... It's
> a commonplace that bad writers imitate and great writers steal
> ... nothing flowers without a history (Russ, *To Write Like a
> Woman*, 86)

Trained in the conventions of genre writing, Russ works without
romantic illusions about originality and individual creation. *The Two
of Them* weaves an effective fabric from fragments of borrowed stories
about women, participating in discourses which emphasize the political impact of a female body-community. In my discussion of this broken fabric, I focused on the most obvious and *acknowledged*
intertextualities in the novel, untangling some of the intertwined stories. This process of untangling also made apparent the ways in
which the intertexts partially interfere with the essentialist-feminist
agenda. Yet these interferences or undesired implications of the patriarchal stories ultimately also work for the text as a whole because
they ensure that the coalition with monolithic essentialism remains a
partial affiliation. In positioning women's bodies and women's stories as primary to the narrative, *The Two of Them* thinks essentialist
strategies to their logical conclusion, but does not create closure at
this point. The text moves on.

Although *The Two of Them* creates the most elaborate fabric of
woman-based intertextualities, Russ began to develop this strategy
early in her career as a writer. In my analysis of the early short story
'My Dear Emily' I have already discussed her use of such intertextualities. My reading related this story to Mary Shelley's *Frankenstein*
and the names of the protagonists, Emily and Charlotte, to the Brontë
sisters. There is no stability in this lineage since the names also evoke
the writers Emily Dickinson and Charlotte Perkins Gilman. Later
texts of Russ's explicitly feminist period specifically weave in patriarchal stories of women in their narratives. This section will discuss
how *The Female Man* and *On Strike Against God* implement and transform the stories of women characters whose creation goes back to
ancient oral traditions, similar to those that were the basis for *The
Arabian Nights*, and some of which have become stock characters in
literature. In this discussion, I will re-examine the biblical stories of
Jael and Ruth, and will explore how Russ's texts make use of the fem-

inist potential of such characters as Brynhild and Sleeping Beauty.

Brynhild or Brunhild is a character from the *Nibelungenlied*, a heroic epic written in the early thirteenth century, but drawing on a much older oral tradition. Her supernatural physical strength is tied to her virginity. I would argue that all women characters in the Western literary tradition who are represented as powerful as long as they stay away from romance with men are direct relations of Brynhild. Irene Adler exemplifies this tradition. Yet Brynhild does not give up her virginity as readily as Irene does. Only through deception and with the help of Siegfried, who makes himself invisible with a magic hood and wrestles her down, can her husband win her agreement to copulate with him. The act of penile penetration deprives her of her magic powers. Jael in *The Female Man*, whose powers also lie in her physical strength, identifies with the virginal Brynhild: 'I tied my first sparring partner in enraged knots, as Brynhild tied up her husband in her girdle and hung him on the wall ...' (192). Jael is able to retain her virginity, if 'virginity' denotes the state of someone whose hymen was never destroyed by the entering penis of a male, as it does in compulsory heterosexuality. However, she does not have sex with women either, since, as she points out, she is 'an old-fashioned girl' (196). Her sexual partner is an android, a machine in the shape of a beautiful, blue-eyed, blond youth: 'He's a lovely limb of the house. The original germ-plasm was chimpanzee, I think, but none of the behavior is organically controlled any more' (199).

With her reference to the legend of Brynhild, Jael as a narrator unravels one of the foundational narratives of patriarchy: the woman relinquishes all of her power in the act of heterosexual intercourse. The content of this myth, however, is generally obscured in dominant discourse by promises of romantic love or motherhood (as it is in Irene's case in *The Two of Them*). The legend of Brynhild therefore represents an interstice in the fabric of patriarchal discourse, one of those loopholes in the system which make the development of a subversive feminist counter-discourse possible. The story of Jael, as a stage in the development towards a feminist utopia, uses this gap and maps out an escape route for women from the disempowering, deflowering penetration.

Joanna, one of whose alter-egos Jael represents, takes a different course, since she, in contrast to Jael, disrupts the power of compulsory heterosexuality: 'Brynhild hung her husband on a nail in the wall, tied up in her girdle as in a shopping bag, but she, too, lost her strength when the magic shlong got inside her' (*The Female Man*, 207). Accepting the whole story of Brynhild, Joanna both connects to and distances herself from Jael. While Jael speaks with anger and pain, Joanna is free to be quite irreverent, and can therefore also rewrite the story of Brynhild: she names her erotic fantasies about her girlfriend-to-be Laura Rose 'Brynhildic' (208). A Brynhild who sleeps with women keeps her strength, a story which quite upsets the heroic fabric of the *Nibelungenlied*. Thus, the novel evokes the heterosexual configuration just to break the stifling power it exerts over all protagonists with the exception of the utopian woman Janet.

What renders this process of reshaping patriarchal stories so powerful is that it does not rely on the utopian vision of a fixed space beyond patriarchy, but remains within the logic of patriarchal discourse. Merely denying the validity of such stories, as many radical feminist utopian visions do, precludes the creation of alternative stories. The available languages are, after all, patriarchal symbolic systems and need to be subverted because there is nothing to replace them with. Consequently, Russ's subversions work with the assumption that a utopian space beyond the existing social and symbolic systems is unreachable. Once more, it is the combination of different, even contradictory, intertextualities that ultimately allows her fiction to stay clear of each of these links' inherent determinism.

Russ thus uses Brynhild in the *Nibelungenlied* as a resource for a woman-based rereading of patriarchy. Another such resource in her work is the Bible, also a text which preserves an older oral tradition, presumably from a time when patriarchy as we know it took its shape. As in the legend of Brynhild, *The Female Man* seeks interstices in the biblical discourse which enable Russ to re-interpret the images of women produced by the Bible. Joanna as speaking subject refers to a female prophet and judge in the Old Testament, whose story is also significant for Jael: 'I won't tell you what poets and prophets my mind is crammed full of (Deborah, who said 'Me, too, pretty please?' and who got struck with leprosy)' (136). Deborah in Judges 4 and 5 leads the Israelites in a successful revolt against Canaanite domination and refers to another Israelite woman, Jael, in her song of victory. Jael kills the leader of the Canaanites, Sisera, thus ending the struggle against the oppressors:

> Judges 4:
> Then Jael Heber's wife took a nail of the tent, and took an hammer in her hand, and went softly unto [Sisera], and smote the nail into his temples, and fastened it into the ground: for he was fast asleep and weary. So he died.

Judges 5: 24–27 [from Deborah's song of victory]
Blessed above women shall Jael the wife of Heber the Kenite
be, blessed shall she be above women in the tent. [Sisera]
asked water, and she gave him milk; she brought forth butter
in a lordly dish. She put her hand to the nail, and her right
hand to the workmen's hammer; and with the hammer she
smote Sisera, she smote off his head, when she had pierced
and stricken through his temples. At her feet he bowed, he fell,
he lay down: at her feet he bowed, he fell: where he bowed,
there he fell down dead. (King James Version)

When Jael, who is also the speaking subject at that point, kills Boss,
she uses a direct quote from Deborah's song of victory, thus confirm-
ing the immediate connection to her biblical namesake:

He fell on me (you don't feel injuries, in my state) and I
reached around and scored him under the ear, letting him
spray urgently into the rug; he will stagger to his feet and fall,
he will plunge fountainy to the ground; at her feet he bowed,
he fell, he lay down; at her feet he bowed, he fell, he lay down
dead. (182)

In the Bible, the prophetess Deborah and the killer Jael do act, but
they act in concert with the patriarchs of their own clan against an
outside enemy. Deborah is a wise woman, respected for her abilities
as a judge, yet she defers to 'the law of the father' and to Barak, the
patriarch. Relating Jael to women rather than to another male authority, *The Female Man* effectively reconstitutes Jael as a warrior in her
own right.

The Bible itself invites such a subversive rereading, narrating as it
does two versions of Sisera's death which contradict each other in
several instances. Deborah's song of victory, attributed to Deborah
herself, gives a much more detailed account of the killing, which—
most importantly—does not mention that Sisera was asleep when
Jael killed him. On the contrary, since he 'fell down' dying, he cannot
have been in a horizontal position previously. Deborah's version
allows room for a Jael who actually fights against Sisera, instead of
coming to him 'softly' and killing him in his sleep. This biblical reference therefore author-izes women on yet another level: Deborah is
one of the few women in the Bible who is an acknowledged author of
part of the holy text. Again, Russ subtly creates a subtext of female
authorship.

The Female Man takes this hidden story of the warrior woman, narrating a new Jael who acts of her own accord. The new Jael's companions in struggle are members not of a patriarchal clan, but of a
nation of women who defy patriarchy. This partial restaging of the
biblical story assigns men collectively the role of the Canaanites,
whose irrevocable fate it is to lose, while the Israelites, the women,
must win by historical necessity. This analogy shows the particular
force of this kind of reference to the Bible in an American context. One
of the core narratives of justification in the development of American
democracy is based on a typological reading of the Bible. This reading identifies the new Americans with the Jews in the Old Testament,
who escaped oppression in Egypt by fleeing to the Promised Land.
However, while in their journey to Canaan, a patriarch, Moses, leads
the Israelites to freedom, in Judges 4 and 5, two women finalize their
liberation, one of them brutally killing the leader of the opposing
army. Thus reconstituting a core American cultural narrative, Russ's
text once more confronts patriarchy where such a confrontation is
most effective: on its own ground.

In *On Strike Against God* (1980),⁵ linking female characters to other
women on every level of experience has become the leading principle.
This novel makes the re-creation of the Bible even more explicit than
The Female Man: 'Queen Esther, my namesake, got down on her knees
to save her people, which is no great shakes, but Ruth—whose name
means Compassion—said Whither thou goest, I will go too. *To her
mother-in-law*' (*On Strike Against God*, 24, italics in original). Ruth in the
biblical book of the same name indeed loves the mother of her late
husband so much that she decides to stay with her, but she submits
herself to the law which makes her the property of her dead husband's nearest male relative and becomes Boaz's wife. Similarly, in
the Book of Esther, it is Vashti, King Ahasuerus's first wife, who
defies patriarchal power and is divorced to set an example for all the
would-be-wanton wives in the kingdom. Russ's text refers to Esther
who in the Bible replaces the transgressor and becomes Ahasuerus's
wife—and proceeds to fulfil this role to his complete satisfaction.
Thus, *On Strike Against God* uses a new, quite different pattern of
relating to women and images of women to the earlier novel: while
the intertextual references in *The Female Man* still look for strong
women as role-models, the references in *On Strike Against God* seek
out the 'weak' and the 'collaborators' to listen to *their* voices and
stories.

In its reference to the biblical Esther, *On Strike Against God* makes use of the contradictions within patriarchy by pitting science against biblical and literary discourse:

> Big news for all the Esthers and Stellas in the audience—your name means 'star.' Forget Hollywood. Stars, like women, are mythologized out of reality. For example, the temperature at the core of Y Cygni ... is thirty-two million degrees Centigrade ... If you're really ambitious, you might try to be a nova ... Moreover, a supernova is visible from Earth every three centuries and we're about due for one. Just think: *You might be it.*
>
> Did you hear that, Marilyn? Did you hear that, Natalie, Darlene, Shirley, Cheryl, Barbara, Dorine, Lori, Hollis, Debbi? Did you hear that, starlets? You needn't kneel to Ahasuerus. You needn't be a burnt offering like poor Joan. Practice the Phoenix Reaction and rise perpetually from your own ashes!—even as does our own quiet little Sun, cozy hearthlet that it is, mellow and mild as a cheese, with its external temperature of 6000 degrees Centigrade (just enough to warm your hands at) and its perhaps rather dismaying interior, whose temperature may range anywhere—in degrees Centigrade—from fifteen to twenty-one million. The sun's in its teens, fifteen to twenty-one. The really attractive years. The pretty period.
>
> And that, says *my* bible, is what they mean by my name. That's an Esther. That's me. (24–25, italics in original)

Using scientific discourse, the text turns images of weakness into images of immense power. The conventional star metaphor's vehicle is the star as an innocuous, cold and passive entity, something to behold and admire from a distance, a thing without a life of its own. In this passage, the speaking subject uses scientific knowledge, also produced by patriarchy, to claim the star as an image of power and action, in command of a vast amount of energy. Even the sun, conventionally a symbol of absolute (masculine) power and the energy source for all life on this planet, is just a 'cozy little hearthlet' by comparison. In this passage, the narrator also sends out an appeal to an imaginary 'audience', which is not addressed as gender-class, but as a group of individual women, referred to by name. The listed names echo the names of Hollywood stars such as Marilyn Monroe, Natalie Wood and Shirley Maclaine, those emblems of the 'feminine' role which is continuously recreated in infinite variations by the media.

On Strike Against God thus supplements the materialist feminist rhetoric of class warfare by a language of personal relations which refers to a community based on shared womanhood. Russ's text extends this textual community of women to the projected reader in the text, who is also constructed as female (see also Lefanu, 178). Russ's writing therefore becomes more and more woman-centred through what I call her 'explicitly feminist' phase which approximately spans the 1970s. Her work increasingly represents or projects protagonists, narrators and fictional authors as female. The readers are addressed as (white American middle-class) women. Men appear relegated to a passive position in which not only are they denied their own voice in the text, they are also barred from the text as readers.

Such strategies of empowerment and exclusion show how Russ's writing is contiguous with the feminist moment that Julia Kristeva identifies with a cyclical notion of time. Diverse feminist texts such as Mary Daly's classics *Gyn/Ecology* (1978) and *Pure Lust* (1984) as well as Adrienne Rich's influential essay 'Compulsory Heterosexuality and Lesbian Existence' (1980) all participated in this moment. Cyclical time corresponds to a notion of history which allows contemporary feminist writers to connect to women's experience across time, regardless of historical and cultural differences. Since history in such writing does not progress along a straight line, feminist utopian visions affiliated with this moment, such as Daly's and to some extent Rich's, privilege space over time to metaphorically mark their distance to patriarchy. Russ's utopia Whileaway, which stands at the beginning of her explicitly feminist phase, exemplifies her position as participant in both moments: Whileaway exists in the future, but also in another, parallel universe.

Furthermore, this moment in feminist literary criticism shows a primary concern with plot, that is with stories about women and women's life stories. Russ's essays in Susan Koppelman's *Images of Women in Fiction* (1972) attest to this concern. Reading the stories of the Brynhilds in patriarchal literary tradition from the position of this type of feminism maps out a simple strategy of resistance: the refusal to relate to men on a sexual-emotional level. An Irene Adler who simply says 'no' to the advances of Godfrey Norton would make a formidable foe for Holmes. Killing the male lover, as Irene does, has a similar effect. In 'What Can a Heroine Do', Russ points out that while the literary tradition is full of images of women, there are no 'Women who have no relations with men (as so many male characters in American literature have no relations with women)' (81). Within the logic of this feminist moment, one can extrapolate from Brynhild's story why this may be so. Women without men are just too dangerous.

In order to authorize or empower women as writers, narrators, readers or characters in her fiction, Russ activates intertextual links to both feminist and patriarchal stories. A plot of liberation which operates within her text is the 'rescue of the female child', an important topos in feminist utopian writing, particularly writing affiliated with Kristeva's second moment, feminism which focuses on sexual difference rather than equality.

CHAPTER FIVE
Patterns of Innocence:
The Rescue of the Female Child

> If women are the earliest sources of emotional caring and physical nurture for both female and male children, it would seem logical, from a feminist perspective at least, to pose the following questions: whether the search for love and tenderness in both sexes does not originally lead toward women; *why in fact women would ever redirect that search*; why species-survival, the means of impregnation, and emotional/erotic relationships should ever have become so rigidly identified with each other; and why such violent strictures should be found necessary to enforce women's total emotional, erotic loyalty and subservience to men—Adrienne Rich ('Compulsory Heterosexuality', 637, italics in original)

Rich's 'lesbian continuum' incorporates multiple forms of woman–woman relationships that give first priority to emotional links to women. This community of women differs significantly from the materialist notion of a sex-class, revealing as it does the intimate connection between women's role in reproduction and compulsory heterosexuality. Patriarchal discourse, according to Rich, has produced a social system of coercion, which demands that women form primary relationships with men and sever their original ties to the mother. The different ways of associating with women covered by the lesbian continuum reach from rediscovering images of women in literature and history/historiography (as delineated above) to revealing the possibility of erotic relationships among women. Joanna Russ's texts experiment on this continuum, exploring the liberatory potential of consciously inhabiting the female body and connecting to others—precisely because this body is produced and reproduced by the patriarchal discourses that feminist thinking seeks to disrupt.

In her essay 'Recent Feminist Utopias' (1981) Russ identifies a theme in contemporary feminist utopian writing which she calls 'the rescue of the female child' (79). In these utopias, the following narrative pattern emerges: an older woman, who has struggled to an awareness of her position within a patriarchal culture, rescues a younger woman or girl from her initiation into a mature life fully determined by patriarchy. Russ explains this pattern:

> Puberty is an awakening into sexual adulthood for both sexes. According to Simone de Beauvoir in *The Second Sex*, it is also the time when the prison bars of 'femininity,' enforced by law and custom, shut the girl in for good. Even today entry into woman's estate is often not a broadening-out (as it is for boys) but a diminution of life. Feminist utopias offer an alternative model of female puberty, one which allow [sic] the girl to move into a full and free adulthood. All the novels described [in 'Recent Feminist Utopias'] not only rescue the girl from abuses which are patriarchal in character; they provide something for her to go to, usually an exciting and worthwhile activity in the public world. (80)

This rescue pattern is one of the most pervasive themes throughout Russ's own writing. From 'Bluestocking' (1967), which I have already discussed, to 'The Little Dirty Girl' (1982) and 'The Mystery of the Young Gentleman' (1982), her texts continually rework this narrative pattern, which spans a whole range of possibilities along the lesbian continuum.

Russ's critique of patriarchy in this vein intersects with psychoanalysis in significant ways, even though she severely attacks the policing effect of traditional psychoanalytic therapy. It was psychoanalytic discourse which articulated the different psychosexual development of boys and girls. According to classical psychoanalysis, a woman's life is structured around the demands of heterosexuality and reproduction: via 'penis envy' and her role in the Oedipus complex, the little girl supposedly shapes her feminine identity, simultaneously dissociating herself from and identifying with the mother. Her adolescence is determined by her first menstruation (which makes her a potential mother) and she reaches 'sexual maturity' when she is ready for her first *heterosexual* genital contact and thus able to bear a child. The structuring events for the mature woman are marriage (or a similar relationship with a male), child-birth and menopause. The key event for the male adolescent, on the contrary, is his first (self-induced) ejaculation (Person, 623). The resolution/repression of the Oedipus complex, which for the girl is characterized by lack and loss, confers the power of the father to the son, a power which is confirmed through marriage (or a similar form of ownership-relation to a woman). Thus, the moments of decreasing power for the female as constructed by patriarchy are the moments which empower the male. Brynhild's penis envy results in her *desiring* the male to deflower her; safely hooked to a penis, she ceases to inspire fear.

Within the logic of psychoanalysis, these mechanisms make heterosexuality crucial for the functioning of patriarchal societies. From this perspective, lesbianism, since it disrupts normative heterosexuality, emerges as a powerful threat to male hegemony. The site of the threat, however, is not sexual intercourse between women, but the conscious decision to put men second and to primarily associate with women. In her novel *On Strike Against God*, Russ characterizes this particular weak spot in patriarchy as follows: 'Sleeping with women is all right if it's just play, but you must never let it interfere with your real work, which is sleeping with men' (85).

Kathleen Spencer in her thoroughly researched essay 'Rescuing the Female Child: The Fiction of Joanna Russ' (1990) expands on Russ's own definition of this feminist rescue motif in her analysis of selected novels and short stories. Spencer's article, which originated in a paper presented at the Popular Culture Association Convention in 1988 (184, n. 1), marks a significant shift in Joanna Russ scholarship towards the end of the 1980s. Together with Sarah Lefanu's seminal chapter on Russ in *In the Chinks of the World Machine* (1988), it moves the focus of attention away from the search for wholeness and unity towards acknowledging the remarkable complexity of Russ's oeuvre. However, while Lefanu celebrates the deconstructive elements in Russ, Spencer expresses her puzzlement: 'This is another of those uncomfortable books which Russ regularly produces, her analysis of the sex-gender system increasingly complex' (178). The categories Spencer establishes in her article serve to contain and control these disturbing complexities:

> In Russ's fiction, the rescuer is always a woman in early middle age (35-45 years old); the child is either about 12 (that is, on the edge of puberty), or more commonly, about 17 (on the edge of sexual awakening). (167)

Leaving aside her problematic placement of the age of 'sexual awakening' for the moment, I agree with Spencer about the significance of this narrative pattern for a reading of Russ's fiction. This pervasive rescue motif consistently rests on an intimate intergenerational relationship between a mature woman and a young girl which also has erotic overtones. According to Spencer, five stages of increasing complexity can be identified:

(1) physical removal from a patriarchal culture ('Bluestocking', *The Two of Them*);
(2) rescue from the psychological crippling in patriarchy (*Picnic on Paradise, The Two of Them*);
(3) rescue from 'compulsory heterosexuality' (*The Female Man*);
(4) rescue of the younger self ('The Little Dirty Girl');
(5) rescue of the mother ('The Autobiography of My Mother').

As useful as such a delineation undoubtedly is, it also conceals significant overlaps—and complexities that are relevant for my readings in this study. Most of the identified elements are simultaneously present in Russ's stories of mutual rescue, and I would even argue they are present in most if not all intimate relationships between women in Russ's texts. Alyx in 'Bluestocking', for example, does facilitate Edarra's physical escape from marriage and virtual or even literal death, yet the text does not create an imaginary 'elsewhere' outside patriarchy where the two could go after a rescue from the 'patriarchal culture'. As they turn towards each other, Edarra becomes both Alyx's younger self and her daughter, who in turn can 'rescue' the elder from her isolation as exceptional woman. Similarly, when Irene rescues Zubeydeh from Ka'abah in *The Two of Them*, she has to do more than just physically remove the girl from the restrictive culture, since the value system and patterns of behaviour of this culture are etched into the young Ka'aban's mind. Again, the destination of their escape is not a clearly female space free of patriarchal impurities (although Irene's final dream projects the desire for such a space), but another patriarchal culture with which both have to contend.

In her readings of the individual texts, however, Spencer does account for some of the ambiguities that remain unaccounted for by her categorization. She points out the reciprocity of the relationship between Irene and Zubeydeh (as well as of all other such rescue operations): 'If Irene clearly rescues Zubeydeh, Zubeydeh also in a sense rescues Irene' (178). Yet although Spencer mentions the reciprocity of the process, her categories retain the (ultimately patriarchal) idea of the unilateral rescue operation, which the text already transcends.

Moreover, Spencer tacitly accepts the conventional structuring of a woman's life by placing the edge of sexual awakening at the age of seventeen, which coincides with the age at which a young woman becomes a potential bride in a capitalist patriarchy. Seventeen is not the age when the girl's own sexual feelings 'awaken', but the time when her body is mature enough to conceive and bear a child. It is about the time when the Prince can finally kiss Sleeping Beauty awake into motherhood. 'Sexual awakening' in this definition thus equals the first genital contact with a person of the opposite sex and positions the woman as a womb ready to receive the inseminating penis. Spencer inadvertently reinscribes the very categories of patriarchy that the liberatory politics of her essay aim to displace. Zubeydeh at the age of twelve is far from being asexual:

> Irene feels small fingers on her face. Zooby-dooby has sat up and is saying in a shocked tone, 'Why, Irene, you're *crying.*' Zubeydeh flings herself into Irene's lap, a little too actively compassionate for comfort. The kisses are nice, but the knees and elbows dig in. (*The Two of Them*, 155, italics in original)

Although Zubeydeh rejects an overtly sexual relationship to Irene, she is certainly aware of the possibility: 'I don't think you and I should get into an arrangement like that because we're friends and I would hate to do anything that would put our friendship in jeopardy' (156). Irene suppresses a snicker about the cliché but is quick to agree: 'Zubeydeh, dear, I prefer you as my daughter. Truly I do. I'm not one of those ladies [she uses Zubeydeh's term for lesbians], at least I think I'm not, but if you meet one later and want to go away with her, it'll be fine with me. When you're older, I mean' (156). In accepting the lesbian continuum, that is in putting relationships to women first, both Irene and Zubeydeh escape *compulsory* heterosexuality.

These texts operate with the implicit assumption that emotional and erotic relationships to men would become thinkable to the degree in which a culture rejects heterosexuality as the norm. In the story 'Bodies', which is part of Russ's larger project *Extra(Ordinary) People* (1984), Russ envisions the possibility of such a post-patriarchal culture, in which the body has ceased to be the site of power struggle and the basis of social organization. In 'Bodies', paradoxically, the sexual and racial category which the individual's body may fit in patriarchal societies is irrelevant in economic terms as well as in erotic relationships. Yet the characters mimic and parody types from patriarchal times (e.g. the handle-bar moustached cowboy Harriet), again exemplifying the impossibility of imagining a space *completely* beyond. 'Bodies', as Part Three will demonstrate, explores the political potential of camp and other gender incongruities that contradict the identity politics of the female body traced in Part Two. Ultimately, what is representable is not the unspeakable space beyond the entangling web of oppressive mechanisms in patriarchy, but the desire for such an extra-patriarchal space.

In Russ's feminist utopian writing, the rescue of the female child is a topos which addresses such a desire for a space free from oppression, without activating a monolithic narrative of liberation. The recurrent rescue story upturns the relationship between mother and daughter in the patriarchal context, in which the daughter is expected to separate from the mother and simultaneously become like her. By reconstituting women's intergenerational relationships, the rescue story reinforces a girl's emotional tie to a maternal friend, yet resists the daughter's identity with the mother. As the example of Irene and her foster daughter Zubeydeh has shown, accepting the self as 'mother' and recognizing the 'daughter' as independent individual are both inextricably linked to a reconciliation with one's own mother. Irene does not become Rose, Zubeydeh remains distinct from Irene. Yet they connect, effectively shutting men out.

Morlocks, Mothers, Mirrors: 'The Second Inquisition'

In much of Russ's fictional work, the female narrator-protagonist occupies a central position in the text's resistance to patriarchal story patterns. 'The Second Inquisition' (1970) exemplifies this strategy. The short story concludes *The Adventures of Alyx*, yet one looks in vain for a trace of the quick-witted sword-and-sorcery pick-lock—Alyx does not appear as a protagonist or even a minor character in the story. This absence raises the question of why Russ included 'The Second Inquisition' in the collection. Apparently one needs to look for more indirect connecting elements in the text. Russ herself gives the following answer:

> The Second Inquisition *is* an Alyx story—the character in it is Alyx's great-granddaughter. I wanted the stories to form a sort of closed piece, a Klein-bottle thing, with its tail in its mouth, to imply that the protagonist of the Inquisition went on to write the other stories. That's impossible, of course, but I did like the tail-in-mouth effect. (Letter to the author, 21 September 1995, emphasis in original)

Russ here conjures up an image of a paradoxical space which both closes and opens the story sequence as a whole. In 'The Second

Inquisition' itself, only the last sentence conflates the protagonist with the narrators of the other Alyx stories, all of which are told by a covert narrator not involved in the tale. The statement 'No more stories' (192) concludes the text, implying that all the stories were told by a single narrator. Thus, the frame provided by the other texts in the collection opens up a reading of the short story which locates the (partial) 'rescue' of the young woman in the act of narration itself.

However, while the act of narration emerges as pivotal, the bond between two women which the story narrates is what makes this act possible. The two protagonists, an older woman from 450 years in the future and a 16-year-old girl growing up in a nondescript American town in the 1920s, develop a relationship that is both maternal and erotic, although there is no explicit sexuality between the two. Each woman becomes in a way 'mother' to the other. The visitor from the future boards in the house of the narrator's parents in the guise of a circus performer. She is extraordinarily tall and of thoroughly mixed descent (a common device in the science fiction of the late 1960s and early '70s to imply a society in which race has ceased to be a distinguishing factor). Whereas *The Two of Them* narrates the events primarily from the perspective of the older woman, in 'The Second Inquisition' it is the younger woman, as the narrator, who takes centre stage.

The erotic tension between the women is generated by the narrator's desirous gaze at the visitor's body, as the following passage, the very first paragraph in the short story, illustrates:

> I often watched our visitor reading in the living room, sitting under the floor lamp near the new, standing Philco radio, with her long, long legs stretched out in front of her and the pool of light on her book revealing so little of her face: brownish, coppery features so marked that she seemed to be a kind of freak and hair that was reddish black but so rough that it looked like the things my mother used for scouring pots and pans. (165)

The visitor's body as an object of observation thus becomes one of the central themes in the text. The narrator-protagonist repeatedly runs her eyes over the surface of the visitor's body, keeping her under constant surveillance. For example, she reminisces: 'She would lower herself into the chair that was always too small, curl her legs around it, become dissatisfied, settle herself, stretch them out again—I remember so well those long, hard, unladylike legs—and begin again to read' (165–66). When the visitor gets involved with a man, the narrator closely observes their conversation as well as their physical interactions: 'There was a great deal more of the same business and I watched it all, from the first twistings to the stabbings, the noises, the life-and-death battle in the dark' (185).

The text keeps this lavishly detailed description of the visitor's body in tension with an unsettling uncertainty about her physical existence. Disrupting her story, the narrator unexpectedly negates her primary protagonist's presence: 'It was almost a pity she was not really there' (172). This incision in the narrative flow comes precisely at the moment when the text introduces a parallel science fiction story line. The narrator desires to interact with the stranger, who represents a possible escape from her future in male-controlled domesticity. She watches the boarder closely and sneaks by the older woman's room, hoping for a meaningful conversation:

> Sometimes the open book on the bed was Wells's *The Time Machine* and then I would talk to the black glass of the window, I would say to the transparent reflections and the black branches of trees that moved beyond it.
> 'I'm only sixteen.'
> 'You look eighteen,' she would say.
> 'I know,' I would say. 'I'd like to be eighteen. I'd like to go away to college. To Radcliffe, I think.'
> She would say nothing, out of surprise. (171)

This passage makes it uncertain for the first time whether the narrator-protagonist is talking to her own transparent reflection in the windowpanes or to someone who is physically present. The grammatical construction used here suggests repetition ('would talk', 'would say'), but the fact that the dialogue occurs only once contradicts this interpretation. Plausibly, one can only be surprised once by the same incident. From the repetitiveness of everyday life the narrative thus surreptitiously slides towards the subjunctivity of a science fiction story. The ambiguous subjunctive is sustained throughout the section which ends with the statement quoted above: 'It was almost a pity she was not really there' (172). The narrative avoids a clear distinction between 'realistic' discourse and fantasy or science fiction in the text, making the presence and even the existence of the visitor a matter of supreme uncertainty. The text links the material experience of the narrator in her ordinary adolescent life with the excitement of a science fiction plot in which the same young girl participates in a life-and-death struggle of historical significance for a society 450 years in the future. On one hand she is utterly alienated from her own mother, on the other she is able to form emotional and erotic ties to a maternal stranger, who turns out to be a possible far-future progeny of herself.

As in many of Russ's later texts, the narrator, who makes herself part of the story, is endowed with greater control over plot and narration than a conventional 'first-person' narrator. In making the process of creation part of the story, that is in placing a significant part of the story in the narrator's imagination, the text gives her an authority and autonomy that is not available to a narrator who merely recalls events from her own experience and must by implication be controlled by a superior authorial consciousness. This enhanced status of the narrator counteracts the pervasive 'heterosexual' writing plot that subjects a female narrator to a male authorial consciousness (Lanser, *Fictions of Authority*, 34–35), even if the author of the text is a woman.

As in the other Alyx stories, the killing of a man is crucial for the development of the story, but also for the relationship between the two women. The living body of the visitor serves as a major site of the interwoven science fiction plot. As much as the narrator makes the visitor's physical presence unstable, it is nonetheless central to the story. When her opponents in the far future track her down to her hiding place, the agent, who comes alone, invades the innocuous space of a small town dance which the visitor and the narrator are attending together. This agent, for the benefit of the people at the dance, acts as the visitor's cousin. When he shakes her hand in a mock gesture of friendship, he penetrates her palm with a minuscule explosive, which turns her body into a live bomb and is meant to immobilize her. The alien object in her body, which is clearly analogous to the penetrating penis, forces her to act—at least on the surface—as he commands. Only her ingenuity and deviousness allow her to circumvent the power of the penetrator, and only her ability to kill him ruthlessly saves her life:

> When he fell, she kicked him in the side of the head. Then she stepped carefully away from him and held out her hand to me; I gave her the poker, which she took with the folded edge of the tablecloth and reversing it so that she held the cold end, she brought it down with immense force—not on his head, as I had expected, but on his windpipe. (181)

I refer back to the discourses of agency discussed in Part One here to demonstrate the ways in which contradictory concepts of feminist textual politics interlace in Russ's texts. At the same time as the text 'unearths' a female physicality and sexuality independent from opposition to the male, Russ refers to the concept of class struggle, which rests on this opposition. Similarly, the 'unearthed' body does not appear as a rigid and stable whole, but is wrought with uncertainty and remains unstable.

It is at this juncture precisely that I would go beyond Kathleen Spencer's reading of the 'rescue' theme. In none of the cases she analyses is there a clear-cut rescue from a state of oppression to one of freedom. While she does address the complexities and uncertainties of the texts, she expresses her desire for an unambiguously safe haven for the young girl in 'The Second Inquisition' to go to: 'It is an appallingly bleak ending to a remarkable story, one which shifts unpredictably from the discourse of realism to the discourse of SF and back again' (172). Based on this assessment, Spencer describes the rescue of the narrator in this story as abortive: 'In 1970, the attempt to rescue the self can be imagined, but not carried through successfully' (173). While I would concede that one can identify different types of rescue, possibly even a development towards a 'higher degree' of liberation in the later stories, to my mind none of the texts presents an unequivocally successful rescue operation. It is exactly this indeterminacy that shapes the utopian space—the destination of each escape—as a process rather than a stable state of being.

'The Second Inquisition', much like 'Life in a Furniture Store' (1965), utilizes the act of narration as liberatory practice. However, while the narrator in 'Life in a Furniture Store' resorts to ultimate solipsism, the young woman who tells the story of 'The Second Inquisition' creates an enduring link to another woman and envisions a life beyond the limitations of her own. At the end of the story, she faces her parents alone, but she is able to give new shape to the visitor's body through her tale and to envision an undomesticated future for herself: 'Someday I would join a circus, travel to the moon, write a book: after all, I had helped kill a man. I had been somebody' (192). She did not kill the man alone. As in 'Bluestocking' (1967), the two women rely on each other's strength and cooperation.

Physical violence, escape from patriarchal domesticity and storytelling interrelate in complex ways in this short story. A reading in the context of Russ's other texts makes these multilevelled interrelations tangible. In the passage from 'The Second Inquisition' quoted above the maternal friend of the narrator, who also remains a stranger, kills a man from her own culture. The passage repeats a theme in Russ's writing which links androcide, agency and the ability to speak. Once more it is the body, in this case the male body, that serves as the site where these connections are performed. A return to the central killing scene in *The Female Man* highlights the multiple significance of the murderous act and the way in which the woman performs it. Jael, when she kills, routinely bites out her victim's instruments of speech. Matter of factly, she declares: 'the best way to silence an enemy is to bite out his larynx' (*The Female Man*, 182). 'The Second Inquisition' makes the connection between physically destroying the man's ability to speak and his death even more emphatic. The narrator makes a point of expressing her surprise at the fact that, instead of hitting his head, the visitor smashes her opponent's windpipe, effectively silencing him in more than one way. In the chapter on androcide, I pointed out that killing men in this context is by no means an empty image of raving violence, but has a crucial function as a narrative device that confirms or establishes the agency of a female character. The way in which Russ fills the act itself with metaphorical depth adds further weight to this interpretation. Both narratives make the very organ which women had been barred from using central in the death of the man. Significantly, these stories are told by female narrators.

While the story resonates with the voice of a young woman telling her own story, communication between the protagonists is far from being smooth or unbroken. The most significant bond between the two remains unspeakable:

> 'Did you ever think to go back and take care of yourself when you are little? Give yourself advice?'
> I couldn't say anything.
> 'I am not you,' she said, 'but I have had the same thought and now I have come back four hundred and fifty years. Only there is nothing to say. There is never anything to say. It is a pity, but natural, no doubt.' (190)

This passage reveals the narcissistic desire contained in the pedagogical eros which runs through such intergenerational relationships between women. The science fiction element in the story lets the protagonist play out this desire, just to confirm the impossibility of its fulfilment. Moreover, her ineffectual attempt to speak to her own self in the child, who is her 'great-grandmother', also demonstrates the circularity of such time-travel. Although she cannot communicate her knowledge to the girl in which she seeks her self, however, she does enable the girl to speak her own story.

These paradoxical dynamics within Russ's metaphorical mother–daughter bonds further demonstrate how her texts reach into the moment of feminism that radically emphasizes sexual difference. As Mary Daly has pointed out, the metaphor of choice for the feminist movement in history is the spiral, not the circle, which only brings one back to the same. Daly's definition of radical feminism which she gives in the 'First Passage' of *Gyn/Ecology* clarifies how Russ activates this feminist moment in her rescue of the female child theme:

> Radical feminism is not reconciliation with the father. Rather it is affirming our original birth, our original source, movement, surge of living. This finding of our original integrity is re-membering our Selves. Athena remembers her mother and consequently re-members her Self. Radical feminism releases the inherent dynamic in the mother–daughter relationship toward friendship, which is strangled in the male-mastered system. (39)

The woman from the science fictional future in the girl's story attempts such a remembering return to her origin. The impossible point of the operation is to rescue the self in rescuing the other. The text also brings out one of the paradoxes which destabilize the maternal relationship between the two women. While the young girl looks up to the tall and skillful stranger as a maternal role-model, she is herself the foremother of the time-traveller. This reversal flips the two women's roles, the 'mother' becoming the 'daughter' and vice versa.

Like Russ's other stories of rescue, some of which I will discuss in the following sections, 'The Second Inquisition' explores the paradoxical relation of feminism to motherhood, or rather the contradictions between what Adrienne Rich has called 'the institution of motherhood' vs. the 'experience' of motherhood. The two short stories discussed in the following section revisit this site of contest between selfhood and maternal or filial relationships, illustrating how these texts' 'personal' narrative voices correlate with the stories they tell.

My Mother in the Mirror: 'The Autobiography of My Mother' and 'The Little Dirty Girl'

Spanning the crucial decade of the 1970s, Russ published a circle of texts which combine science fictional elements with a personal narrative voice that borrows from autobiographical writing. This circle echoes themes from the earlier short story 'Life in a Furniture Store' (1965) and includes the stories 'Old Pictures' (1973), 'The Autobiography of My Mother' (1975), 'Daddy's Girl' (1975),[1] 'The Little Dirty Girl' (1982), the coming-out story 'Not for Years but for Decades' (1980) and the novel *On Strike Against God* (1980). I have already mentioned Russ's strategy of making a fictional author part of the text as narrator. This fictional author often shares characteristics with Russ herself, sometimes even her name. In Part One, I discussed this narrative device in terms of women's agency as authors. Such an autobiographical or quasi-autobiographical narrative voice in Russ's writing nevertheless also dovetails with creating stories of rescue within what Rich has called the lesbian continuum. For what combines all of these 'autobiographical' texts is that their narratives revisit, or 're-member' in Daly's terms, the self and/or the mother as a child. Among the stories mentioned above, 'The Autobiography of My Mother' and 'The Little Dirty Girl' most explicitly deploy and reformulate the rescue of the female child as a theme. Like 'The Second Inquisition' these two short stories connect the rescue of the self to a reconciliation with the mother and motherhood.

Kathleen Spencer reads 'The Autobiography of My Mother' as another story of failed rescue (176), but I would argue that such a reading passes over the multiple liberatory power of the text. Since absolute 'liberation' is utterly impossible, partial 'failure'—if that term applies at all—is always part of the paradoxical project of feminism. Indeed Russ's reformulations of the rescue motif question the usefulness of imagining such a completely non-patriarchal space. Furthermore, in my interpretation it is not so much the mother, as Spencer suggests, but the narrator herself who ultimately becomes the escapee. She 're-members' her (narrated) self through her own narrative.

The narrator in 'The Autobiography of My Mother' represents a series of scenes in which she encounters her own mother in various stages of the mother's life. Through telling the story of these encounters, the narrator, as fictional author, rewrites the story of her own self. Of course such an encounter is impossible in autobiography, but science fiction is a more pliant genre. Although the narrator's ability to travel freely through time is not explained, the narrative follows basic science fictional premises about time-travel. It is these conventions (and plain logic) which highlight the narrator's dreadful dilemma.

She desires to protect her mother from a denigrating life in marriage, a life which forces her to abandon ambitions of becoming a poet, but if the narrator were to succeed in this 'rescue', she would instantaneously destroy herself. Paradoxically, the precondition of her own existence is her mother's succumbing to the very situation from which the narrator desires to rescue her, namely motherhood as institution. Thus, the interactions with her mother are fraught with contradictions and ambivalent emotions, which the narrator frames in an ironic reference to the cliché values of white suburban domesticity with which her mother had brought her up:

> 'Consider what you gain by not marrying,' I said. We walked out onto Columbus Avenue. 'All this can be yours.' (Be the first one on your block; astonish your friends.) I told her that the most sacred female function was motherhood, that by her expression I knew that she knew it too, that nobody would dream of interfering with an already-accomplished pregnancy (and that she knew that) and that life was the greatest gift anybody could give, although only a woman could understand that or believe it. I said:
> 'And I want you to take it back.' (209–10)

The distinction between the narrator and the other woman breaks down in similar ways to those in 'The Second Inquisition'. The mother is chronologically the narrator's senior, but through the text's speculative time loop into an imagined past, she is also the child. Temporarily merging the two female protagonists enables the narrative to reconstitute the relationship between them. Unlike in Gertrude Stein's *Autobiography of Alice B. Toklas*, in which authorial consciousness and narrator are clearly distinct if interwoven, the narrator of 'The Autobiography of My Mother' modulates between becoming the mother and being herself. She does not speak for her mother, she becomes her mother.

In Lacanian psychoanalysis, upon entering the 'symbolic order', the language and social structure of patriarchy, the child is forced to repress the imaginary bond to the mother. Since in theory the heterosexual model is absolute, this means that the female loses the possibility of establishing physically and emotionally intimate bonds to women. While the little girl now becomes the mother to desire the father, the boy enters the Oedipal triangle and, repressing it, matures to desire women. Reaching back into her mother's childhood, the narrator in 'The Autobiography of My Mother' seeks an alternative to this identity (sameness) with the mother. Reconstituting this link to the mother through her narrative then allows the daughter to initiate a process of individuation that enables rather than precludes love. In order to be able to find the mother as a person, the narrator strips her of institutionalized motherhood, turning her into a little child:

> I was visiting friends in Woodstock; you may find it surprising that I met my mother there for the first time. I certainly do. She was two years old. My mother and I live on different ends of a balance; thus it's not surprising to find that when I'm thirty-five she's just a little tot. (206)

The narrator seeks to recover her mother's original self in the child, yet the necessary reconciliation is not only with the mother as a person, but with the concept of motherhood itself.

Once more, Adrienne Rich's categories become productive points of intersection in exploring Russ's feminist narrative strategies. In *Of Woman Born* (1976), Rich draws a clear distinction between the 'experience' or potential of motherhood and the patriarchal institution of motherhood, which is useful in this context. As Rich points out, 'All human life on the planet is born of woman' (11). Yet, in 'the most fundamental and bewildering of contradictions, [motherhood as institution] has alienated women from our bodies by incarcerating us in them' (13). What links Russ to Rich here is that her short story fictionalizes precisely the paradoxical split of motherhood into institution and lived experience which Rich's analysis makes explicit as vital in the struggle for/with the female body. The institution of motherhood forces the mother to give up her own ambitions to give birth to her daughter.

In Part One, I demonstrated how Russ dismantles motherhood as patriarchal institution through artificial reproduction, which serves as a foundation in her feminist utopian vision very much like in Firestone's study *The Dialectic of Sex*. However, artificial reproduction, while it frees the woman of motherhood as a mechanism of control over her body, ultimately does not face the feelings of pain and guilt in which this institution entangles women. Explaining sex-class, gender and reproduction in economic terms, as Firestone did, can tell only one of many stories that make up the kaleidoscope of cultural meaning. For the institution of motherhood generates feelings of resentment and loss between mothers and daughters which the same institution requires them to deny.

'The Autobiography of My Mother' shows both mother and daughter caught in such strangling webs of guilt and self-denigration. In a series of unconnected scenes the narrator and her mother enact a variety of possible relations between women. The narrator encounters the mother as an infant, as a younger sister at play, as a niece, a cousin, a stranger, a lover. She meets her in a restaurant when she is 19: 'At that time I wasn't born yet. I'm not even a ghost in her thought because she's not going to get married or even have children; she's going to be a famous poet' (208). The narrator's mother does not become a poet. Instead, she gives birth to the narrator. Whether or not the two events are causally linked is irrelevant, since the institution of motherhood predetermines that connection. Put simply, the mother exists to give her life to her offspring. She feels guilty because her self-effacement cannot be complete, and she is resentful because of the opportunities she lost and the creative potential she wasted.

Telling the speculative tale of her mother's original child self, however, transforms the narrator's relationship to her mother, releasing both positive and negative emotions between the two from their institutionalized prohibitions. She faces and demystifies the animosities between herself and the image she has of her mother, at least on the level of narrative:

> An unspoken rule between us has been that I can hate her but she can't hate me; this breaks ...
>
> 'I think,' says my mother thoughtfully ... 'that I'm going to get married.' She looks at me, shrewdly and with considerable hatred.
>
> '*That way,*' she says in a low, controlled voice, '*I will be able to get away from you!*' (214, italics in original)

The narrator also moves beyond facing the hatred between herself and her mother and braves another hideous taboo, incestuous love. When the narrator meets her mother as a 19-year-old in a Chinese restaurant, she courts the perplexed young woman with what must be the most ridiculed come-on line of all times: 'Do you come here often?' (209) The tension between the two is erotic enough for the narrator to lapse into ironic denial: 'It may occur to you that the context between us is sexual. I think it is parental' (209). The irony stems from the fact that the two are clearly not mutually exclusive. At 19, her mother is not a mother yet, she is just a young girl with dreams. Staging an encounter with her mother as not-a-mother expresses her desire to see the woman without the barrier of guilt:

> Here's something else I like: when I was twenty-nine and my mother—flustered and ingenuous—told me that she'd had an embarrassing dream about me. Did she expect to be hit? It was embarrassing (she said) because it was incestuous. She dreamed we had eloped and were making love.
> Don't laugh. I told it for years against her. I said all kinds of awful things. (215)

In this rewriting of the Oedipus story, the narrator recalls her mother's dream not as an imaginary scene between a juvenated mother and herself, but as an event from her lived experience. By telling the many stories of female–female relationships, the narrator reinterprets the dream, adding her own incestuous desire to the plot.

The mother's dream thus serves as a point of transition in the short story. The narrated scenes unfold successive stages of liberation away from culturally predetermined and sanctioned paths for the mother–daughter relationship towards recognizing the necessity to love. The text explores the possibility of hating the mother, the luxury of being able to hate the daughter, and the even greater luxury of mutual love. The last sentence in the short story recalls the chorus of a popular song by The Beatles which places the link to the mother in the context of heterosexual romance: 'All you need is love' (217).

Consequently, the liberating potential lies not so much in the plot of rescue, but once more in the act of telling. The daughter cannot literally rescue the child that will become her mother, not even in science fiction. As in 'Life in the Furniture Store', the telling is by no means therapeutic. Psychic health is not an objective. The pivot is power: the power of the narrator to tell her own stories of existence and to experiment with anti-psychoanalytical stories of daughterhood which enable the lesbian continuum, rejecting compulsory heterosexuality.

In this rewriting of the psychoanalytical story of individuation, 'The Autobiography of My Mother' partially reunites the image of the mother with the original goddess. The text thus participates in the feminist search for an unmarred female body through the symbolic power of such a mother-goddess. The end of the short story comes around to a reference to the ancient Babylonian myth of creation, in which Tiamat, the goddess of chaos, is defeated by the male god Marduk. In the *Enuma Elish*, Marduk creates order from chaos and thus becomes the supreme god of the universe. He creates earth and sky by splitting Tiamat's body in two halves. Rosemary Radford Ruether in *Gaia & God* describes Marduk's victory over Tiamat as symbolic for the defeat of the matriarchal idea in this society (16-19). Russ's narrator instead establishes a bodily connection to the mother, going back to a changed myth of creation, in which the male god is displaced by the original mother-goddess:

> This is what comes of re-meeting one's mother when she was only two—how willful she was! how charming, and how strong. I wish she had not grown up to be a doormat, but all the same what a blessing it is not to have been made by somebody's hands like a piece of clay, and then he breathed a spirit in you, etc., so you are clay and not-clay, your ingredients fighting each other like the irritable vitamin pill in the ad—what a joy and a pleasure to have been born, just ordinary born, you know, out of dirt and flesh, all of one piece and of the same stuff She is. To be my mother's child. (Your pleasures and pains are your bellybutton-cord to the Great Mother; they prove you were once part of her.)
> I asked, Why couldn't my mother have been more like You!
> (216)

Having travelled back to the moment when the future mother is just recognizing herself as an individual, the narrator of the short story here expresses the wish that she could interfere with her mother's entrance to the patriarchal symbolic order. But the solipsistic time-traveller cannot change history. What she can do, however, is to manipulate the story she tells. Russ's text provisionally reinstalls the original goddess in the body of the mother and ridicules the Judaeo-Christian male god as supreme symbolic creator. The rule of the mother, assumed to be creative, non-linear and non-repressive, supersedes the law of the father.

The goddess as a symbol corresponds to Rich's concept of the 'experience of motherhood.' The text does not represent maternity as an accessible entity outside patriarchy, but, in a manoeuvre similar to the one which I analysed for such characters as Brynhild, consciously grounds it in existing narratives. Via a narrative reconciliation with the mother and with a reconstituted concept of motherhood, the narrator comes to terms with herself as a daughter. Like 'The Second Inquisition', the story thus transforms and complicates the rescue pattern in various moves of reversal. Ultimately, the rescued 'child' is the adult daughter whose narrative invents a youthful image of her mother and circles back to rescuing herself.

'The Dirty Little Girl' is more solipsistic and direct in disclosing the self as protagonist in its rescue of the female child theme, but the story uses similar time loops back into childhood. This time, however, it is the childhood of the narrator that serves as a point of reference and it is the child who travels to the time and space of her adult self.

This adult is also the autobiographical narrator and fictional author of the story. Her autobiographical narrative voice is enhanced by the fact that she shares a number of central characteristics with the author. Like Joanna Russ, she is a writer, teaches creative writing in Seattle, and has severe, incapacitating chronic back pain. Yet it is crucial to point out that the text is by no means an autobiography. As 'The Autobiography of My Mother' relies on science fictional elements in the development of the narrative, 'The Little Dirty Girl' uses genre elements from fantasy, specifically from ghost stories, which are out of place in clear-cut autobiography. Neither does the story tell an anecdote from the author's, Joanna Russ's, life. But the autobiographical elements in the text lend credibility to the intimately personal narrative voice. Thus identifying the narrator with the author in the text both makes the narrator clearly female and invests her with the authority of an author who writes with confidence of her own life. What is more, the story is framed as a personal letter, which also draws in the reader as female addressee in a circle of intimate communication between women. Thus, the story exemplifies Russ's move towards an ever more personal narrative voice. In this move, major concerns in Russ's oeuvre—particularly after 'When It Changed'—coalesce: writing, reading and reformulating the stories of women's lives, resistances and revolutions.

The severe health problems of the narrator, which link her to the author, also provide the basis for connection and reconciliation with the girl self as the main theme in the story. The first encounter with this girl self combines both the ordinary and the unusual. On a shopping trip, the narrator meets a strange eight-year-old girl, who offers to help her carry her groceries and comes to take up more and more room in her life. Throughout the story, the back pain is always present. The narrative moves from the body of the narrator, via the body of the child, to the body of the mother, to come full circle to a transformed image of the body of the narrator herself.

Going through similar oscillations to the visitor in 'The Second Inquisition', the body of the girl is the site of another transformation. On one hand she is materially and physically present, an unsanitary, smelly child's body. The narrator finds the girl physically repulsive: 'Here was a Little Dirty Girl offering to help me, and smelling in close

quarters as if she hadn't changed her underwear for days: demand-
ingness, neediness, more annoyance' (5). On the other hand, however, the body of the child is also unstable. On each successive visit,
she becomes physically smaller, and the incongruities between the
child's body and her intellectual capabilities become greater. Gradually, the narrator realizes that the girl is a ghost, more specifically the
ghost of her own self which she has rejected, 'messy, left alone,
ignored, kicked out, bedraggled, like a cat caught in a thunderstorm'
(3). The girl's body disappears little by little. Her sometimes unpleas-
ant physical presence is thus accompanied by an almost complete
disembodiment:

> And as surely as A.R. had been a biggish eight when we had
> met weeks ago, just as surely she was now a smallish, very
> unmistakably unnaturally knowledgeable five. But she was
> such a *nice* little ghost. And so solid! ... If the Little Dirty Girl
> was a ghost, she was obviously a bodily-dirt-and-needs ghost
> traumatized in life by never having been given a proper bath or
> allowed to eat marshmallows until she got sick. (13–14, italics
> in original)

The conflict between the narrator and her child-self is resolved
when she embraces the small, dying, dirty body for its own sake,
without the detached sense of utility that had governed their interactions previously. It is not disgust but fear of the alien self that has pre-
vented her from sensually, lovingly accepting her infantile alter-ego: 'I
imagined the Little Dirty Girl sinking her teeth into my chest if I so
much as touched her. Not touched for bathing or combing or putting
on shoelaces, you understand, but for touching only' (16). The
moment they get into bed together to sleep, the externalized self of
the narrator becomes part of her and disappears: 'She said sleepily,
"Can I stay?" and I (also sleepily) "Forever." But in the morning she
was gone' (17). The photograph of the Dirty Little Girl referred to at
the end of the story is the pictorial representation of the narrator's
own aged body.

'But that's not the end of the story' (18), as the narrator points out.
The reconciliation with the self does not conclude the plot. As the
narrator faces her own child-self, she also faces the maternal in herself, and conversely, once she is able to mother her own self, she can
brave the confrontation with her mother:

> Well, this is the woman who came to visit a few weeks later. I

> wanted to dodge her. I had been dodging academic committees
> and students and proper bedtimes; why couldn't I dodge my
> mother? So I decided that *this time I would be openly angry* (I'd
> been doing that in school, too). (18, italics in original)

The mother recognizes the change in her daughter and this recognition triggers her to revisit the narrator's childhood: 'When you were five, I had cancer ... I kept it from you. I didn't want to burden you' (20). Again, it is the mother's physical illness that determines their relationship.

However, these bodily illnesses do not serve as metaphors for the women's psychological condition. Such a reading would reinforce the very dichotomy between the body and the mind which is displaced by the text. Through physical pain and physical pleasure the body manifests itself as material reality. Representations of sickness and sensuality thus reinforce the body's presence in the text. In 'The Second Inquisition' the curious and desirous gaze of the young narrator on the older woman's body, as I have shown, makes a similar connection to the body's materiality that serves as the basis of the story's liberatory impulse. The narrator in 'The Autobiography of My Mother' embraces her own body as part of her self, which in turn enables her to connect with her mother's physical being. Yet Russ once more makes neither rescue nor reconciliation unambiguously complete: 'I wish I could go on to describe a scene of intense and affectionate reconciliation between my mother and myself, but that did not happen—quite' (21).

The narrator's tale thus transforms her own body from an external substance alien or even hostile to her self to an entity which is an integral part of her self. The narrative parallels this transformation in a sustained metaphorical link between her body and the image of a horse. Referring to the time before the Little Dirty Girl came into her life, the narrator explains her physical pain by the way in which she had treated her body as other. She uses the image of a plough horse:

> Besides, that was no worse than my flogging myself through
> five women's work and endless depressions, beating the old
> plough horse day after day for weeks and months and years—
> no, for decades—until her back broke and she foundered and
> went down and all I could do was curse her helplessly and beat
> her the more. (19)

With the wisdom of hindsight, the story makes a causal link between the way in which the narrator treated her body like a utility and her illness. The narrator thus reconnects her physical and her psychological pain, which she represents as caused by the separation of her body from the work of her mind. At the end of the text, however, the plough horse has become the horse of a king and referred to in the first person. Speaking to the addressee of the epistolary text, the narrator concludes the story with a transformed quotation from Shakespeare: 'the one thing you desired most in the world was a photograph, a photograph, your kingdom for a photograph—of me' (22). The quotation here contains a concealed reference to a horse desperately needed by the anonymous recipient of the letter that frames the narrative. The split between the narrator and her body has shifted. The photograph represents not just the body but is represented as a mirror image of the narrator herself.

Both 'The Autobiography of My Mother' and 'The Little Dirty Girl' thus explore the transformative power of storytelling. As the narrators in these texts confront the stories of their own selves, they retell the story of motherhood. In 'The Little Dirty Girl', the rescue of the female child as a plot pattern has moved to the explicit rescue of the narrator's self through her own narrative. The pattern is similar if less explicit in both 'The Second Inquisition' and 'The Autobiography of My Mother'. The impossible desire which all these stories express is ultimately to travel back in time and to rescue the child-self. While the stories confirm the impossibility and paradoxical character of this desire, the potential for 'rescue' pops up in a place different from where the trajectory of desire had seemed to lead the narrators. The act of narration itself turns out to be the site where a more process-oriented kind of rescue can take place. Whereas in these three 'autobiographical' stories, the 'rescued child' is either the narrator or a protagonist, the novel *Kittatinny* brings in the reader as part of this rescue pattern.

Warrior Woman and Girl Love: Kittatinny

Kittatinny was published in 1978 by Daughters Press with illustrations by Loretta Li, as a book for young girls. The protagonist is the eleven-year-old girl Kittatinny who goes on a magical journey through a landscape of rewritten myths and fairy tales. On her journey, Kit meets Taliesin, the beautiful female dragon who gives her the power of the sword, she fights the deadly 'slonches', finds a book which contains an alternative story of the mermaid Russalka, watches the Warrior Woman fight, and finds the real Sleeping Beauty, who is an ageless girl vampire. In an enchanted forest, she picks up the newly born B.B., a satyr who accompanies her on the rest of the trip. B.B. is physically marked as male: 'So Kit was not surprised to see, peeping between the baby's hairy little legs (which he was waving vigorously in the air as if he were on a bicycle) a rod of flesh with a bag of skin under it' (15). The two from then on live a symbiosis: when the girl carries B.B. who lives off her heartbeat, she has no need to eat.

As Kit lives through a succession of adventures, the little satyr becomes more human and grows to be her own size. Eventually, B.B. 'goes out like a candle' (80) and momentarily disappears from Kit's life. Like the visitor in 'The Second Inquisition' and A.R. in 'The Little Dirty Girl', he is slowly revealed as the protagonist's alter-ego, whose physicality and gender are both subject to uncertainty. Returned from her fantastic journey, Kit is startled to find her lost travel companion at her home. He has become fully human, but 'it couldn't be him because this person had bumps on her chest that looked like breasts (and were) and where B.B.'s little flesh-roll had hung between his legs this person had a tidy mound of hair exactly like Kit's' (87). B.B. thus confronts Kit with her own conventional concepts of sex and gender-roles, which have limited her imagination. Only through B.B.'s intervention is Kit able to overcome the cultural restraints her society put on her and to experience the rewritten children's stories:

> B.B. shouted furiously, '*Boy*? I was never a *boy*! What do you mean, *boy*? You're as bad as the master printer with your *boy*! That's all you can think about is *boy*!'
>
> 'Now look here—' Kit said.
>
> 'Look here yourself!' yelled B.B. 'I *told* you about legendary creatures, didn't I? I told you I would turn into whatever you were. Is it my fault you've got stupid ideas and a limited imagination? Is it my fault you think only boys can lose their tempers and have adventures?' (87, italics in original)

B.B. is represented as the part or aspect of Kit's self which rebels against the limitations of patriarchal valley life. At the very moment when the girl chooses the love of the woman Rose Bottom over that of the man Ondry Miller, the text destabilizes the sexed body and the link between masculinity and maleness. As in 'The Second Inquisition', the two selves merge in the mirror image of the protagonist's body: 'Kit put her fingers out to touch B.B.'s and B.B. put *her* fingers out to touch Kit's. Kit's fingers did not meet the faun's. Instead they met a flat surface, hard and cold, like glass' (89, italics in original).

As B.B.'s presence enabled Kit's masculinity, s/he also facilitates the link to the other woman: 'And in spite of Kit's being the adventurous one and Rose the stay-at-home in the lovely dress, they were the same' (86). Although sexual desire is not represented as exclusively directed towards women, the text authenticates/privileges lesbian love over the love of men:

> Kit felt as if B.B. were at her again, though she didn't know why, and she wanted to put her arms around her friend [Rose]—so she did—and then suddenly she felt just as she had with Ondry Miller, which was extremely confusing as you weren't supposed to feel that way with another woman. Only it was coming over her in waves, and this time it wasn't just fun but something that made her heart hurt. And then they were kissing each other, which was worse. Kit kept on kissing the soft skin on Rose's face and neck and feeling Rose's breasts press against her own until the confusion got to be too much, and then she stopped. (86–87)

As the narrative 'rescues' Kit from compulsory heterosexuality, the text opens a door for the reader. The maternal voice of the narrator replaces the plot of heterosexual romantic love and normative female passivity with stories which celebrate women who actively pursue their sexuality and the desire for the female body.

However, as in the other stories of rescue in Russ's oeuvre, *Kittatinny* resists definitive closure and static utopian spaces. The narrator, unapologetically didactic, makes this principle of the shifting, process-oriented utopia explicit in an image that parallels Kit's subversive journey through children's literature: 'once you've changed, you have to go out again on adventures that never end because all of it's an adventure and all of it constantly changes. So there's no home, really, and no end to traveling ...' (92).

In these four representative texts, the short stories 'The Second Inquisition', 'The Autobiography of My Mother' and 'The Little Dirty Girl' and the novel *Kittatinny*, the rescue of the female child is inextricably linked to the narrative act as well as to the act of reading. The reconciliation and connection with other women in these creative acts are not parts of a confessional therapy, but rather assertions of power, specifically the power to endow women's strength and the love of women with symbolic meaning. In these texts, the power to tell one's own story thus correlates with woman's erotic desire for the female body and a reconciliation with motherhood and with the woman who gave birth to the protagonist.

This connection of intergenerational (erotic) tensions and (utopian) desires points to fundamental contradictions within contemporary feminist discourses on sexuality. Intergenerational relationships in Russ's fiction utilize the contradictory nature and instability of the mother–daughter relationship, as the discussion of the 'rescue of the female child' model illustrated. From the perspective of the younger woman, the elder is a mother, a teacher and a role-model, who represents a potential future, as well as the guardian of the past. In patriarchal societies, it is the mother who is positioned to enforce the young woman's initiation to motherhood, and the daughter is always also a potential mother. The image of the mother thus represents both a link with women's history and with feminist utopian desire. Similarly, from the point of view of the older woman, the female child or young woman represents her desires for a changed past, for liberating the child-self from debilitating discourses of the self. The younger woman/girl looks with admiration at the power and independence of the older woman, and the older woman desires to teach and advise the younger woman as her younger self. The following discussion will analyze how the inherent erotic tensions in this intergenerational rescue pattern function in explicitly sexual relationships between women in Russ's work.

CHAPTER SIX
Lesbian Existence: Impossible Dreams of Exteriority

> Let's be reasonable. Let's demand the impossible—Russ, (*On Strike Against God*, 107)

> There is no one person in or out of fiction who represents a stronger challenge to the Judeo-Christian tradition, to patriarchy and phallocentrism, than the lesbian-feminist—Elaine Marks (282)

Radical feminist thinkers affiliated with Kristeva's second moment in feminism, such as Adrienne Rich, Mary Daly or Andrea Dworkin, base their cultural criticism on the idea that heterosexual intercourse serves as one of the central sites of women's oppression in patriarchy. Therefore, from this perspective, it is only from within patriarchal conceptualizations of sexuality that feminist interventions can displace this oppression. As Chapter Five demonstrated, attaining agency does not complete the processes of feminist utopian speculation in Russ's fiction. Russ simultaneously explores how women's economic position in patriarchy is linked to their bodies and their sexuality through a complex system of mutual interaction.

Russ's central 'heterosexual' protagonists, Alyx in the short story collection *The Adventures of Alyx*, Jael in *The Female Man* and Irene in *The Two of Them*, assert their agency by killing a man, but this act by itself does not make these women subjects of their sexual desire. Alyx, the woman who kills a man she hates without so much as winking, she who never hesitates to act, becomes an instrument of her lover's pleasure in copulation:

> 'Forgiven,' Alyx managed to say as he plunged in, as she diffused over the landscape—sixty leagues in each direction—and then turned into a drum, a Greek one, hourglass-shaped with the thumped in-and-out of both skins so extreme that they finally met in the middle, so that she then turned inside-out, upside-down and switched right-and-left sides, every cell,

> both hands, each lobe of her brain, all at once, while someone
> (anonymous) picked her up by the navel and shook her vio-
> lently in all directions, remarking 'If you don't make them cry,
> they won't live.' She came to herself with the idea that
> Machine was digging up rocks. He was banging her on the
> head with his chin. (*Picnic on Paradise*, 121–22)

The narrative of Alyx's own sexual pleasure buries this pleasure in
images of passivity which remove her from her self. Only after what
may be her orgasm does the text have her 'come to herself'. Such passivity, which normative heterosexuality makes necessary for women,
is impossible for Jael. She uses an android for her sexual gratification
not simply because passivity does not turn her on sexually, but also
because compulsory heterosexuality endows each sex act with political significance. Similarly, Irene, once she realizes 'I don't know any
women' (*The Two of Them*, 120), ceases to relate to Ernst sexually. She
'kick[s him] out of bed' (153). Therefore, while killing Ernst affirms
her agency, identifying with the lesbian continuum opens a process
which enables her to decide that heterosexual intercourse impedes
her liberatory political acts: she chooses 'not to'. Since patriarchal
narratives of sexual relations operate in structures of ownership and
submission, female characters' ownership of their own bodies is a
central image in radical feminist rewritings of women's sexuality.
Claiming their bodies as their own by refusing to give men access to
them, celibate and lesbian women in these rewritten stories break up
the complexly interrelated system of patriarchal economics and compulsory heterosexuality, and create a utopian space for a revolutionized concept of sexuality (partially) beyond the gender dichotomy.

Masturbation: My Own Body

> I will tell you my own, recently-developed theory of sexuality,
> proven by years of experimental masturbating: i.e. you feel
> your climax most whenever you are being most stimulated.
> This opens surprising fields of research to those of us with
> suckling infants or three hands or other situations like that.
> Honest (*On Strike Against God*, 55)

This passage from *On Strike Against God* sums up the attitude towards
sexuality implicit in Russ's writing since the 1970s, her 'explicitly
feminist' phase. Participating in the discourse of body ownership,

these texts counter the theories of lack projected by psychoanalysis. Russ's work after 'When It Changed' shifts from an appetitional model of sexuality based on psychoanalysis to a model which untangles sexuality from the system of libidinal economy. In his essay 'Orders of Chaos: The Science Fiction of Joanna Russ', Samuel Delany analyses this central paradigm shift in Russ's writing:

> The model that Russ constructs is a process model: sex is a process that two or more persons of different sexes can assist one another through, that two or more persons of the same sex can assist one another through, or that one can indulge in by oneself. (95)

Delany's analysis, however, does not account for the very different functions which the various types of sexuality, homosexuality, heterosexuality and autosexuality, fulfil in Russ's novels. Moreover, by sweepingly dismissing psychoanalysis as 'clearly unscientific' (122), he overlooks Russ's heavy reliance on the categories of psychoanalysis in the creation of her alternative models.

Autoeroticism in Russ's work is a case in point. Post-Freudian psychoanalytic research has related masturbation in adolescent girls to their sense of autonomy and self-esteem. Clinical evidence shows that girls who masturbate during adolescence are more likely to actively pursue career goals later in their lives, which indicates a close connection between assertiveness and the exploration of sexuality (Person, 624).[1] Again, this is not to say that there is any form of essential or 'natural' tie between agency and autoeroticism but rather that a psychoanalytic view on late capitalist patriarchal culture makes this connection. The interviewees in any research project obviously also operate within the system of dominant cultural narratives. In psychoanalytic discourse, masturbation is also a direct indication of the level of active involvement in sexual intercourse:

> So-called low drive [in women] is manifest in the low rates of female adolescent masturbation, the tendency to tie sexuality to intimacy, and the ability to tolerate anorgasmia. Here the tacit assumption is that male sexuality constitutes the norm and that women perform at a deficit. (Person, 623)

Russ's post-1970 novels clearly respond to this model, constructing images of women who know exactly what they want from sexual encounters because they have claimed their bodies and their sexuality as their own through masturbation.

Dorothy Allison articulates the connection between masturbation and power, sex and agency in her essay 'Puritans, Perverts, and Feminists' published in her essay collection *Skin* (1994), recalling her adolescent reading of science fiction:

> The honest-to-god truth is that I spent most of my adolescence—and I'll admit it, even my twenties—jacking off to science fiction books, marvelous, impossible stories full of struggle and angst.
> As a girl I read Robert Heinlein's *Podkayne of Mars*, C.J. Moore's *Jirel of Joiry*, the Telzey books by James Smith, *More Than Human* by Theodore Sturgeon, and all of the Alyx Stories by Joanna Russ ... I would orgasm to the adventures I conjured up for myself in those worlds, but more important was the constant excited satisfaction of imagining myself so far away and different. (93–94)

What makes masturbation liberatory in these texts is not the act itself, but telling a story about it. Framing the act in a self-affirming narrative, feminist clinical psychoanalysis, Dorothy Allison and Joanna Russ participate in the same feminist oppositional practice.

Russ's novel *And Chaos Died* (1970), on the contrary, still primarily operates with a concept of sexuality which relates masturbation to an immature and unfulfilled love life. The novel creates a voyeuristicly erotic scene between the two protagonists, Jai Vedh and Evne, and another character, in which Jai and Evne observe the other woman's sex play with herself. Because the two protagonists can read the woman's mind, the observation encompasses her accompanying sexual fantasies.

However, one may at the same time read the novel as a site of transition in respect to sexuality. *And Chaos Died* does experiment with gender discontinuities and sexual deviations, disrupting the normative heterosexual plot of romance. Jai Vedh, the main character, similar to Cal in *The Female Man*, does not correspond to conventional concepts of masculinity, particularly in science fiction. Since most of the plot takes place in his mind, his body also remains unstable. Similarly, space and time appear distorted through the narrative. Jai Vedh, as a result of an interstellar accident, encounters a utopian planet whose population has acquired the skill of extra-sensory perception. The social structure on this planet is vaguely matriarchal. Since the inhabitants can manipulate matter with their minds, they can do without technology, which makes the culture seem primitive to an outsider (Delany, 'Orders of Chaos', 113).

Like his body and gender, Jai Vedh's sexuality is unfixed. Although he claims he is homosexual, Evne, who is a genetic surgeon, seduces him effortlessly. In the mid-1970s, Russ playfully disowned the way in which *And Chaos Died* represents homosexuality, but in her most recent stories, such as 'What Did You Do During the Revolution, Grandma?' (1983) or 'Bodies' (1984), she comes back to similar sexual discontinuities. In her review of *The Dispossessed* in *The Magazine of Fantasy and Science Fiction* of March 1975, Russ criticizes Le Guin's heterosexual bias: 'We are told that one (male) character is homosexual: yet he acts asexual' (42). She adds in a footnote: 'A mistake made in *And Chaos Died* by Ross—um—Roos? Rouse? Somehow I forget' (42).

Jai Vedh, however, is far from leading an asexual life. In fact, sexuality constitutes the main theme, the leitmotif, in the novel. But more often than not, the eroticism remains disguised or subdued and the sexual acts discontinued. Evne teaches Jai to develop his own extrasensory powers. Combining their mental capacities, the population of the idyllic planet transport Jai Vedh and Evne to a spaceship bound for Earth. The two end up in a room that belongs to one Mrs Robins, a character reminiscent of Mrs Robinson of *The Graduate*. Jai and Evne are about to make love, when they sense her coming back. In their extra-sensory minds, the image of Mrs. Robins's body appears as an assembly of artificial parts: 'She had milk-blue eyes, cropped straw hair, a butcher's smock, and spiked sandals. She had enormous breasts, two wells of silicone jelly, enormous buttocks, a faked, crowded waist, dyed eyes, dyed hair and no uterus' (93).

Samuel Delany reads Mrs Robins's 'hysterical absence' as a symbol of emptiness, a 'social vacuum' which is 'permanent, unchangeable, appeasable only in fantasy' ('Orders of Chaos', 114). Such an interpretation leaves little room for Mrs Robins's own voice. The culture in which she lives is a dystopian extrapolation from contemporary capitalism in which the alienation of the individual is carried to an extreme. Mrs Robins's name, in addition to its reverberations of sexual frustration and insatiable hunger from the movie, recalls a hero from the very beginnings of capitalism: Robinson Crusoe. Deprived of human relationships, she is alone even if she does leave her insular room. She is completely isolated, and cultural standards of beauty mould her body. Evne senses Mrs Robins's alienation, and her own, Evne's—unalienated—body responds with a violent reaction: she has to vomit. Without invalidating Delany's reading, I would interpret Mrs Robins's body as an emblem not just of emptiness but also of an overload—weighed as it is with the artefacts of a culture that has made the woman's body a commodity.

On entering the room, Mrs Robins immediately assumes that the two nude people have been placed there to perform for her amusement, and she expresses her disappointment when they refuse to do so. Ironically, she ends up performing for them. She takes out an elaborate sex toy, an 'exercycle' designed to assist her in masturbation and proceeds to operate it with determination, while Evne and Jai witness the image of a man forming in the woman's mind:

> The exercise seat plunged and rose, plunged and rose. The woman herself stiffened, knees together.
>
> It was a real, true idea. It was a real thought. It was inside her head. She couldn't think of herself but only of a man, not of her own body, her lovely twin sister, but only of a man who had skin, bones, teeth, fingers, a penis, a brain, and whose lungs were breathing air into her own. (96)

Here, masturbation appears to confirm the woman's alienation from her body. In her imagination, Mrs Robins reproduces sexual intercourse with a man, positioning herself as the passive recipient of pleasure. However, such a reading of Mrs Robins as sexually deprived only confirms the limiting interpretation of the two protagonists through whose voyeuristic eyes the narrator represents Mrs Robins's pleasure. Neither Jai and Evne nor the narrator avert their eyes from the scene which they purportedly disapprove, but rather vicariously savour every detail of the woman's autoerotic pleasures, freely sharing them with the reader. These pleasures are, after all, Mrs Robins's own.

While the narrative of *And Chaos Died* disavows the titillating effect of such scenes of spectatorship and autoerotic pleasure, Russ's later novels, specifically *The Female Man* and *On Strike Against God*, explicitly explore the liberatory potential of masturbation scenes. Sex toys emblematically represent the emancipation of masturbation in Russ's work. On Whileaway, the feminist utopian society in *The Female Man*, girls receive vibrators as gifts in their initiation ceremony:

> these charming dinguses are heirlooms. They are menarchal gifts, presented after all sorts of glass-blowing, clay-modeling, picture-painting, ring-dancing, and Heaven knows what sort of silliness done by the celebrants to honor the little girl whose celebration it is. There is a tremendous amount of kissing and

hand-shaking. This is only the formal presentation, of course; cheap, style-less models that you wouldn't want to give as presents are available to everybody long before this. (148)

Whileawayans use these devices by themselves and when more than one person is involved. The distinction between masturbation and 'real' sex has been dissolved. Similarly, in *On Strike Against God*, when the speaking subject is sexually aroused by the first erotic interplay with the woman she loves, and it does not result in copulation, she simply masturbates:

> I kissed Jean on the cheek and said a trembly good-by.
> And staggered to the bedroom, kicked off my shoes mechanically, sat down on the bed. Pulled the curtains to, pulled down my pants, reached in the bottom drawer of the bureau for the vibrator.
> A little voice cried, *You'll wear yourself out!*
> But ah, that was impossible. (52, italics in original)

The shape and function of these sex toys, which are expressly non-penetrative, once more confirm the stories' dependence on the psychoanalytic narrative of sexuality. In this narrative, the clitoral stimulation corresponds with active sexuality, whereas vaginal penetration expresses passivity. Since sexuality in this logic serves as the basis for social structure, passive sexuality is directly related to a submissive social role. Here, Russ's explicitly feminist texts show a concept of sexuality contiguous with *And Chaos Died*. Mrs Robins's exercycle is penetrative and denigrating rather than liberating, whereas Whileawayan vibrators are non-penetrative and correspond directly with the character's active sexuality. Thus making vaginal penetration a forbidden act, both texts perpetuate the idea that such penetration is necessarily an act of domination. The stories Russ published in her 'critically feminist phase', particularly 'What Did You Do During the Revolution Grandma?', partially shift this symbolic meaning, giving dominance and submission a slightly different twist. Part Three will analyse this shift in greater detail.

It is this patriarchal erotic symbolism, then, which ensures that the act of masturbation for Mrs Robins confirms her position in the patriarchal order. For the autoerotically inclined women in *The Female Man* and *On Strike Against God*, on the other hand, masturbation correlates with their freedom from patriarchal sexuality. Through masturbation these women get in tune with their own sexual fantasies and pleasures, thumbing their noses at compulsory heterosexuality. In Russ's later novels, masturbation is therefore directly linked to what must be the most radical sexual acts of resistance in the logic of psychoanalysis: lesbian lovemaking.

Copulation: Our Bodies, Our Selves

> ... while it is easy enough to show women doing men's work, or active in society, it is in the family scenes and the love scenes that one must look for the author's real freedom from our most destructive prejudices (Russ, 'Images of Women in Science Fiction', 89)

I have already discussed two major strategies of liberation in Russ's texts: androcide and entering the lesbian continuum. Another such strategy is deploying scenes of sexual/erotic interactions between/ among women which deliberately exclude men. Lesbian existence as represented in Russ's novels is such a formidable force in the struggle against the oppressive mechanisms of patriarchy because it combines claiming women's own sexuality with the assertion of agency in a way which deprives patriarchy of one of its most crucial foundations. This foundation is the heterosexual family arranged around the phallus and within this arrangement woman's role as object of trade among men and receptacle of semen. Although *We Who Are About To ...* and *The Two of Them* contain lesbian sexuality as a potential, the two books which most explicitly explore sex scenes among women as a narrative strategy are *The Female Man* and *On Strike Against God*.

In placing this immense revolutionary significance on lesbian sexuality, I do not want to indicate that Russ's texts represent it as merely a political act. But it is an old feminist truism that since patriarchal power rests on the most intimately personal, this is where a feminist revolution can be most effective. This truism is especially relevant for radical feminisms of Kristeva's second moment. As I pointed out earlier, it is not lesbian lovemaking as such that opens up a space for revolution, but ignoring men as sexual partners. Women who turn to women for sexual pleasure disrupt the story which traditional psychoanalysis presents as the norm.

I have been using the term 'lesbian' as if it were an uncontested term. However, it is perhaps the prevailing uncertainty of what precisely constitutes a lesbian that contributes to the threat which the concept poses to the heterosexual contract. Furthermore, the concept is as fragmented and heterogeneous as it is contested. In the short time of its existence since the late nineteenth century, there has been 'natural', 'converted', 'political', 'genetic' and even 'ludic' lesbianism and many more variations on these themes. However, for my reading of Russ here, the contours of lesbian existence remain comparatively clear, if only for the moment of analysis. A lesbian, then, is a twentieth century woman in a Western patriarchal culture who desires other women. This definition is not meant to exclude women from non-Western cultures or lesbians who do not identify as 'woman', but is strictly limited to the specific textual interpretation ventured in this study. According to this provisional definition, Joanna in *The Female Man* and Esther in *On Strike Against God* are lesbian characters, but Jael and Irene, even though they come to primarily associate with women politically and emotionally, are not.

Nevertheless, not all critics agree with this assessment. Marilyn Hacker has argued, for example, that there are no feminists and no lesbians in *The Female Man*. Janet, according to Hacker, is not a lesbian since 'her sexuality is, in her world, the norm, and indeed the only possible orientation' (75). I agree with Hacker in that Janet is not a lesbian. In Part Three I will even go further and claim that she may not even be a *woman* (another contested term) because in her society, with the absence of men, this category has ceased to carry meaning. However, in Part Nine of the novel, 'The Book of Joanna', it is Joanna, not Janet, who dis-covers her sexual attraction to Laura Rose—and is very much aware that she is venturing into territory outside the norm: 'bringing my fantasies into the real world frightened me very much. It's not that they were bad in themselves, but they were Unreal and therefore culpable ...' (208).

Joanna's apprehensions and doubts about the cultural validity of her desire point to the political implications of lesbian sexuality for feminism. Joanna, the tenderfoot refugee from compulsory heterosexuality, experiences the erotic relationship between herself and another woman not primarily as orgasmic pleasure, but as a radical break with patriarchal constructions of reality:

> I can't describe to you how reality itself tore wide open at that moment. [Laura Rose] kept on reading and I trod at a snail's pace over her ear and cheek down to the corner of her mouth, Laur getting hotter and redder all the time as if she had steam inside her. It's like falling off a cliff, standing astonished in

mid-air as the horizon rushes away from you. *If this is possible, anything is possible*. Later we got stoned and made awkward, self-conscious love, but nothing that happened afterward was as important to me (in an unhuman way) as that first, awful wrench of mind. (208, my emphasis)

Patriarchal articulations of reality do not allow for satisfying sexual experiences for women outside the heterosexual framework. Making 'Real what was Unreal' (208), Joanna and Laura are committing a crime against what structuralist psychoanalysis calls 'the Law of the Father', which is 'the crime of creating one's own Reality, of "preferring oneself"' (*The Female Man*, 208). The text is also careful to distinguish between the actual act of lovemaking and the *possibility* of lovemaking between women—of the two the latter causes the radical break. Nevertheless, to open up this possibility and to recognize it as real, Joanna and Laura do have to actually sleep with each other. Merely fantasizing about it is not enough: 'having Brynhildic fantasies about her was nothing—I have all sorts of extraordinary fantasies which I don't take seriously ...' (208).

On Strike Against God has a straightforward plot and does not—in contrast to *The Female Man*—employ multiple narrative layers, but the two books are nevertheless closely related. In respect to lesbian sexuality, *On Strike Against God* is a continuation of the earlier book. *The Female Man* delineates the liberation process of one of the speaking subjects. The end point of this process, lesbian lovemaking, marks the beginning of a new, more subtle revolutionary process. This is where *On Strike Against God* starts off:

> Clumsily I put my arms around her, twice-clumsily I kissed her on the neck, saying hoarsely, 'I love you.' (Which was something of an over-simplification, but how are you going to explain it all?)
> *She went on reading.*
> She blushed delicately under me, like a landscape, I mean her neck, she just turned red, it was amazing.
> Reality tore itself in two, from top to bottom. (49, italics in original)

Here, the radical break with patriarchal constructions of reality occurs early in the novel, propelling the speaking subject into another process of liberation, which leads her away from the patriarchal concept of love as possession of the other and to an acceptance of her self: 'The world belongs to me. I have a right to be here' (58).

Having broken with the 'Law of the Father', Esther and her lover Jean begin to explore and compare their bodies 'like little girls'. The two women stage an imaginary journey back into their early puberty, a time when 'the prison bars of femininity' had not yet completely closed in on them. Referring to childhood gives them a conceptual space in which to find new meaning and a new language for their bodies:

> Then she took off her sunglasses and smiled at me, so that tears rose to my eyes. She unhooked her dress (home-made so no zipper) and let it drop to the floor, then with crossed arms shucked her slip and did a little victorious dance around the room, waving the slip in the air. We took off all our clothes, very soberly, and then had a cup of tea, sitting politely on the couch, naked; I went into the kitchen to fetch it in my bathrobe. We looked each other over and I showed Jean the mole on my hip; so she lifted her hair and showed me the freckles on the back of her neck. We compared our 'figures' like little girls. We sat on the two ends of the couch, our knees up, feet to feet, and talked about the ecstasies and horrors of growing breasts at twelve, of bouncing when you ran, of having hairy legs, of being too tall, too short, too fat, too thin. There is this business where you think people end at the neck; then gradually as you talk, as we talked, *as we reconstituted ourselves in our own eyes— how well we became our bodies! how we moved out into them.* I understood that she felt her own ribs rise and fall with her breathing, that her abdomen went all the way into her head, that when she sat, she felt it, I mean she felt it in herself, just as I did. Until she looked—as she had felt to me before—all of one piece. (59, my emphasis)

Returning to their childhood selves allows them to make their bodies, which had formerly been the property of their husbands or male lovers, their own. Talking about their initiation to womanhood, for both a painful experience, they try to undo the damage caused in their puberty. Like the protagonists in 'The Autobiography of My Mother' and 'The Little Dirty Girl', Esther and Jean find remnants of an uncommodified body and physical pleasure in their childhood selves.

The way in which reference to the female body operates in Russ's writing once again demonstrates that her development as a radical feminist writer does not directly parallel the development of radical feminist discourses, even as she employs some of the same strategies and images. While her short stories and novels do intersect with Rich's lesbian continuum and lesbian existence and are concerned with the correlations between motherhood, daughterhood and the female sense of self in ways similar to Mary Daly, her fiction also emphatically undermines these categories. Russ draws the female body into her texts through a number of narrative strategies which all closely link the body, sexuality and the act of narration. Part One analysed how androcide establishes or confirms women's agency, but the killing scene also brought the woman's body in focus. In 'The Second Inquisition', *The Female Man* and *On Strike Against God*, on the other hand, sexual acts and/or erotic glances exchanged among women celebrate the female body in the text without the presence of a counterpart that is not female. Other texts, such as 'The Little Dirty Girl', bring in the female body through its illness and pain. Thus fictionalizing androcide, erotic acts or physical suffering allows Russ's texts to perform the act of narration through and on the surface of the body. But it is a body whose contours remain as uncertain and unfixed as agency in her materialist thread. Her texts consistently resit attempts by critics to pin them down to any one affiliation. They revel in the many.

PART THREE
Indeterminacy

One of the best things (for me) about science fiction is that—at least theoretically—it is a place where the ancient dualities disappear. Day and night, up and down, 'masculine' and 'feminine' are purely specific, limited phenomena which have been mythologized by people. They are man-made (not woman-made). Excepting up and down, night and day (maybe). Out in space there is no up or down no day or night, and in the point of view space can give us, I think there is no 'opposite' sex—what a word! The Eternal Feminine and The Eternal Masculine become the poetic fancies of a weakly dimorphic species trying to imitate every other species in a vain search for what is 'natural'—Russ (in 'Commentary', *Khatru*, 43)

Introduction to Part Three

Radical materialist feminists and feminists concerned with sexual difference have demanded that images of women in literature speak to the actual experience of women in 'real life'. Parts one and Two explored ways in which Russ's fiction intersects with these concerns. The readings showed that while Russ's work does develop from pre-feminist to explicitly feminist and critically feminist interpretations of social power and sexuality, both concerns are present in most texts and in tension with each other. However, those readings also indicated that there is a third strand in her writing, which undermines and contradicts the foundations of these first two moments in feminism. Feminist theory affiliated with this third moment, which corresponds to Kristeva's third generation, has in various ways criticized the first two moment's investment in universalizing enlightenment categories. Such thinkers for example examine the way in which the category 'woman' itself is produced in (patriarchal) discourses. Since to these theories there is no such thing as the essentially female/feminine outside the symbolic order, woman's 'authentic' experience does not exist except as a utopian dream—a line of argumentation which at first sight might look like a clever anti-feminist plot. If 'woman' is just a product of discourse, anything connected to a universal 'women's cause' becomes an essentialist regression and a corroboration of the binary gender system: every time a woman acts to fight for the rights of her sex-class, she actually perpetuates and justifies the system of categorization that created the oppression; every time a woman decides to form primary relationships with women and to put men second, thinking she can 'escape' patriarchy, she confirms the expulsion of women from the symbolic order. On the other hand, merely deconstructing patriarchal discourse in a language and medium inaccessible to people outside academia does not change the economic position of women, nor does it release their sexuality from their economic role in reproduction. Russ ingeniously manoeuvres her texts out of this apparent impasse: consciously working with these contradictions, she creates an open subject position for her female characters. This open subject position enables identities that destabilize the closed systems of sex class and sexual difference, without relinquishing the political force of these categories. Thus, for the purpose of gaining agency and claiming their own sexuality, women in Russ's texts in part act as if the categories produced by patriarchy were, in fact, stable categories. In the following, I will further explore how Russ activates narrative possibilities offered by science fiction as a genre which allow these texts to use and simultaneously counteract the essentialism inherent in the materialist feminist position.

Part Three will revisit certain spaces of intersection between Russ's work, feminist theory and genre fiction that have already been discussed in the previous chapters. I will, however, foreground the disruptive elements in Russ's novels and short stories, elements which destabilize the very sexual and political categories established by the texts. So far I have focused on intersections with such feminist texts that were largely contemporaneous with Russ's own writing and closely tied to feminist activism. In the 1980s, however, radical US feminism took part in the large-scale 'turn towards theory'. Particularly the 'French' theories of Hélène Cixous, Luce Irigaray, and Julia Kristeva became integral parts of feminist reflections on writing, the body, and sexual difference. Toril Moi's book *Sexual/Textual Politics* (1985), in which she criticized much of American feminism for its implicit biologism and essentialism and for its reductive concepts of patriarchy, played an important role in this transformation. In the 1990s, theorists such as Judith Butler who grew up in this climate of more theory-oriented feminism are analysing the instability and discursive formation of gender and sexuality. The following discussion will examine the ways in which Russ's fiction meets with these more recent feminist theories, which most of her fiction predates.

Radical feminist theory in the 1990s, participating as it does in many different academic disciplines, has assumed a significantly different role in relation to the women's movement. Many universities have (however reluctantly) established Women's Studies programmes; feminism has become accepted in many academic fields. The academic branches of feminism have further added to its diversity and made its theories increasingly complex. The following analysis focuses on spaces of intersection between Russ's fiction and more recent feminist theories such as Judith Butler's idea of 'gender performativity' and Donna Haraway's cyborg identities. Again, I emphasize continuities as well as departures from earlier concepts of feminist politics.

Therefore, the following readings will demonstrate the ways in which Russ's work, even as it participates in radical materialist and essentialist feminist discourses, moves beyond concepts of victimization. Russ's texts painfully disclose oppression and subordination of women as a group and vividly elucidate the deadly opposition between oppressor and oppressed. Yet she simultaneously always also envisions overcoming these dichotomies. She undermines the idea of the essential, 'pure' lesbian at the same time as she celebrates women's sexual love for women. Criticizing universalizing narratives about sexuality such as the psychoanalytic and anti-psychoanalytic stories of women's passivity in 'patriarchy', Judith Butler says in 'Against Proper Objects' (1994):

> Feminist positions such as Catherine MacKinnon's offer an analysis of sexual relations as structured by relations of coerced subordination and argue that acts of sexual domination constitute the social meaning of being a 'man,' as the condition of coerced subordination constitutes the social meaning of being a 'woman' ... But that deterministic account has come under continuous criticism from feminists not only for an untenable account of female sexuality as coerced subordination, but for the totalizing view of heterosexuality as well—one in which all power relations are reduced to relations of domination—and for the failure to distinguish the presence of coerced domination in sexuality from pleasurable and wanted dynamics of power. (7)

Butler here emphasizes the distinction between power and dominance. In Parts One and Two, I focused on the intimate connection between sex, gender, sexuality and agency. In these analyses, the social power of males over females was conceptualized as dominance within an all-encompassing system of patriarchal capitalism. In such reductive systems of analysis, men would be the perpetrators and women the victims—until they can kill the man and claim their body as their own. The third moment in feminism explicitly resists such totalizing views of sexual relations and power, pointing out the historicity and multiplicitous constructedness of all discourses. These theories no longer conceptualize women as the universal victims of patriarchal domination. Furthermore, they problematize time as a concept, showing that both the linear model of time, which was the basis of the materialist project, and the cyclical model of time, which provided a symbolic connection to the female body cycles, are historically produced and reproduced within a web of related discourses.

Thus, participation in 'patriarchal' discourses and practices is not culpable but inevitable, and the task is not to try to overthrow the 'system,' but to utilize existing spaces of incongruity. In her earlier book, *Gender Trouble* (1990), Judith Butler uses a childhood story to illustrate this feminist strategy, which turns its fundamental conundrum and dilemma into a major asset:

> Contemporary feminist debates over the meanings of gender lead time and again to a certain sense of trouble, as if the indeterminacy of gender might eventually culminate in the failure of feminism. Perhaps trouble need not carry such a negative valence. To make trouble was, within the reigning discourses of my childhood, something one should never do precisely because that would get one *in* trouble. The rebellion and its reprimand seemed to be caught up in the same terms, a phenomenon that gave rise to my first critical insight into the subtle ruse of power: The prevailing law threatened one with trouble, even put one in trouble, all to keep one out of trouble. Hence, I concluded that trouble is inevitable and the task, how best to make it, what best way to be in it. (vii)

Russ participates in discourses of gender indeterminacy which enabled theories such as Haraway's and Butler's, even as she espouses the materialist project which rests on a clear and stable model of gender opposition, superseded by a similarly stable model of the gender-less society.

In my discussion of *The Female Man* in Part One, I showed how age displaced gender as a basis for social structure in the utopian society of Whileaway. The following chapter will expand on the ways in which Russ in all phases of her development uses age differences as a means to represent pleasurable power dynamics in erotic relationships which do not lapse into rigid patterns of domination. These texts do more than simply reject the link between sex and power. Merely envisioning a sexuality without absolute dominance of one over the other (the age-old paradox of all utopias) would just confirm the power structures it negates. In using age rather than a binary system of reference as the force that generates power differences between women, Russ faces power in sexual interactions rather than simply negating it. What women find erotic in sexual relations with women is as much implicated in dominant discourses about sexuality as the most traditional and misogynist images of heterosexual intercourse. Working with these mechanisms, Russ's texts partially break up the rigid determinism of essentialist notions of female sexuality, rescuing the erotics of power for a reconstituted concept of sexuality.

CHAPTER SEVEN
Patterns of Experience: Sappho and the Erotics of the Generation Gap

Sappho and her island Lesbos are omnipresent in literature about women loving women, whatever the gender or sexual preference of the writer and whether or not Sappho and her island are explicitly named. Through her own poetic fragments she is the unwitting initiator of three apparently distinct models, which have, in fact, a common origin: the older woman who seduces beautiful young girls, usually in a school or by extension in a convent or bordello; the older woman who commits suicide because her love for a younger man is unrequited; the woman poet as disembodied muse—(Marks, 273)

In Part One of this book, which focused on agency, I discussed the relationship between rescuer and rescued in 'Bluestocking' (1967) in terms of Elaine Marks's 'Sappho model.' The tensions between Alyx and Edarra develop from the antagonistic through the maternal to the sexual, at which point they are diverted through a mysterious appearance of two *male* sexual partners. From this perspective, I would argue that Russ's rescue stories, which affect all of her intimate relations between women, are closely affiliated with the 'Sappho model'—at least in the subtext. In these rescue stories the maternal, the erotic and the 'autoerotic' between two women of different generations emerge as reassuring yet unstable female spaces. The 'mother' easily shifts to becoming the lover (as Alyx becomes Edarra's lover—if only in the subtext); the daughter becomes the former self (as in 'The Little Dirty Girl'); the mother or the great-grandmother become daughters (as in 'Autobiography of My Mother' and 'The Second Inquisition' respectively). At the same time, Sappho always also stands for women's power to write, which is probably the strongest red thread which runs through Russ's fiction as well as her criticism.

Kathleen Spencer has also positioned the 'rescue of the female child' motif in the larger context of feminist writing: 'Tracing this motif through Russ's writing not only reveals the development of the pattern in one writer's works, but helps illuminate what can be seen as the central issue for many feminist writers and theorists, and not just within SF' (167). I would argue that putting this rescue motif in the even larger context of the Sappho myth both reveals the ways in which concepts of sexuality develop in Russ's oeuvre and shows how the myth of the woman-loving female poet may serve as a powerful paradigm for feminist writing and theory.

The Sappho myth has traditionally served to domesticate women's bodies and their relation to language in circumscribing the woman who loves women in a discourse that reduces her to her sexuality (Marks, 273, 276). Elaine Marks demonstrates the emergence of a new, woman-centred mythology through the writing of women who search for a Sappho *before* domestication. Russ, however, does not go on a quest through history for the isle of Sappho as the locale of an authentic, 'undomesticated' female sexuality. With the Sappho plot, Russ's texts *disclaim* original femaleness within a narrative practice that emphatically asserts the need to link to women/lesbians and to find a voice for the unspeakable. This unbearable contradiction allows her Sappho to fully enjoy the sexual/political act of depoliticizing sex.

The following discussion will analyse the dynamics of sexual relationships between women, one of whom is significantly older. These relationships follow patterns similar to those described for the 'rescue of the female child', yet the texts make the erotic tension explicit, using the representation of the sexual act between the two women both to show the initiation of the younger to the pleasures of the female body and to destabilize the concepts of gender and sexuality as well as their interrelations.

Although Russ wrote only a few actual plays and says about herself, 'I was NOT a good playwright' (letter to the author, 21 September 1995), many of her earlier narrative texts contain strong dramatic elements, as the example of the short story 'My Dear Emily' has shown. Russ's most distinct reformulations of the Sappho model function within such contexts of the theatrical. In my discussion of sapphic intergenerational erotics, I will focus on four texts ranging from the late 1960s to the early 1980s. This delineation will also supplement my (provisional) categorizations of Russ's career as a writer. The first short story, 'Scenes from Domestic Life' (1968), is roughly contemporaneous with the Alyx stories and represents an 'early' phase, before the formulation of an explicitly feminist agenda. *The Female Man* (1975) asserts the anger and politics of explicit lesbian-feminism, without however glossing over the contradictions and instabilities of this stance. Finally, 'The Mystery of the Young Gentleman' (1982) and 'What Did You Do During the Revolution, Grandma?' (1983) belong to most recent developments, in which her texts systematically reach beyond the politics of woman-identification, foregrounding the deconstruction of binary conceptions of 'woman' and 'man'. My discussion of these developments will also demonstrate the continuities between these phases, highlighting the postulated provisional character of the categorization. Especially the reading of 'Scenes from Domestic Life' will show that even in her early, supposedly 'proto-feminist' phase, Russ's texts already destabilize gender and the female body as bases of identity.

A Queer Kind of Love: Drag of Age

> The repetition of heterosexual constructs within sexual cultures both gay and straight may well be the inevitable site of the denaturalization and mobilization of gender categories. The replication of heterosexual constructs in non-heterosexual frames brings into relief the utterly constructed status of the so-called heterosexual original. Thus, gay is to straight not as copy is to original, but, rather, as copy is to copy. (Judith Butler, *Gender Trouble*, 31)

'Scenes from Domestic Life' came out in 1968 in the small magazine *Consumption* and was not—unlike most of Russ's other short stories— reprinted in any of her collections. In similar ways to 'My Dear Emily' it is formally close to a play, the narrator reduced to a few comments in between the dominating discourse of the characters. Like this vampire story it is concerned with play-acting and performance in relation to sexuality.

The scene is Greenwich Village, presumably in the 1920s, a time when popularized Freudianism had reached the American middle class, initiating heated talk about 'aberrant' sexual practices. Lillian Faderman says about this time and place in *Odd Girls and Twilight Lovers:*

> While a lesbian identity was impossible for many women to assume during the '20s, sex with other women was the great

adventure, and literature and biography suggest that many women did not hesitate to partake of it ... The era saw the emergence of little areas of sophistication or places where a laissez-faire 'morality' was encouraged, such as Harlem and Greenwich Village, which seemed to provide an arena in which like-minded cohorts could pretend, at least, that the 1920s was a decade of true sexual rebellion and freedom. (67)

The two protagonists of the story, Miss Jones and Miss Edward, play out a drama of romance on such an imaginary arena of sexual freedom, simultaneously asserting female sexuality and denaturalizing the pleasures of the body. The two women meet in the seemingly innocuous atmosphere of an outdoor café. Within their first few speech acts, the two women are clearly placed in the typology of the Sappho model. The text casts the older woman, incidentally a teacher of literature, as the sexual aggressor who clearly lusts after the feminine and 'fragile' Miss Jones:

> 'I believe you got that hat at Peck-and-Peck,' murmured Miss Jones.
> 'I never think about clothes,' replied Miss Edward, leaning mesmerically forward—a dry, keen, remarkably lifelike fifty.
> 'Don't you?' said Miss Jones, looking at her sidewise, 'I do, I'm afraid. All the time.' (22)

The two women play a ritualized game of seduction, mocking and mimicking heterosexual romance, much like the impersonations of the vampire Guevara in 'My Dear Emily'. Miss Edward, after the first initiating sentences by Miss Jones, plays the part of the older seductress. In the first five scenes, she is the one who propels the plot through her insistent verbal advances, cleverly disguised as polite attempts at pleasant small talk. In these first scenes, Miss Jones only meekly reacts to Miss Edward's questions and demands, displaying artful airs of refusal when she is asked to Miss Edward's apartment. "'I couldn't think of it. I hardly know you." ... "No, no, no," said Miss Jones, shrinking away. "Never. Don't even talk about it"' (23). Thus, the power to move their romance forward is clearly with the older woman.

Miss Jones's elaborate refusal points to the underlying content of Miss Edward's speech acts. The two converse in code, enacting double roles, constantly evading a textually fixed self which could be identified as 'core' beneath the mimicry. Even though possible sexual activities are never mentioned explicitly, both understand what polite invitations such as 'I would ask you to my *pied-à-terre* on Eighth Street but ...' signify. The two women's speech acts are thus charged with an excess of eroticism which runs counter to their commonplace surface content.

These erotically charged interactions define the younger woman as sexually inexperienced, and the older woman as the teacher of unspeakable lesbian pleasures. Miss Edward marks the younger woman as 'child' who is helpless and has to be taught the ways of the world. Reading Miss Jones's palm, she predicts that the young woman will go on a trip soon, accompanied by a friend. '"A very dear friend," said Miss Edward, sweating a little, "Who will teach you a *very great deal*"' 24, italics in original). Again, the supposedly innocent 'girl' understands the message: 'I don't think I want to learn anything' (24). What is significant in their role-play is therefore not their respective physical age, but the age and experience they project through their performance.

Miss Jones heats the atmosphere by affecting complete innocence in sexual matters. When Miss Edward suggests speaking about love, 'true love', ostensibly as an abstract concept, Miss Jones exclaims with exaggerated shock: '"Oh, don't" . . . "It's so . . . fleshly"' (25). Miss Edward wickedly points to the cherry on Miss Jones's cake. Again, the sexual implications of the speech act remain undecoded or half-decoded:

> 'You eat it,' said Miss Jones, frowning slightly.
>   'I beg your pardon,' said Miss Edward, laughing a short, masculine laugh of bitter irony ... (26)

Miss Edward here takes the part that Alyx cannot play. The 'rescue of the female child' here is the object of ridicule, in which the rescued merely impersonates a child and the rescue operation is a theatrical performance. The older woman—in a way similar to Alyx—acts the male part in the romance, whose passionate courtship initiates the virgin in the pleasures of the body.

Thus, this early story clearly retains a reference to a model of sexual interactions which presupposes two complementary genders. The two women's role-playing, though resting on their age difference, is reminiscent of pre-Stonewall butch/femme codes of dress and behaviour, in which each woman had to assume one of two roles, 'masculine' or 'feminine'. The butch/femme relationship then functioned within gender patterns that were modelled on idealized images of courtship as projected by fiction and Hollywood (Faderman, 170). Lillian Faderman maintains that butches in the 1950s 'followed that chivalric behavior, as real men often did not outside of romance magazines and movies' (170). Thus, Faderman represents the lesbian copy of the supposed 'original' as superior to the heterosexual performance.

Miss Edward and Miss Jones both relish the power dynamics and tensions of their lovemaking, which remain, however, disguised by the pretence of celibate spinsterhood. The older woman exclaims:

> I realized then that I would be the happiest person in the world if only I could devote my life to serving you. I thought perhaps you did need me, even with your beauty and your glowing personality, that you needed a friend, someone to care for you, a *cavalier servante*. (27)

Miss Jones is less imaginative in her replies: '"No, no," said Miss Jones, shrinking away, "No, I couldn't"' (27). But Miss Edward, insistent, continues her courtship unthwarted: 'I swear a life of service like a wandering knight!' (27)

In spite of Miss Jones's consistently negative replies, the next scene shows the two in Miss Edward's apartment and the younger woman stripped to her slip. Her verbal refusal becomes more aggressive as if amplified by her nudity: '"I hate you!" . . . "I detest you!" ... "What you want is *dreadful*!" ... "I never heard of such a thing in my life ... I'm distracted, I'm frantic"' (29). At this point, the text introduces the first discontinuity in the flow of the performance. Instead of using physical force and/or displaying her sexual prowess, as a male suitor in a romance novel might have (and as Martin Guevara does), Miss Edward challenges the younger woman to leave, passing the power over to her: 'Either you make up your mind to stay and take the consequences or you take your dress and that idiot hat and get out. I've had enough!' (30). Miss Jones, wishing to return to the original plot of romance with its promise of unspeakable orgasmic pleasures, walks into the bedroom 'with her head hanging and with a slow step, with the cross, sad, bored, noble expression of a martyr' (30). The following scenes place Miss Jones's 'submission' clearly in the realm of pleasurable role-play, in which she chooses to relinquish the situational power to heighten further erotic pleasures.

In the morning after the act, Miss Jones's behaviour has changed completely. Again the plot is disrupted. Instead of having become the possession of the deflowering agent, she demonstrates her independence from Miss Edward. In this scene, Miss Jones has thoroughly relinquished the role of the child. Coolly putting on her make-up, she gets ready to leave—with no intention of returning. The plot of romance to her is completed. Miss Edward, continuing her part uninterrupted, enacts the disappointed lover, who wonders why he/she is being left:

> 'You're overwhelmed with guilt. Aren't you?'
> 'Oh dear, no,' said Miss Jones ...
> 'Well, it's *over*, isn't it?' [Miss Jones] produced a dazzling smile. 'It was wonderful,' she said, 'Don't worry. You were marvelous. Such a drama, you know, with love and death and pursuit and forever and all the rest of it.' (31–32)

In this scene, the two women perform within puzzlingly shifting and skewed patterns of mimicry. Miss Jones acts a meta-role in which she represents Miss Edward's performance of courtship as an expertly played imitation, while Miss Edward still plays within the patterns of courtship that Miss Jones refers to as titillating game.

When the younger woman thus locates the essence of their sexual relation solely in the play-acting, Miss Edward appeals to the pleasures of the female body:

> What about the rest? What about love? What about passion? What about pleasure? You felt that passion and that pleasure, don't deny it! Don't pretend about the deepest experiences of your soul. Don't deny your body. (32)

Miss Jones, unmoved and consistent in her new role, responds: 'I should think that if you wanted the *real* thing, you'd get a man' (32). Perfectly in accord with the discourses of her time, Miss Jones now poses as the bisexual experimenter, who has no intentions of identifying as lesbian. The rescue from compulsory heterosexuality here seems to be abortive. However, the reference to the 'real thing' here ironically positions it as the less desirable pleasure. Although Miss Jones acknowledges the privileged status of heterosexual intercourse in dominant discourses of what counts as 'real', she clearly prefers the supposed 'copy' as the more pleasurable performance. Because the sexual act is recognized as play (as well as thoroughly divorced from reproduction), the power she artfully relinquishes remains solely situational and does not leave the bedroom.

Miss Edward, who had seemingly opened her heart and poured out her innermost emotions about the sanctity of the female body, however, does not plunge herself into suicidal contortions of grief as the Sappho model would suggest: 'It took Miss Edward fully two hours to recover from the experience' (33). She is ready to pick up her next date, resuming an almost identical game. The full extent of the intricate and multi-layered performance thus does not become apparent until this last scene, in which Miss Edward meets the *next* girl in the same café, responding to the same cues with precisely the same code:

> 'I believe,' said the girl in a murmur, 'that you got that lovely suit at Henri Bendel."
> 'I never think about clothes,' stated Miss Edward dogmatically. (33)

This new break with the conventional plot of 'true love' not only mocks all that is sacred to heterosexual romance, it also questions the valorization of the woman and the female body. Yet Miss Edward's missing penis, which would tie the deflowered woman to her/him and close the plot with marriage and motherhood, does not emerge as a substantial lack. Quite to the contrary, she is able to continue her game, continuously mocking the promise of 'true love' as the essence of female sexuality. Her sexual pleasures are entirely her own, operating as she does in a utopian women-only space, where her ability to act is not challenged by the presence of a male. When Miss Jones, evoking the spectre of 'the *real* thing', penetrates this space, Miss Edward's sexuality may momentarily seem devalued, but playing on, she emerges victorious. To her erotic enjoyment, what counts as 'the *real* thing', is irrelevant. Her *performance* is not only equal to but exceeds that of heterosexual males.

Furthermore, the story irreverently reworks myths of female sexuality that are an integral part of the plot of heterosexual romance. The aged, post-menopausal spinster, who is completely negated as a sexual being in the dominant story of heterosexual erotic interactions, is the one who commands the most exquisite orgasmic pleasures. These pleasures are represented as unattainable for the heterosexual male, whose sexual performance is limited by his static link to the 'real thing', his penis. He is thus demoted from possessor of supreme power to object of supreme ridicule, making him expendable in the (supposedly unlimited) arena of female sexuality.

This non-science fictional short story allows a freedom with plot and sexuality that was not available to Russ as a science fiction or fantasy writer at the time. Only one year later, Russ published 'When It Changed', a story which indeed marks a change in her representations of lesbianism, taking its sexual practices out of the closet. This year, 1969, was also the year of the 'Stonewall Rebellion', the first gay riots in American history. Stonewall assumed a significance for male gays and lesbians that reached far beyond its immediate effects on the media, which began to accept 'homosexuals' as a marginalized minority who legitimately claimed their rights as citizens (Faderman, 196). Without intending to establish any direct relationship between 'When It Changed' and Stonewall, I do believe that Russ's work proves to be at the forefront of the rapidly changing discourses on sexuality in the late 1960s and '70s. Yet even in participating in these discourses, Russ remains critical of their essentialism, prefiguring crucial feminist/queer debates of the 1990s. However, 'Scenes of Domestic Life' uses a model of sexuality which relies on two opposing genders, with the older woman clearly occupying a masculine position. Later references to the 'Sappho model' in Russ's work abandon binary coding altogether. The reference to age makes power even more fluid and subject to instant change and reversal.

A Female Genghis Khan in the Windowpanes: Power, Ghosts and Cunnilingus

In my discussion of Whileaway, I argued that its all-female utopian society displaces gender in favour of age as a basis of social power. Whileaway privileges sexual relations between individuals of equal power; intergenerational sexual acts are one of the greatest taboos in this utopian society. However, the sexual scenes narrated in *The Female Man* thrive on unequal yet dynamic power distribution, similar to the one in 'Scenes from Domestic Life'. These sexual acts momentarily abandon the concept of 'equality', deriving pleasure from playing with precisely what is forbidden. Both of these texts resist the conflation of self and other which proved so central to the 'rescue of the female child' stories. Instead, these representations of sexual intercourse unfold an arousing dynamic of seizing and relinquishing provisional power, which allows them to sidestep equilibrium and stasis. I use 'power' in this context to signify the potential ability to determine and move events in the story of copulation. Unlike the stable and ultimately monolithic power associated with agency as discussed in Part One, this notion of power is not based on the individual's material, socio-economic position but on her actions at a particular moment in the plot. In this section, I will return to *The*

Female Man, specifically the relationship between two characters, Janet, the woman from a utopian future, and Laura, the teenager from Anytown, USA, in 1969. Janet initially has power over Laura, because she *acts* as the more experienced, not because she has a higher social position as the elder. From this perspective, power is created and re-created with each new action (represented linguistically in the text as a verb).

In *The Female Man*, the section directly preceding the passages in which multiple narrators relate the sexual encounter between Laura and Janet makes the central theme of this encounter explicit:

> Dunyasha Bernadetteson (the most brilliant mind in the world, b. A.C. 344, d. A.C. 426) heard of this unfortunate young person and immediately pronounced the following *shchasnï*, or cryptic one-word saying:
> 'Power!' (68)

The power dynamic generated by the erotic activities between Laura and Janet displaces the notions of empowerment through sexual relations between women as discussed in Part Two. Laura is released from compulsory heterosexuality as all-encompassing concept of normality, yet her acts of resistance are not directly equivalent to the 'rescue of the female child'. The 'rescue of the female child', rests on a partial conflation of the rescued with her rescuer as well as on a simultaneous reciprocal rescue of the older woman. Janet has no need of being rescued. She can empathize with the pain of the adolescent, but she cannot share the experience of this pain.

Paralleling the shifting power positions of the two lovers, the narrative voice is of uncertain origin, produced as it is by indistinct and changing agents. The narrators, implicitly and loosely identified as Jael and Joanna, witness the scene as disembodied presences. As in 'Life in the Furniture Store', 'Sword Blades and Poppy Seed', and other fictional texts by Russ, the narrator who speaks as a ghost renders her own body as well as those of the other characters unstable. The narrators move in and out of Janet's body and mind, relating the physical interactions with the young girl partially as their own experience. The text disembodies the narrators, but does not make them completely body-less. However uncertain the presence of their bodies, they are clearly identified as women.

Janet is first to explicitly recognize the erotic tension between herself and the young girl, who acts—somewhat like Miss Jones in 'Scenes from Domestic Life'—younger than she is. One of the narra-

tors remarks: 'We noticed the floss and dew on the back of her neck—
Laur is in some ways more like a thirteen-year-old than a seventeen-
year-old' (*The Female Man*, 62). Her (half-hearted) rejections of Janet
are also reminiscent of Miss Jones: 'Never—don't—I can't—leave
me!' (71) However, while Miss Jones is fully aware of the part she
plays, Laura is still 'the victim of ventriloquism' (62), the act of heterosexual, 'true' womanhood forced on her by her family.

The narrators, who are present in Janet's body and mind at the
time, share the Whileawayan's explicit sexual fantasies, but represent
them in the third person: 'In the bluntness of her imagination she
unbuttoned Laur's shirt and slid her pants down to her knees' (63).
This strategy puts a definite distance between the lesbian sexual acts
and the narrative voices, yet allows the engaged eavesdroppers to
experience these acts directly through the body of the perpetrator.
Janet, initially being in a position of superior power, keeps her own
emotions and sexual desires for the young woman in check. Finally,
however, it is Laura who takes the initiative, claiming the power to
move the action: 'Then she [Laura] put her hand on Janet's knee, a
hot, moist hand with its square fingers and stubby nails, a hand of
tremendous youthful presence, and said something else, still inaudi-
ble' (70). The subtle power struggle between the two continues,
Janet in her actions emphasizing the youth and inexperience of the
other: 'Janet pulled her up on to her lap—Janet's lap—as if she had
been a baby' (70). Laura, counteracting this reduction of self-determination and control, attempts to manifest herself as an adult and
sexually mature woman:

> Janet—I—held her, her odor flooding my skin, cold woman,
> grinning at my own desire because we are still trying to be
> good. Whileawayans, as has been said, love big asses. 'I love
> you, I love you,' said Laur, and Janet rocked her and Laur—not
> wishing to be taken for a child—bent Miss Evason's head
> fiercely back against the chair and kissed her on the mouth. Oh
> my goodness.
>
> Janet's rid of me. I sprang away and hung by one claw from
> the window curtain... (71)

Here, the narrator is temporarily disembodied to change places in the
scene of desire; turned into a feline ghost, she continues to watch—
and to narrate her observations—from outside in third-person narrative. She thus remains part of the scene, adding her voice to the
chorus of narrators.

In addition to the tensions created by the age difference, there are also cultural differences which govern the erotic desires of the two women. Laura, for lack of other models, relies on stories of hetero-sexual romance in moments when she has the power to determine the 'plot' of their lovemaking, assuming, however, the freedom to play the role of the male. Thus, whereas Miss Edward and Miss Jones referred to a single set of roles, masculine and feminine, Laura and Janet move within a field of possibilities. The Whileawayan has no concept of gender in sexuality and is thus able to create space for Laura to play out her fantasies.

The passage quoted above also shows the way in which the ghosts or disembodied narrators merge in Janet's body, physically leaving her in crucial moments of the lovemaking. These moments always also coincide with shifts in power between the two lovers. The narra-tor who flees Janet's body here is recognizable by her physique. The claw loosely identifies her as Jael, the fierce killer of men, whose body is an assemblage of lethal weapons (such as steel claws and teeth, as well as artificially re-enforced muscles). When Laura kisses Janet in a gesture of assumed adulthood, Jael, who hates men but does not desire women, flees Janet's body.

The second narrative consciousness, however, remains in Janet's body until the Whileawayan proceeds to assume control over the younger woman's sexual pleasure through cunnilingus, giving her 'the first major sexual pleasure she had ever received from another human being in her entire life' (74). The narrator says:

> So I fled shrieking. There is no excuse for putting my face between someone else's columnar thighs—picture me as washing my cheeks and temples outside to get rid of that cool smoothness (cool because of the fat, you see, that insulates the limbs; you can almost feel the long bones, the *architectura*, the heavenly technical cunning. They'll be doing it with the dog next). I sat on the hall window frame and screamed.
>
> Janet must be imagined throughout as practicing the extremest self-control. (74)

In her description of the bodily object of oral stimulation, the narra-tor here betrays her physical enjoyment of the act that she explicitly resists. Another, more distanced narrative voice, the one who speaks of Janet's self-control, intervenes at this point, encouraging such a reading. The titillating oscillation between embodiment and disem-bodiment is accompanied by a profound ambiguity about the body itself as well as who is speaking to whom at a particular moment.

This disjunction between what is said explicitly and the implicit sexual pleasure shows a continuity between *And Chaos Died* and *The Female Man*. The voyeuristic scene of masturbation in the earlier novel also works with a narrator and protagonists who experience the sexual arousal of the masturbating woman directly through her mind. However, there are also significant differences which highlight the shift in the way in which Russ represents sexuality. While in *And Chaos Died* the sexual pleasure of the narrator and the observing protagonists remains concealed, the later text deliberately lifts the veil of the narrator's explicit rejection of and resistance to these sexual pleasures. *The Female Man* opens the doors to the closet, making this process an integral part of the narrative and the act of narration.

The love scene between Janet and Laura which is narrated in the passage from which I quoted above unites all of the characters in *The Female Man* who at one point in the book also speak up as narrators. The only protagonist excluded from the act here is Jeannine, who is also the only one who never assumes the authority of the narrator. This controlled exclusion further underpins the significance of how telling the story interacts with the (female) body in the text and the erotic activity performed with the body. Such playful self-referentiality is of course not unique to feminist science fiction. Yet I would argue that feminist science fiction makes serious political use of it in specific ways. Science fiction and fantasy, because of their speculative potential, can make use of disembodied narrative voices, characters who speak as ghosts or read other characters' minds and body pleasures. Thus, the act of narration itself becomes science fictional and radically feminist in Russ's work.

In the scene of copulation narrated here, Janet and Laura do not come together as equals. The age difference creates a dynamic of power and restraint. The very experienced older woman wilfully keeps her desires for wild abandon in check to teach the younger woman basic yet unspecified techniques. Whereas Laura continually acts out scenes that draw on the same narratives as normative heterosexual romantic love does, Janet's concept of sex does not rely on such fantasies. From Janet, Laura learns to expand her restrictive imagination: '[Laura] had learned from a boy friend how to kiss on top, but here there was lots of time and lots of other places' (74). Representing sex as pleasurable activity that requires certain acquirable skills, the text denaturalizes sexuality and divorces it from its normative connection to romantic love.

The two invisible characters present at the scene of Laura's first sexual encounter with another woman are also reminiscent of Siegfried in the legend of Brynhild, who is present in the bedroom and invisible through his magic hood. However, the effect is the reverse: while intercourse deprives Brynhild of her power and initiates her into the patriarchal order, it places Laura outside this oppressive system, conferring to her agency and possession of her own body. Lesbian sexuality thus reverses the disempowering deflowering of the virginal woman through the patriarchal myth, empowering her to commit new revolutionary deeds against the oppression. In 'The Book of Joanna', the final chapter in *The Female Man*, the fictional author Joanna enters a sexual relationship with Laura without the mediation of Janet as an imaginary other. Through this integrative character, who is recognizable as a white, middle-class woman in an America of 1969, the text is able to connect the liberating vision of the science fiction narrative to the world of the implied white middle-class reader, making it directly relevant to her life.

Janet, in order not to exploit the young girl's inexperience, gives up the power that she could exercise in the act, deliberately creating a space for Laura to explore possible sexual performances. Although Laura refers to familiar patterns of heterosexual love, the underlying 'Sappho model' simultaneously breaks this connection. The roles she takes up are not determined by her anatomy. In her sexual encounter with Janet, she learns to claim power as contingent and situational rather than a fixed and unyielding capacity.

The link between her desire for power and her sexual desires crystallizes in her adolescent daydream, in which she envisions herself as Genghis Khan (60). If she were, according to this dream, a powerful woman, she would be excluded from heterosexual romance because she had 'never met a man yet who wanted to make it with a female Genghis Khan. Either they try to dominate you, which is revolting, or they turn into babies' (67). For her, not being able to relate sexually to a male is thus less determined by an unwillingness to give up her virginal independence, but rather by an incompatibility with her own sexual power fantasies. Since Janet's power rests on knowledge not biology, in the act of teaching this knowledge, power may pass over and shift freely between the two women. The achievement of orgasm reshuffles their power differences, but there is no sense of closure:

So it was easy. Touched with strange inspiration Laur held the interloper in her arms, awed, impressed, a little domineering. Months of chastity went up in smoke: an electrical charge, the wriggling of an internal eel, a knifelike pleasure.

'No, no, not yet,' said Janet Evason Belin. 'Just hold it. Let me rest.'

'Now. Again.' (74–75)

Both 'Scenes from Domestic Life' and *The Female Man* thus represent lesbian sexual practices as superior to the supposed 'original'. Both texts create an implicit comparison between heterosexual intercourse and sex between women in which the latter emerges as more pleasurable, varied, open and multiplicitous. This section has focused on the pleasure of the acts, revealing that their link to the female body is—though crucial—only provisional. This perspective adds to the political implications of representing lesbian sexuality in Russ's fiction the sheer enjoyment of talking about it. While texts such as *The Female Man* and *On Strike Against God* first have to narrate the ground on which lesbian sex becomes thinkable, the more recent short stories 'The Mystery of the Young Gentleman' and 'What Did You Do During the Revolution, Grandma?', which I will discuss in the following section, take sex between women as a given. This starting point allows them to avoid representing sex between women as 'better' or more pleasurable than sex between women and men and to explore finer nuances of intergenerational pleasures. Furthermore, Russ's later work also expresses the desire to move beyond the concepts 'woman' and 'lesbian', the latter being, after all, a category firmly embedded in twentieth-century dominant discourses.

He's a Not-So-Young Lady:
Invisible Folks and Unnatural Lusts

'The Mystery of the Young Gentleman' (1982) was first published as an independent short story, but later became part of Russ's collection/novel *Extra(Ordinary) People*. The story continues major themes in Russ's work, but shifts the focus from the struggle for an independent self to the instabilities and pleasures of writing, sex and gender. The previous sections showed how 'Scenes From Domestic Life' and *The Female Man* already make use of subversive play-acting and gender performance to destabilize these concepts. 'The Mystery of the Young Gentleman' moves a step further and makes acting the predominant factor in the relationship between the two protagonists. They have no other identity than the one they perform, and—more importantly—they are aware of it.

Specifically, the story reformulates the 'rescue of the female child' theme and its relation to the Sappho model, critically echoing scenes from Russ's earlier work. The narrator, who travels as 'Joe Smith of Colorado', is on his/her way from Europe to the US. He/she is accompanied by the enigmatic young girl Maria-Dolores, 'a fifteen-year-old from the slums of Barcelona' (64). The text has the form of a travel journal/letter addressed to a fellow member of the 'telepathic minority' who have formed a secluded community up in the mountains of Colorado—the destination of 'Joe Smith' and Maria-Dolores. The young girl shares the gift of extra-sensory perception, but has not learned how to use it properly. Both the 'rescue of the female child' theme and the 'Sappho model' as well as the way in which they interact have been transformed in this story. As in 'Scenes From Domestic Life' and *The Female Man*, the explicit sexuality between the two protagonists prevents a conflation of selves.

While their personal interactions become more intensely erotic, the two protagonists continuously improve the act which they play to the world: much of the two travelling companions' time and energy is spent in the attempt to create the best possible appearance and to perfect their performance of gender and class roles. Maria-Dolores travels as Joe Smith's little twelve-year-old female cousin, but her body does not necessarily tie her to a specific role: 'Next time I travel as your son!' (70) The narrator, performing the part of the maternal teacher, shows her how to play the feminine role but without identifying this role as the girl's essential self. After all, Joe Smith's access to motherhood rests only on her/his performance since s/he is not clearly a woman. This training in subversion corresponds to another transformation of the maternal role from a model in which the mother is a combination of victim and perpetrator to one in which she serves as a collaborator in resistance. With this transformation of the maternal, the short story continues yet another theme from Russ's earlier work.

This troublesome 'mother', even as she teaches her foster daughter how to perform upper-class femininity, makes sex and gender uncertain. Although Maria-Dolores is 'one of them', a telepath, she has a great deal to learn about how the telepathic community functions:

> She says, being a real pest, 'I bet there are no women in the mountains.'

'That's right,' I tell her. (She's also in real confusion.)
'But *me!*' she says.
'When you get there, there will still be no women.'
'But you—is it all *men?*'
'There are no men. Maria-Dolores, we've been over and over this.' (70)

The underlying logic in this dialogue is that since the members of the isolated community interact through controlled telepathy, they do not depend on categories such as gender, class or race. Thus, this story links a materialist utopia with a liberation from certain limiting categories in the symbolic order. The telepathic community, then, represents the desire for an ungendered, classless society, which in itself is unrepresentable in language. This (provisional) loyalty to the necessity of utopian visions, even if they are impossible, demonstrates that even in Russ's latest work the affiliation with deconstructive discourses is as partial as the one with materialist and essentialist feminism.

Although the gender of the narrator/protagonist Joe Smith remains ambiguous and unstable throughout, the interactions with the young girl consistently follow the Sappho model. As in *The Female Man*, the older partner possesses the knowledge necessary for satisfying sexual intercourse and the younger is more than eager to learn. Sexual desire is thus not represented as desire for an external object but for the pleasurable process itself. This process follows patterns reminiscent of the interactions between Alyx and Edarra in 'Bluestocking,' between the two protagonists in 'The Second Inquisition', or between Irene and Zubeydeh in *The Two of Them*. The crucial difference from these earlier texts, however, is that 'The Mystery of the Young Gentleman' makes the sexual tensions between the two characters explicit. When the narrator says, 'I get up and go in to where I have a view of her white-kid calves and her child's dress' (65), s/he seems to steer dangerously close to stories of child abuse and sexual exploitation. But such a reading would deprive the young woman of the very self-determination that is the utopian goal of the rescue theme and turn her into a passive victim. What is more, the text itself counteracts such a reading. Maria-Dolores is not entirely uninitiated and, like Laura in *The Female Man*, wants to prove that she should not be considered a child: 'I've done it before. With girls, too; girls do it with girls and boys with boys; everybody knows that' (71). Like Laura, it is ultimately Maria-Dolores who initiates explicit erotic interactions with 'Joe Smith'.

Moreover, the power that knowledge gives the elder is transferable and unfixed, and the desirous gaze on the other does not reduce her to permanent availability. The narrator tells Maria-Dolores that sex among telepaths requires extreme self-control and distancing because it opens the channels that normally protect them from the chaotic mass of thoughts and emotions of other people. S/he explains that one has to prepare for these sexual encounters:

> 'Because,' I say, 'this is how it happens when one is young,' and knowing so much more than she, sit down, knees giving away, with my face in my hands. The two mirrors so placed that they reflect each other to infinity, as you see in a barber-shop, each knowing what the other feels. That remembered fusion which opens everything, even minds. (72)

The crucial point in these sexual interactions is to resist the fusion of selves yet to come close enough to recognize oneself in the other. The narrator fantasizes about sex with the young girl in the solitude of the Colorado mountains: '"Joe Smith" of "Colorado" slides his hands under the little girl's shirt—a process I'm sure he could describe very well—but his face will never be reflected in her eyes' (90). Again, the fantasy represents the potential sexual act as a process of teaching that rests on the self-control of the older and her/his ability to relinquish the power that knowledge gives her/him over the young girl:

> As I bend slowly down to the nubbiness, the softness, the mossy slipperiness, the heat, that familiar reflection begins back and forth between us, a sudden scatter-shot along the nerves, its focusing on the one place, the echoes in neck and palms and lips, the soles of her feet, her breasts. Maria-Dolores is breathless; 'Don't stop!' forgetting that I know. She closes her eyes, sobs, grabs inside, clutches my head with her hand: overwhelming! And sees me, all I remember, all I feel, all I know: overwhelming! And then, out of the things I know—and can't help knowing—she sees the one thing as strange and terrible to her as the dark side of the moon: herself. (90)

As Janet in *The Female Man*, the narrator here ultimately takes pleasure in restraining her/his sexual desires, making space for the young girl to exercise her power and to explore her own sexuality. This passage also evokes the image of a core self that Maria-Dolores can perceive in the mirror of the other. Telepathy enables the lovers to sidestep the mediation of culture and the symbolism of language—a concept which clearly contradicts the idea that their identity is coextensive with their performance. Thus, while 'The Mystery of the Young Gentleman' makes the identities of the protagonists unstable and based on the acts they perform, it also grounds them in a self that is independent of the symbolic context in which it exists. However, this self is not, as for instance in Mary Daly's work, an original home that women need to recover, but rather an unattainable, fearful space. As unattainable as the hidden side of the moon without a space programme. Again, the text keeps a securely grounded stability in tension with the instability which is its focus.

This instability primarily centres on the narrator/protagonist 'Joe Smith'. S/he is never clearly identified as a woman, although the text towards the end points to the possibility. Referring to one of the many books that Maria-Dolores reads, the narrator says: 'It's called *The Mystery of the Young Gentleman* (he's a not-so-young lady, we find out)' (92). Even though the text leaves Joe Smith's sex uncertain, her sexuality is comparatively unambiguous. Her sexual fantasy suggests cunnilingus and clitoral stimulation rather than penetration, her/his role in the sexual act resembling that of Janet in *The Female Man* rather than that of Machine in *Picnic on Paradise*. Orgasm, rather than being represented as a loss of self, becomes a moment of supreme self-knowledge. The narrator's imagined sexual encounter with the young girl thus demonstrates that, in spite of the foregrounded gender uncertainties and the destabilization of the category 'lesbian' in 'The Mystery of the Young Gentleman', the female body at the same time remains a privileged site of pleasure and empowerment.

The narrator also engages in—quite different—sexual acts with an elderly physician on the ship to divert the interest this man had taken in the strange couple Joe Smith and Maria-Dolores. While sex with the narrator for the young girl is potentially empowering, it completely disempowers 'Dr Bumble', in part because he is unable to recognize gender as purely performative. At first he is fascinated with 'Joe Smith' of Colorado and the young girl travelling with 'him', and he begins to write up an account about the narrator's supposed homosexuality under the title 'A Hitherto Unconsidered Possibility: The Moral Invert' (78). To protect her/his and Maria-Dolores's travelling act, the narrator now performs for the doctor, always slightly shifting her/his role to the utter confusion of her/his victim. Acting as a woman disguised as a man, s/he seduces the old physician and coolly 'handles his secret self' to give him an unceremonious orgasm: 'For a moment he comes back to himself to see his wife—no, the Col-

orado gambler—no, the actress—in one dim, ambiguous person'
(85). Unable to recognize the various selves of the narrator as performances, 'Dr Bumble' loses himself in the search for 'essence'. The
narrator tells him:

> But it's perfect nonsense, my dear fellow, a woman pretending
> to be a man who pretends he's a woman in order to pretend to
> be a man? Come, come, it won't work! A female invert might
> want to dress and live as a man, but to confess she's a woman—
> which would defeat her purpose—and then be intimate with
> you—which she would find impossibly repulsive—in order to
> do what, for heaven's sake? Where's the sense to it? No there's
> only one possibility, and that's the truth: that I have been
> deceiving nobody, including you, but that you, my poor dear fel-
> low, have been for a very long time deceiving yourself. (88)

Using the doctor's own rigid and limited gender-categories, the narrator here does nothing more than put labels on her/his various performances—which can only make sense if they are recognized as
such. To the doctor the only possible—and logical—conclusion is the
one implied in this passage, namely that the narrator is, in fact, a male
invert who was able to tap his, the doctor's, own hidden homosexual
desires. To maintain face, he unwittingly proceeds to return to his
male heterosexual role performance and, negating the discontinuities, burns his account of the 'invert'.

Thus, 'The Mystery of the Young Gentleman' retains a trace of the
idea of lesbian sexuality as preferable to normative heterosexuality,
even as lesbianism loses its political function as centrepiece of a liberation story. Joe Smith in spite of her/his unfixed sex and gender
shares fundamental characteristics with the maternal teacher in the
Sappho model. Yet the story also departs from Russ's earlier work in
significant ways. In this particular adaptation of the model, the passing on of knowledge moves to the centre and becomes thoroughly
tied in with the erotic interactions between the older and the younger
protagonist. Furthermore, the story emphasizes distance and difference between the two, rather than establishing sameness. Maria-
Dolores in no way represents a younger version or former self of Joe
Smith. Joe interacts with her as an independent individual. Neither
does she carry the weight of the struggle for a better, less oppressed
future since the utopian vision in the text is spatial rather than temporal: the society of telepaths exists parallel to the rest of the narrative world—in the mountains of Colorado.

The story thus exemplifies a central paradox in Russ's writing, particularly of the late 1970s and 1980s, namely the impossibility of and necessity for a utopian vision. The text both creates and deconstructs its utopian visions and desires for a society in which neither race, class, nor sex or gender have symbolic meaning and social function. The 'Young Gentleman' may or may not be female, but since her/his performance in the sexual act convincingly parallels that of lesbians in Russ's oeuvre and elsewhere, this question is ultimately irrelevant. Furthermore, regardless of whether s/he has a male or a female body, s/he can convincingly pass as either in the world outside the utopia.

Another story which combines explorations of gender play-acting with a version the sapphic plot is 'What Did You Do During the Revolution, Grandma?' The story was first published in 1983 in *The Seattle Review* and is also incorporated in *Extra(Ordinary) People*. Like 'The Mystery of the Young Gentleman', it is an epistolary story in which the central protagonist and narrator disguises herself as a male. Her disguise, however, also includes cosmetic surgery, an incomplete sex-change operation (incomplete because the narrator refuses to let the surgeons attach a penis). This surgery uses as a model Asmodeus, a demon character from Jewish legend. In this disguise, the narrator takes on a masculine name and—among other things—enters an erotic relationship with a significantly younger protagonist, who is unmistakably female.

Like Joe Smith in 'The Mystery of the Young Gentleman', this male impersonator is sent on a mission for which she has to travel to another culture. The 58-year-old protagonist is an agent of the leftist United Front, an organization reminiscent of the Trans-Temporal Authority in *Picnic on Paradise* and *The Two of Them*. She learns that she is to go to Ruritania in the role of Issa, a demonic male character from Ruritanese mythology who resembles Asmodeus, to help instigate a revolution: '*We want you to do this little thing for us: go into Storybook Land and impersonate an ambassador to King Shabriyar ...*' (122, italics in original). However, an unsettling factor disrupts the narrative logic of the text, as well as that of the revolution. This factor is what the narrator calls *Ru*, a measurement which represents the consistency of causality: 'Only at *Ru* 1.0 is there an ironclad relation of cause and effect' (120).

For this reason, the precise object of the narrator's mission in the story remains obscure and she proceeds to act out her own agenda, which she narrates in a series of 'snapshots'. One of these story fragments is particularly significant in this context because it represents

a parodic twist on the Sappho model. Like the other stories of intergenerational relationships in Russ, it is grounded in a scene of teaching. In her role as Issa, the narrator gives mathematics lessons to the
King's 13-year-old daughter, who promptly tries to seduce the alien
'Prince'. To the young seductress's disappointment, however, Issa
claims, as part of 'his' elaborate disguise, that 'his' fiancée at home
had cast a spell over 'his' genitals so 'he' would not be able to use
them for copulation. But 'he' is imaginative and ultimately finds a
way to circumvent this handicap:

> '*Can* you take me?' she says, and I, 'Alas, lady'—and she—and
> I—and she—and I—and then a very awkward silence.
>   Then I say, 'There's a way—'
>   Very incautious of Issa, no doubt, but how can you throw a
> lady out of bed? . . . I didn't come here to masturbate a thirteen-
> year-old.
>   On the other hand— (137)

In contrast to the stories discussed above, 'What Did You Do During the Revolution, Grandma?' thus reads like an ironic comment on
the liberating potential of the 'Sappho model'. The self-mocking voice
of the narrator reveals sheer lust for the young girl rather than the
wish to 'rescue' her as motivation for the sexual act. Ruritania is on a
parallel universe which functions on an even lower level of consistency than the basic narrative world. Since in this world events are
not necessarily causally related, a story of rescue as well as a utopia
becomes an absurdity. Thus, instead of worrying about her assign-
ment, the narrator pursues her pleasure and impersonates a pirate for
the erotic entertainment of the Princess:

> And she sheds the Princess, red all over and face averted, and
> having found nakedness even more deliciously shameful than
> pirates, lies there while I violate her with my mouth, which
> (thank God!) makes talking impossible ...
>   I put my finger inside her; she groans and then, moving her
> hips from side to side, 'Oh no. Oh, don't. Oh, please don't.'
>   So it begins all over again. (137–38)

The presence of digital penetration in this scene is remarkable only
when read in conjunction with the absence of such sexual practices
in representations of lesbian lovemaking in the texts discussed previously. This sexual fantasy of violation, enjoyable as it may be for the
Princess, echoes the exploitation of the lower *Ru* worlds by the world

of the narrator. In this variation of the Sappho model, sexuality is once more the site of a power struggle, but here the older woman gives in to the pleasure of acting out the girl's fantasy of submission instead of 'rescuing' her from a patriarchal arch-enemy.

The narrative that frames the narrator's adventure in Ruritania is in the form of a letter addressed to a 'Beloved Woman'. The writer of the letter is convalescing from serious surgery, presumably an operation that reconstructed her body to its original form before she was turned into Issa. In this frame, the narrator counteracts the effect of the story of her adventure as Issa, which mocks the possibility of utopian visions, by emphasizing their necessity:

> [H]uman pleasures, human pains and human loves are real, not rhetorical no matter on what *Ru* position of what more-or-less Earth they occur; they are the only things that count and would reconcile me to a great deal more than any small nuisance I have to put up with in this newly-emerged, post-revolutionary, stumbling, bumbling, not so very dreadful, indeed rather nice and quite significant Utopia-to-be— (144)

In this text as in her other work, Russ emerges as a consistent radical; all three of Kristeva's feminist moments, which could simplisticly be identified as 'materialist', 'essentialist' and 'deconstructionist' are present to varying degrees in most of her fictional work. This presence also prevents her from totalizing the impossibility of transcending language, as so much poststructuralist feminism is tempted to do. These consistently partial affiliations allow the texts to think feminist oppositional thoughts to their radical conclusion but at the same time to resist universalizing any one of them. *Extra(Ordinary) People* thus engages lesbian-feminism but at the same time puts it in tension with the deconstruction of its utopian premises. Even more so than Russ's earlier texts, this novel/collection acknowledges the power dynamics among women which subvert the woman-identification suggested by lesbian-feminist politics. The following chapter will further examine the ways in which Russ's work simultaneously undermines the categories established by its feminist utopian visions.

CHAPTER EIGHT

The Great, Grand Palimpsest of Me: Fragmented Locations and Identities

To resolve contrarieties, unite them in your own person—Russ, *The Female Man* (138)

The title of *The Female Man* echoes Germaine Greer's *The Female Eunuch* (1970), in which Greer reveals the stereotypical concept of femininity as one of lack, which constructs the woman as a castrated man. Placing the concept of a gendered identity within the cultural context, Greer asks for alternative versions of this identity:

> We know what we are, but know not what we may be, or what we might have been ... Nothing much can be made of chromo-somal difference until it is manifested in development, and development cannot take place in a vacuum: from the outset our observation of the female is consciously and unconsciously biased by assumptions that we cannot help making and can-not always identify when they have been made. The new assumption behind the discussion of the body is that every-thing that we may observe *could be otherwise*. (16–17, italics in original)

The speculative possibilities of science fiction make this genre a dis-cursive space that is excellently suited for narrative experiments with such alternative identities. Placing another version of a genetically identical woman in an imaginary cultural context allows Russ to explore the ways in which culture determines the characters' sense of self and identity. In turn, this speculative freedom also allows the text to experiment with strategies of resistance against this determinism.

Although *The Female Man* contains the most prominent examples of characters with alternate identities, Russ's work is full of such exper-iments. Jael collects her 'other selves out there in the great, gray might-have-been' (160), proving that all they have in common is the same genotype: 'We ought to think alike and feel alike and act alike, but of course we don't. So plastic is humankind!' (162) In *The Two of Them*, Irene as an adolescent makes up an alternate identity for herself and names her Irenee Adler, '*the* woman' (5, italics in original) uninhibited by patriarchal concepts of femininity who can defy the rules of passivity and go out to become an interstellar Trans-Temporal agent. Zubeydeh has a 'Bad Self' (137) which allows her to act outside the rigid confines of Ka'aban gender roles. Similarly, Esther, narrator of *On Strike Against God*, refers to an alter-ego named Joanna: 'One of us who is writing this (we're a committee)' (23). Esther uses the metaphor of the palimpsest (17) to refer to the multiple overlapping texts that make up her self, emphasizing the possibility of change through new stories one writes up for oneself. Such overlapping stories also allow Joanna, the fictional author in *The Female Man*, to enter into a dialogue with herself which provides her with a story of liberation.

Joanna's Story? Jael's Story? Empowering Dual Visions in *The Female Man*

Within the multi-layered narrative of *The Female Man*, two interlaced strands emerge: one in which Jael searches in different parallel universes for other versions of herself as allies in the war against Manland and another in which Joanna negotiates between her own different selves within herself trying to break through the limiting patriarchal narratives that inhibit her mind. But all *four* protagonists, Jeannine, Jael, Janet and Joanna, are part of both stories. For example, Jael may be read as a character in a science fiction story who kills a Manlander in self-defence, but at the same time she is also a product of Joanna's imagination, an alternative personality within Joanna. Joanna is an intermediary between these two narrative levels and has a special status as narrator: '[addressing the reader:] don't think I know any of this by hearsay; I'm the spirit of the author and know all things' (166). As 'spirit of the author', Joanna is able to switch between different narrators, using the 'voice' of Jael, Janet or herself to relate the narrative. This oscillation between different narrative voices breaks down discursive hierarchies in the novel, since different points of view are related directly from the first person perspective. The unstable narrative voice creates a double ambiguity in the text: on the one hand, the reader has to keep track of the two intersecting stories which run through the text, while on the other, she can rarely be sure who is speaking at a particular moment.

Janet, as a narrator, is an exception: her narrative is clearly distinguishable from Jael's and Joanna's, and she gives an immediate, first-hand account of the utopian society on Whileaway. Tom Moylan observes that this head-on confrontation with the utopian world transforms the traditional narrative frame in which a guide shows a non-utopian visitor around (63). *The Female Man* thus blends three different genres: Jael's science fiction, Janet's utopia and Joanna's realistic narrative.

From Joanna's point of view, Janet is one of her possible other selves, one which is completely free from inhibiting patriarchal structures in her mind. Joanna refers to these inhibiting structures as 'the knowledge you suffer when you're an outsider—I mean *suffer*; I do not mean *undergo* or *employ* or *tolerate* or *use* or *enjoy* or *catalogue* or *file away* or *entertain* or *possess* or *have*' (137, italics in original). Janet, in Joanna's mind, 'appears Heaven-high ... with a mountain under each arm and the ocean in her pocket' (213), and transforms Joanna's life when she 'visits' her: 'Before Janet arrived on this planet', Joanna was 'moody, ill-at-ease, unhappy, and hard to be with' (29) and did nothing but 'live for The Man' (29):

> Then a new interest entered my life. After I called up Janet, out of nothing, or she called up me (don't read between the lines; there's nothing there) I began to gain weight, my appetite improved, friends commented on my renewed zest for life, and a nagging scoliosis of the ankle that had tortured me for years simply vanished overnight. (29)

Reading 'between the lines' in spite of or rather because of the narrator's admonitions against it, one detects an intersection between the two narrative levels in this passage. From Jael's perspective it is Janet who visits Joanna as a time traveller between universes. From Joanna's point of view, however, Janet is a daydream, a possibility to interact with a desired aspect of Joanna's own self.

Thus, a mental state which might be treated as multiple personality disorder by clinical psychology becomes a space for liberating acts of power: the dialectic of gender which I delineated in Part One simultaneously takes place in Joanna's mind: 'I'll tell you how I turned into a man. First I had to turn into a woman' (133). She accepts the negation of self through patriarchal discourse, associating with the category 'woman':

> You will notice that even my diction is becoming feminine,
> thus revealing my true nature ...
>
> Very swampy in my mind. Very rotten and badly off. I am a
> woman. I am a woman with a woman's brain. I am a woman
> with a woman's sickness. I am a woman with the wraps off,
> bald as an adder, God help me and you. (137)

Subsequently, she negates the negation within herself: 'Then I turned
into a man' (137). Splitting the image of herself in four distinct personalities, all of whose names start with 'J', allows Joanna to stage
this dialectic in her mind in the framework of a science fiction story
and thereby to propel herself into a state of mind in which she can
confront and reformulate inhibiting patriarchal narratives.

Janet's visit on Joanna's earth surfaces some of the ambiguities
inherent in the text: 'Oh, I made that woman up; you can believe it!'
(30) Joanna's exclamation can be read in two ways: on the one hand
she refers to her efforts to refine Janet's manners and appearance: on
the other she also implies the possibility that Janet is merely a product of her, Joanna's, imagination. Joanna tries to teach Janet the cus-
toms and especially the taboos of her planet, as well as the intricacies
of the English language, one of the main objectives being to find a
male mate for the Whileawayan. But Janet is not in the least interested in men and tells Joanna: 'about this men thing, you must
remember that to me they are a particularly foreign species; one can
make love with a dog, yes? But not with something so unfortunately
close to oneself' (33). Janet is, however, apparently quite interested in
Joanna herself, who at that point is still under the effect of compulsory heterosexuality and rejects her with exaggerated violence: 'She
bent down to kiss me, looking kind, looking perplexed, and I kicked
her. That's when she put her fist through the wall' (33). This passage
illustrates the unsettling ambiguity that runs through the text: in the
science fiction framework, Joanna and Janet are two separate characters who could conceivably sleep with each other. Taken as a daydream, however, the text presents Janet as merely one of Joanna's
personalities, without a physical body of her own. Both readings exist
as possibilities throughout the novel, but none of them in a privileged
position. This simultaneity exemplifies the way in which Western
feminist oppositional politics must deploy multiple strategies to
resist both the socio-economic system which privileges white middle-
class males and the symbolic order which accompanies it.

Other novels by Russ employ similar strategies to connect the science fiction narrative to the life of the fictional author and/or implied reader. Although *The Two of Them* is far less complex structurally, it also splits the narrative into a science fictional and a realistic strand. Irene is thus both a protagonist in the science fiction adventure and a woman from a basic narrative world which corresponds to the world of the implied reader. After having killed Ernst, Irene returns to the world of her childhood and becomes a 'thirty-year-old divorcée with a child to support', a woman who has left her husband and faces the vicissitudes of a world hostile to women, rather than being a well-trained member of an effective espionage organization. *The Two of Them* and especially *The Female Man* make these experiments with multiple identities within the cultural context explicit through the science fiction narrative.

Dissolving discursive hierarchies and the singular narrative voice, *The Female Man* creates an unstable narrator who is at the same time one character—Joanna as spirit of the author—and three *different* characters who are able to move in and out of each other and between their worlds. These ambiguities allow Joanna to tap the anguish that leads Jael to man-slaughter, and, charged with this power, to overcome the cultural training that had made one aspect of her as selfless as Jeannine. The following section will focus on the way in which Joanna negotiates between her multiple selves, without ever attempting to integrate them into a unified whole, which would, after all, inevitably get stuck in essentializing and reified definitions of the self as compact external object—which one could comfortably perceive in a mirror. The continued references to quite different oppositional discourses in Russ's work thus activates permanently shifting, multiple and—above all—contradictory identities.

Welcome Selves, Goodbye!

> Somewhere there is a book that says you ought to cry buckets of tears over yourself and love yourself with a passion and wrap your arms around yourself; only then will you be happy and free. That's a good book. (*On Strike Against God*, 32)

Jeannine, Janet and Joanna in *The Female Man* do not only share the same genotype with Jael, they are also connected via their names, a fact that the text emphasizes repeatedly: 'Janet, Jeannine, Joanna. Something very J-ish is going on here' (148); 'Jeannine, Janet,

Joanna. Something's going to happen' (149); 'Joanna, Jeannine, Janet. What a feast of J's. Somebody is collecting J's' (155). Jael, who otherwise hates everyone else, expresses the deepest affection for her three alter-egos: 'How she loves us! ... She turns the warmth of her smile on Jeannine the way none of us has ever been smiled at before, a dwelling, loving look that would make Jeannine go through fire and water to get it again ...' (158). Jael plans to enlist the other versions of herself to act with her for a single, stable cause: the war that will annihilate the Manlanders. In so doing, she desires to shape a unified identity to integrate all four of them: 'Look around you and welcome yourselves; look at me and make me welcome; welcome myself, welcome me, welcome I' (158-59). As I showed in Part One, Jael makes Whileaway possible, but in attempting to forge a monolithic self, she gets stuck with the phallus. However, of all the other 'Js', only Jeannine is willing to 'do business' (210) with Jael. Janet flatly refuses, without explanation. War, as a patriarchal concept, would be a setback for the open, decentralized society of Whileaway, while to Jeannine it is the only chance to escape her fate as some (any) male's wife. Joanna, being at the same time one of them and all of them, remains indeterminate. She leaves her answer open, and neither fully embraces Jael's war nor rejects it.

The final chapter in *The Female Man* brings the four women together for the last time in a neutral place—a restaurant mostly frequented by women—for Thanksgiving dinner. After the meal, the narrator releases her other selves:

> We got up and paid our quintuple bill; then we went out into the street. I said goodbye and went off with Laur, I, Janet; I also watched them go, I, Joanna; moreover I went off to show Jael the city, I Jeannine, I Jael, I myself.
>
> Goodbye, goodbye, goodbye.
>
> ... Remember: we will all be changed. In a moment, in the twinkling of an eye, we will all be free. I swear it on my own head. I swear it on my ten fingers. We will be ourselves. Until then I am silent; I can no more. I am God's typewriter and the ribbon is typed out. (213)

The disintegration of the subject is a powerful concept in feminist redefinitions of subjectivity. Russ's novels and short stories present the (post)modern trope of the fractured identity not as a source of confusion and disorientation for the narrator, but as an empowering state that allows her to engender stories of liberation within the self.

The concluding section of *The Female Man*, 'The Book of Joanna', in which Joanna brings together her various selves and bids them good bye, shows her as a transformed character. Not only does she 'come out' as a lesbian, she also takes her place as the dominant narrator and fictional author. Thus, the text intertwines the character's coming to terms with the reality of fragmentation, acknowledging her own deviance from the sexual norm, and the act of narration or authoring. As in other texts by Russ, authoring allows the woman engaged in it to manipulate and subvert the discourses of patriarchy and to create her own narratives against the stifling narratives that define her as a member of her sex. Two other novels, The *Two of Them* and *We Who Are About To* ..., further explore the way in which women cope with the patriarchal narratives of femininity which mute their voices and inhibit their access to the process of signification.

So It All Cancels Out: *We Who Are About To...*

'My religion,' said I ... 'says a lot about power. Bad things! It says thou owest God a death. It says that the first thing a sane civilization does with cryogenic corpses is to pull the plug on those damned popsicles, and if you want to live forever you are dreadfully dangerous because you're not living now. It says that you must die, because otherwise how can you be saved? It says that without meaningful work you might as well be dead'. (*We Who Are About To...*, 31)

This passage, put forth by the narrator of *We Who are About To...* (1977),[1] brings to the point one of the key premises of Russ's work: productive activity as prerequisite for an existence that is meaningful within the cultural context. Writing constitutes one such productive activity. Russ writes within the tradition in feminism which claims that, since dominant discourse has constructed the author as male, a female writer is faced with a paradoxical situation: the language available to her defines her as artistic object, not as creator of art, which means that either she cannot write or she must become not-a-woman, placing herself outside the social fabric. The statement quoted above, however, links a meaningful existence to the system of production. Paradoxically, the commitment to language and writing places a significance on the text that partially contradicts such a materialist analysis of society, upon which this statement is predicated.

This contradiction, which is paralleled in the concept of history that prevails in Russ's work, is at the centre of *We Who Are About To* .... The novel's primary themes are the paradoxical interactions between narrating, political activism and history. Such a relationship between women's writing and their access to the writing of history also motivates much of Russ's critical work. In *How to Suppress Women's Writing*, for instance, Russ shows how women and women's writing have been silenced and excluded from history, tracing these forms of suppression from early women writers such as Aphra Behn up to the present. Russ argues that even though there are no longer any formal prohibitions against writing for women, women are just as effectively silenced in the late twentieth century as they have been in history. Misogynist discourse thus still responds to a woman who writes with what Russ calls 'denial of agency' or with the diagnosis that the woman has mental problems: '... *she couldn't have written it ... she stole it, she's really a man, only a woman who is more-than-a-woman could have done it or she did write it but look how immodest it makes her, how ridiculous, how unlovable, how abnormal!*' (36, italics in original). Russ quotes Anaïs Nin, who was told by her psychoanalyst: 'When the neurotic woman gets cured, she becomes a woman. When the neurotic man becomes cured, he becomes an artist ... [T]o create it is necessary to destroy. Woman cannot destroy' (14).

Although these claims may not apply to the diverse positions occupied by women writers in the late 1990s, particularly not to white middle-class women in the West, they do intersect with Russ's work in significant ways. In her fictional writing more so than in her criticism, Russ is able to play out the contradictions between the existence of oppression and its fragmentary and elusive character. Power does not have a single location. To maintain political radicalism in the face of this realization is one of the great accomplishments of Russ's fiction. I have, so far, stressed the liberation narratives in her writing, which contain utopian hope for successful resistance and transformation. However, the story of authoring in such novels as *The Two of Them* and *We Who Are About To* ... simultaneously also strikes a less optimistic note: Zubeydeh escapes the fate of being locked up as a madwoman, but she carries an image of herself as other to her exile. The narrator in *We Who Are About To* ... does create a text, but, since there is no hope that anyone will ever read it, she still remains completely isolated and outside history—sharing the fate of Charlotte Brontë's 'madwoman in the attic' from *Jane Eyre* and of Charlotte Perkins Gilman's narrator in 'The Yellow Wall-Paper'.

Depicting the group's dying instead of their survival, *We Who Are About To* ... satirizes and reverses the science fictional cliché in which a group of hardy pioneers colonize a planet, re-enacting the myth of Adam and Eve on a virgin world (Lefanu, 180). The text of the novel is presented as a transcript from a 'pocket vocoder' recording produced around the year 2055 by a 42-year-old musicologist who does not reveal her name until page 105 when she refers to herself in passing as Elaine. She is shipwrecked on a desolate, uninhabited planet together with three other women, a 12-year-old girl and three men. The narrative is the diary of the group's dying.

In this respect the novel is a reversal of *Picnic on Paradise*, in which the protagonist is left on a barren planet to help a group of people survive. The narrator in *We Who Are About To* ..., who is as alien to the group as Alyx was to the tourists, 'helps' her companions die. The miniature microcosm in the vastness of space had started out in the best Crusoean fashion: as soon as their little rescue shuttle landed, all of them, with the exception of the narrator, busied themselves with setting up a plan of survival and colonization, including a programme for reproduction. To Elaine this plan is downright absurd: when one of the men tries to convince her that she has to think of herself as a 'child-bearer' since 'Civilization must be preserved', she responds laconically: 'Civilization is doing fine ... [w]e just don't happen to be where it is' (31). She continues:

> I said, '... we *are* dead. We died the minute we crashed. Plague, toxic food, deficiency diseases, broken bones, infection, gangrene, cold, heat, and just plain starvation. I'm just a Trembler. My God, you're the ones who want to suffer: conquer and control, conquer and control, when you haven't even got stone spears. You're dead.' (46–47, italics in original)

In spite of this caustic criticism, the three men, with the collaboration of the three other women, proceed to reinstitute a primitive form of patriarchy which reduces the women to walking wombs. Thus, while the rest of the group try to enforce a crude Darwinian narrative of survival, the sole dissenter confronts them with a troublesome counter-narrative in the language of twentieth century medical science. This counter-narrative reveals that the science fictional plot template of unlimited space exploration and colonization is predicated upon the erroneous notion that humans are made to master the universe.

The novel accentuates its critical reference to such science-fictional stories of colonization through the violent confrontation between the two opposing positions. The narrator leaves the group to die by herself in a cave up in the barren mountains, but the new self-defined colony cannot allow this kind of dissent because it undermines the story on which they intend to live. Four members of the group track her down to either force her to agree or—if necessary—kill her. Without hesitation, Elaine in turn kills them all, except for the ones who are already dead (one of the men had a heart attack and one of the women has committed suicide). Slowly starving in her cave, she thinks about her past: 'And now I have to live with this awful, awful woman, this dreadful, wretched, miserable woman, until she dies' (155). Literally even more isolated than the narrator in 'The Yellow Wall-Paper', the dying narrator moves further and further inside herself, since this, for her, is the only place to go.

In this isolation, the act of narration becomes synonymous with life. Because all the others are dead, Elaine is the only one left to make up the history of the failed colony—and the story of her life. She is dying and what will remain of her is only her text: 'Everything's being sublimed into voice, sacrificed for voice; my voice will live on years and years after I die' (128). She owns the only voice left on the planet and has therefore in a sense reached the centre of power. However, while the narrator is at the centre of her own narrative, she is completely outside the rest of human history: 'Far, far away from the cutting edge of change. God knows I'm private now. And on the periphery now. As far from anything as one can get. Outside the outside of the outside' (119).

In this situation of complete and irreversible marginalization, the absent reader paradoxically receives central importance. Starving alone on a desolate planet in outer space, Elaine knows that the chances of anyone finding her recording are virtually nil. Unlike the narrators in Russ's work who are also the fictional authors of the text, such as Joanna in *The Female Man* or the narrator in 'Life in a Furniture Store', Elaine has no access to a story which would give her control over the act of publication. She is recording a diary whose chances of ever finding a human audience are minuscule, yet as she reconstructs the story of her life, she desperately reaches out for a reader: 'What do you know? Do you know anything? ... *Who are you?*' (76, italics in original). 'If neither alien nor human, you're God. Who already knows. So I'm left talking to myself. Which is nothing and nobody' (115). She recalls a nest of fledgelings she once observed which squeaked desperately for their parents: '*Feed me! feed me!*' (157, italics in original). Her narrative shrieks with comparable urgency:

'Read me, read me, read me!' (160).

Parallel to this exploration of the narrator's psychic life, the diary also critically examines her past as a political activist and the way in which she had evaded the double bind of oppositional thinking. In her mind, Elaine conjures up images of people she knew and relates her present isolation to a time when she was a politically active communist. The utopian goal of her activism had been to be 'inside History' (124). But the enormousness of the task had precluded any tangible change as a result of her activism. The revolution did not happen. Her political group was hunted by the 'Civic Improvement Association' (CIA?), put into prison, and the media ignored them. Looking back, she muses:

> My God, how naive we were ...
>
> Although the Civic Improvement Association was worse (or better?); anyway, they still thought they were *at the center*. You have to think that or die. Either you limit what you think about and who you think about (the commonest method) or you start raising a ruckus about being outside and wanting to get inside (then they try to kill you) or you say piously that God puts everybody on the inside (then they love you) or you become crazed in some way. Not insane but flawed deep down somehow, like a badly-fired pot that breaks when you take it out of the kiln and the cold air hits it. Desperate.
>
> So I said Hey, if you're going to send mobs against me, I'll change what I say; I'll say God puts everybody on the inside—and anyway it's true and one must believe it—and I zipped like lightning back to the edge of the board. (118, italics in original)

Getting out of politics because she did not want to die for her convictions paradoxically meant virtual death: 'without meaningful work you might as well be dead' (31). Like the narrator in 'Life in a Furniture Store', she is out of a job and isolated from the rest of humanity. In the story Elaine tells of her past when she was supposedly still 'on the edge of the board', she had only three options, none of which allowed her to lead a meaningful life *within* human history. She could either fight for her politics and be killed—outside history; she could turn inside herself and be considered insane—outside history; or she could compromise and play by the rules—outside history.

These resigned assessments are quite in tune with the fading revolutionary enthusiasm throughout the political left during the latter half of the 1970s. Marilyn Hacker says about *We Who Are About To ...*

in 1977, shortly after the novel came out:

> Baldly—it is a bald book—it is about failure and death. It reminds me of Adrienne Rich's statement that after the critical rejection of her first woman-oriented book, *Snapshots of a Daughter-in-Law*, her next book, *Necessities of Life*, was, had to be, about death—not as a response to critical neglect; as a statement of what is, in our time the ultimate alternative to political commitment. (76)

Still, I would contend that *We Who Are About To* ... is more about the impossibilities of life than about death, even if—undeniably—the narrated events do culminate in the death of all protagonists, including the narrator. It is precisely the analogy to events in Elaine's life which give the narrative of her dying a focus and meaning.

Furthermore, the novel does not culminate in a gesture of closure which would fix the narrator's death and link it to the death of political activism. The text contains multiple stories which destabilize such a reading. Elaine does indeed transform the history of the new colony by preventing it from even starting. Hallucinating, she admits that she did not, as she had claimed before, kill the others out of self-defence or to spare them a slow, painful death:

> I rather enjoyed killing them off and I don't care ...
>   No, I had to. I really had to.
>   But all the same I did. What 'pocket genocide'? I guess so. Up to the elbows in blood. Poetry. (155)

Killing the colony and writing its dying history, she has put herself at the centre. But there is no agency in this centre. The only effect of androcide in this story is that the narrator can die in peace and in the process soliloquize the story of herself and the would-be colony. The history that remains is the text.

Yet this history defies linear logic in ways similar to those in 'What Did You Do During the Revolution, Grandma?' The narrator becomes increasingly fractured and her tale incoherent. As her story progresses, Elaine gives up trying to control what she says, and the text's narrative logic dissolves. Elaine's criticism of the narrative of conquest and colonization demonstrates that history does not progress along a straight line as both idealist and materialist theory presuppose. History is also not cyclical, not even women's history, as radical feminism claimed. History may be both linear and cyclical or neither; the text does not search for conclusive answers. But one painful fragment of certainty emerges from her tale: history may just end arbitrarily, without the consolation of meaning.

Exploring the paradoxes of writing history, *We Who Are About To ...* thus connects with the moment in feminism which Kristeva identifies with a rejection of linear and cyclical temporality. Since history is a fictional text, and death is inevitable, what remains of the individual when she dies is a palimpsest of texts. Even her materialist political activism, for which the link between economic development and history was a necessary one, is ultimately just that, a story. For Elaine the stories of the world are told by music, which conveys meaning without directional logic: 'All the music in the world says all the things in the world—I mean the universe, of course—and that's everything there is. So it all cancels out' (164).

CHAPTER NINE
Vampires, Cyborgs and Disguises: Politics of the Theatrical

> ... laughter in the face of serious categories is indispensable for feminism—Butler (*Gender Trouble*, viii)

Situated within the historical context of postmodern culture in transnational corporate capitalism, feminism(s) have had to reassess all-encompassing theories about 'women' and their 'oppression' in 'patriarchy'. The totalizing claims of the 'information society' over all aspects of lived social relations make it nearly impossible to find discursive spaces from which to argue oppositional politics. Russ's fiction seeks precisely such discursive spaces. As my readings have demonstrated, her work shows an uneasiness with stable identities and sweeping, monolithic political claims from her beginnings as a writer in the late 1950s and early 1960s. Russ shares this searching uneasiness with a number of feminist critics, who have articulated feminist political positions which do not solely rely on the integrity and homogeneity of the category woman.

One of these critics is Donna Haraway, whose cyborg myth, carefully constructed in her classic essay 'A Manifesto for Cyborgs' (1985), illustrates this particular deconstructive stance and as a point of intersection highlights the political significance of non-human or partially dehumanized characters in Russ's fiction. Analysing the complex workings of power and exploitation in what she calls the 'Informatics of Domination', Haraway builds 'an ironic political myth faithful,' as she says, 'to feminism, socialism and materialism' (190). Her *eiron*, her dissembler in this constructed mythical story, is the cyborg, a hybrid creature who takes pleasure in the confusion of boundaries between machine and organism, between human and animal, and indeed between social reality and fiction. Merging human organisms with sophisticated machinery is an invention of science fiction, but also part of social and bodily reality at the end of the twentieth century. Silicon breasts, artificial hearts, prostheses of all kinds, titanium teeth implants, contact lenses and other artefacts have become part of human bodies to the point of being indistinguishable from the 'original'. The cyborg did not choose to become such, but s/he consciously uses this position as political 'myth' which makes possible the weaving of oppositional networks of partial affiliations.

In articulating this destabilizing political concept, Haraway criticizes earlier socialist and radical feminist perspectives—Kristeva's first and second moment—for claiming the status of complete explanation. Both feminist positions in the heat of their revolutionary fervour totalized their own (white, Western) concept of 'woman' as an essentially homogenous group of innocent victims. Throughout this book, I have indicated the ways in which Russ uses the image of vampires and ghosts in similar ways to destabilize the body and gender identities. The following sections will further examine how Russ employs the generic conventions of science fiction and fantasy to explode the concept of the 'natural', 'original' human body. If technology makes it possible to shape and manipulate the body according to cultural definitions or ideological needs, the distinction between bodily reality and discourse about it begins to become leaky.

In Russ's fiction, dehumanized creatures such as vampires and ghosts—like the cyborgs of more recent science fiction—function as impersonators of ironic images of sexed and gendered humanness. Cyborgs and vampires potentially undermine a humanistic concept of 'nature' and destroy its claim to original wholeness and innocence. The vampire Martin Guevara, for example, as a character puts into question the male's biological link to the phallus and power. Ghostly narrators such as Jael destabilize their 'original' female body. Jael's body is artfully crafted as a killing machine for the physical destruction of male bodies; her 'female' body, which was the site of her powerlessness, becomes the site of power. Instead of searching for an all-encompassing concept of humanness which would be universally shared by all people, male or female, white or black, poor or rich, Russ's fiction plays with impersonations and performances of these roles. This play is as serious as it is irreverent, yet it also never exhausts the scope of the text.

A Female Man? Everywoman in Search of a Brand Name

> I sat in a cocktail party in mid-Manhattan. I had just changed into a man, me, Joanna. I mean a female man, of course; my body and soul were exactly the same (*The Female Man*, 5)

Joanna in *The Female Man* and Esther in *On Strike Against God* shape a
story of empowerment for themselves by embracing the category
'woman' as their own, as I demonstrated in Part Two. However, these
two characters simultaneously also reject this category as imposed on
them by a symbolic system alien to the narrative needs of their existence. In *The Female Man*, Joanna as narrator breaks free from the
identity defined for her by patriarchy. She explores possible alternative selves within the discursive framework available to her and
becomes what she calls the 'female man'. Disintegrating the unified
narrator, Russ's texts thus also dissolve the idea of a stable, unitary
self. In *The Two of Them* and *The Female Man*, as well as in *On Strike
Against God*, Russ splits the protagonist into two or more different per-
sonas/personalities, thereby subverting the notion of the stable identity created by revolutionary acts of power such as androcide or the
rejection of men as sexual partners. Russ's writing throughout thrives
on such contradictions.

Materialist feminism has defined gender as a social category distinct from biological sex. This notion of woman as a suppressed
class—in analogy to the proletariat—is crucial in claiming agency in
patriarchal societies and in revealing the constructedness of gender-
role behaviour. However, this analogy also has its limitations because
in these theories gender, unlike economic class, is directly linked to
biology. If you are female in sex, supposedly you are inevitably also
feminine in gender. Within this terminological framework, conceptu-
alizing a genderless society—in analogy to the classless society—is
impossible. The quasi-genderless utopia Whileaway testifies to this
impasse: biological males on Whileaway would be unthinkable. However, even though the text does not project an androgynous utopian
vision, it does produce images of women who contest the biologized
linkage between gender and sex.

Such attempts to find a way out of biological determinism are not
new. As early as the nineteenth century, the American feminist Margaret Fuller struggled to transform patriarchal language to truly
include woman in a genderless generic term:

> By Man I mean both man and woman: these are the two halves
> of one thought. I lay no especial stress on the welfare of either.
> I believe that the development of the one cannot be effected
> without that of the other. My highest wish is that this truth
> should be distinctly and rationally apprehended, and the con-
> ditions of life and freedom recognized as the same for the

daughters and the sons of time; twin exponents of a divine thought. (Fuller, 13)

Margaret Fuller—in the best idealist tradition—could still believe in the power of reason and simply demand 'woman' to be included in what she thought was the generic term, 'man'. To a late-twentieth-century materialist feminist this is not a viable solution, even if she did believe that the heterosexual bond between a man and a woman, 'two halves of one thought', was the prototype designed by 'Nature' herself for 'eternity'. However, for all the theoretical and ideological differences, one central concern of feminist texts like Russ's is the same as Fuller's: to create stories in which women act as equal agents in society and in the process of signification. The materialist, of course, does not rely on reason for change, but on revolution: 'For years I have been saying *Let me in, Love me, Approve me, Define me, Regulate me, Validate me, Support me.* Now I say *Move over*' (*The Female Man*, 140, italics in original). Russ's narrator here could not care less about the well-being of the other sex. Nor is this narrator willing to remain fixed in her own 'half' of the supposedly binary human spectrum. The alternatives she and other gender 'misfits' in Russ's work explore will be the focus of the remaining sections in this study.

Joanna: Not-a-Woman—Everywoman?

If we are all Mankind, it follows to my interested and righteous and rightnow [sic] very bright and beady little eyes, that I too am a Man and not at all a Woman ... you will think of me as a Man and treat me as a Man until it enters your muddled, terrified, preposterous, nine-tenth-fake, loveless, papier-mâché-bull-moose head that *I am a man*. (And you are a woman.) That's the whole secret. Stop hugging Moses' tablets to your chest, nitwit; you'll cave in. Give me your Linus blanket, child. Listen to *the female man*.

If you don't, by God and all the Saints, *I'll break your neck* (*The Female Man*, 140, italics in original)

This passage from *The Female Man* is a twentieth-century radical feminist answer to the concerns politely raised by Margaret Fuller 150 years previously. The concept of the 'female man' expressed here stands in gross contradiction to women acting on behalf of their sex-class and bonding with other women which I have outlined in Parts One and Two. Showing no particular alliance to women as a group, the narrator here expresses the desire to deprive biology of those cultural meanings which specifically affect her as a subject. The 'you' in this passage is not a gendered opponent, but rather anyone, male or female, who denies the narrator access to the process of signification. This example shows how Russ's later novels consciously use contradictory strategies from within patriarchal discourse to undermine the precepts of the oppressive system. The subject her texts try to liberate is gendered because she is oppressed, but, as this passage shows, the system of gender and sex is not taken as an essentially given entity, which points to a—partially—autonomous subjectivity beyond these oppressive categories.

Janet, 'the Might-be of our dreams' (*The Female Man*, 213), represents such a vision of a genetic female who is not a woman. Since there are no men on Whileaway, gender is not a basis of oppression and the category 'woman' is meaningless in the discourses of this culture. She takes no offence at the fact that her last name in English translates as Eva*son* because she does not define her existence in opposition to an other who is male. When she witnesses Jael's impersonation of heterosexual intercourse with the android, Janet—quite unimpressed—remarks: 'Good Lord! Is *that* all?' (198) What radical lesbian-feminism identified as the sources of greatest suffering for women in patriarchy are for her, if anything, sources of mirth.

However, it is the peculiar character of utopian visions that they are not predictions of what the future *will* or *even* should look like, but comments on what is wrong with the present. What distinguishes utopias from other types of cultural criticism is that they are always predicated on an element of hope. Tom Moylan in his book *Demand the Impossible* shows that all utopian writing is a product of its culture:

> [Utopian writing] is, at heart, rooted in the unfulfilled needs and wants of specific classes, groups, and individuals in their unique historical context ... Developed within the context of early capitalism and the European exploration of the new world, the literary utopia has functioned within the dominant ideology that has shaped the capitalist dream and within the oppositional ideologies that have pushed beyond the limits of that dream. (2)

Utopian writing, according to Moylan, always expresses oppressed groups' experience of lack, and is therefore simultaneously critical of and based on dominant ideology. In his chapter on *The Female Man*, Moylan outlines the economic structure of Whileaway as one that 'combines a post-industrial, cybernetic technology with a libertarian pastoral social system. Fulfillment of each person, not accumulation of profit and centralization of power, is the goal of the economy' (67). I would go further and say that what the Whileawayan utopia considers a 'fulfilled life' is shaped by the very capitalist, patriarchal individualism it sets out to dislocate.

This alliance with the culture one wants to revolutionize, far from being a shortcoming, is unavoidable and necessary because otherwise the proposed society would not be recognizable as a viable alternative. Whileaway is thus both a critique of white middle-class American culture and thoroughly grounded in its founding narratives. I have already examined the way in which Russ's texts appropriate for themselves American cultural narratives relating to the Bible. The image of the frontier as formative element in white American individualism and American nationhood provides another such cluster of narratives.[1] These narratives were particularly instrumental in forming the modern American systems of gender, class and race. *The Female Man* uses the Whileawayan utopia to revisit precisely those narratives and to disrupt their continuous reproduction of masculinity and femininity, without, however, touching their implicit assumptions about race and class. The Whileawayan wilderness produces individuals that appropriate elements of 'frontier' masculinity for their culture. These individuals are not explicitly marked by race or class; as a consequence they are, like the original 'frontier man', white by implication. Whileaway also shares the basic assumption of all American frontier narratives, namely that confronting the 'wilderness' by oneself produces and shapes an independence which is largely coextensive with masculinity.

Janet as paradoxical utopian character thus represents what the novel calls a 'female man', a woman who is not a woman and not a man, but still both masculine and female. Like most young adolescents on Whileaway, Janet sets out alone for the wilderness to shape her identity as an individual by surviving in a place removed from society: 'When I was thirteen I stalked and killed a wolf, alone, on North Continent above the forty-eighth parallel, using only a rifle. I made a travois for the head and paws, then abandoned the head, and finally got home with one paw, proof enough (I thought)' (1). Survival in the wilderness, according to the original narrative, turns the individual into a rugged frontier man, who rejects the sophistication and security of urban or agrarian communal living, which is, in turn, associated with femininity. The original version of the survival in the wilderness story gives the man a place in culture and an identity which it denies the woman. On Whileaway, the big, strong male is replaced by a thirteen-year-old girl, who nevertheless retains fundamental elements of his masculinity. Thus parodically evoking the frontier narrative, the Whileawayan utopia functions simultaneously within and outside the dominant ideology that has shaped the capitalist dream, and this is precisely what renders it so effective.

Janet's story of individuation is particularly relevant for Joanna. As I pointed out above, the ambiguity of the narrative connects Janet and Joanna in specific ways which make the Whileawayan's 'masculinity' available to Joanna as well. As a consequence, Joanna's version of the 'female man' reverberates with references to the frontier girl. In the passage quoted at the beginning of this section, Joanna's choice of diction ('If you don't ... *I'll break your neck*') lends her the powerfully independent voice of Janet.

Joanna consciously appropriates for herself an identity that is inherently contradictory: a 'female man' in patriarchal terms does not exist. By naming the unthinkable, she uses a conceptual space in which genders may proliferate and in which she imagines potential selves, such as Janet, outside the patriarchal confines of her sex. Jael, on the contrary, cannot move beyond the gender war, because she cannot name, i.e. conceptualize, the new version of herself after the war. Shaping new, liberating stories from patriarchal narrative raw material is thus a crucial subversive practice which creates a process concept of utopia rather than a fixed image of a 'better' society. Tom Moylan has called this type of subversive utopianism that emerged from the oppositional culture of the 1960s and 1970s 'critical' utopia: 'A central concern in the critical utopia is the awareness of the limitations of the utopian tradition, so that these texts reject utopia as blueprint while preserving it as dream' (10-11). Joanna's concept of the 'female man' and Whileaway represent such open, dynamic utopian visions, which do not—as the static utopian model does—provoke the question: What happens after the revolution? There is no after: the revolution continues.

Esther, Cal and Jai: Something-elses of the World, Unite!

Esther, the narrator of *On Strike Against God*, like Joanna seeks to name herself as other than a woman, at the same time as she connects to women as a woman:

> ... every female friend of mine seems to have accepted in some sense that she is a woman, has decided All right, I am a woman; rolls that name 'woman' over and over on her tongue, trying to figure out what it means, looks at herself in a full-length mirror, trying to understand, 'Is that what they mean by Woman?' ...
>
> I'm not a woman. Never, never. Never was, never will be. I'm a something-else... . I have a something-else's uterus, and a clitoris (which is not a woman's because nobody mentioned it while I was growing up) and something-else's straight, short hair, and every twenty-five days blood comes out of my something-else's vagina, which is a something-else doing its bodily housekeeping. This something-else has wormed its way into a university teaching job by a series of impersonations which never ceases to amaze me ... I do not want a better deal. I do not want to make a deal at all. *I want it all.* They got to my mother and made her a woman, but they won't get me.
>
> Something-elses of the world, unite! (18-19, italics in original)

The way in which Russ modifies the radical battle cry of the political left here crystallizes her strategy of combining existing narratives that contradict each other to make 'queer' new stories for people who do not fully fit the norm—which is ultimately most people. 'Something-else' here is not an economic or social but a symbolic category. The type of patriarchal discourse evoked by the passage quoted above defines the woman as the other, in opposition to the male prototype. Therefore, it is impossible to associate the term 'woman' with the self without the experience of alienation: such a woman's 'own' voice has no place in dominant discourses. The critic Pamela Annas speaks of this alienation as 'dual vision': 'This duality of perception comes ... through the experience of having one's reality defined not by oneself, but by somebody else' (144). The reified concepts of 'woman' and 'man' in the agreed-upon reality of patriarchal cultures force each individual to either accept the reification or to seek out ways of becoming not-a-woman or not-a-man, something-else.

Existing discourses already have such spaces that take up the 'something-elses' of the world; homosexuality has been one of them, at least since the nineteenth century. Ironically, these spaces of deviance or perversion are necessary as the abject other on which the formation and maintenance of the norm depends. Lesbians and gay men thus have a history of being both outside and inside the patriarchal matrix of sex and gender. Making these symbolic categories part of a materialist politics of affiliation, as Russ's work does, is therefore a powerful strategy of resistance. Monique Wittig has claimed that a lesbian, since she does not depend on a social relation to a man, is not a woman: 'We are escapees from our class in the same way as the American runaway slaves were escaping slavery and becoming free' (Wittig, 'One is Not Born a Woman' 20). None of the women in Russ's novels who enter the space of lesbian existence need to kill a man to liberate themselves. Conversely, the women who do commit androcide never proceed to sleep with a woman. Getting away without murder in Russ's texts is possible for lesbians because they are not full members of women's sex-class. The story of Jael in *The Female Man* illustrates the inherent paradox of androcide as an act that affirms woman's existence. A society which eradicates all males loses the chance of eradicating the pernicious sex/gender categorization, petrifying the very system that necessitated the revolution in the first place.

Only as a potential option is androcide therefore useful in the revolutionary process. Lesbian continuum and lesbian existence allow the women in Russ's texts to assert their agency without direct dependence on males, but even if a lesbian could be considered an 'escapee' from 'patriarchy', she would still have to function as part of a culture which remains patriarchal. The category woman is not 'just' an economic, political or even ideological category. It is inscribed by patriarchal discourse on women's bodies and in their minds. Esther in becoming 'something-else' may symbolically escape the gender forced upon her, but she cannot fully escape the cultural meaning attached to her body. Patriarchal discourse defines her uterus and clitoris as a woman's—indeed, every single cell of her body bears the brand of patriarchy: XX. Here, the metaphor of the runaway slave, problematic as it is in the voice of a white European, may be more fitting than Wittig may wish it to be: in the North, the black escapee— although nominally free—was still not considered to be fully human.

Moreover, Russ's fiction does not close these spaces of resistance to males. Cal in *The Female Man* is a closet transvestite who fails to perform the masculine role in the relationship which he dutifully maintains with Jeannine, but who manages to find power and existence on his imaginary stage. He, too, may be read as a version of the 'female man', appropriating as he does the theatrical effeminacy conventionally associated with male homosexuality. His presence in the text disrupts the clear-cut antagonism between men and women which Jael enforces. Similarly Jai Vedh in the earlier novel *And Chaos Died*—another 'J'—rejects most components of masculinity in science fiction. At no point in the novel does he have control over the plot, although most of the text is narrated from within his mind. His partially displaced homosexuality and his unstable physical existence in the text let him occupy a number of different subject positions. Based on his actions and positions in the plot one may read him as a gay man, a bisexual man or even a lesbian woman—ultimately he resists each of these identifications.

Russ's texts thus function within an awareness that the identity of the subject is not tied to her biology, but to the meaning the culture attaches to her body and to her position in her culture. Russ creates images of women and—to a lesser extent—men who search for an answer to the question: Who am I? But this search has as its object not primarily a kernel of truth at the centre of the self, but rather the potentially liberating, quirky multiplicity of selves within the subject. This multiplicitous subject, as I have shown, is always present in Russ's writing from her earliest publications, but her later, critically feminist work brings its disruptive possibilities to the foreground. Donna Haraway's cyborg myth represents the desire to retain a utopian vision while at the same time acknowledging the stark impossibility of a utopian space beyond existing discourses. Russ's impersonators, her cyborgs, vampires, ghosts and aliens are expressions of the same desire.

And *Then* They Saved the World, Right? *Extra(Ordinary) People* and the Utterly Impossible, Positively Necessary Utopic Imagination

A cyborg is a cybernetic organism, a hybrid of machine and organism, a creature of social reality as well as a creature of fiction. Social reality is lived social relations, our most important political construction, a world-changing fiction ... The cyborg is a matter of fiction and lived experience that changes what counts as women's experience in the late twentieth century. This is a struggle over life and death, but the boundary between science fiction and social reality is an optical illusion (Haraway, 191)

Extra(Ordinary) People (1984) is Russ's most recent major work of fiction and self-critically revisits most of the central themes in Russ's oeuvre, such as androcide, authorship and the Sappho model. In terms of form, *Extra(Ordinary) People* enters ground that is both new and familiar. A hybrid between a collection of short stories and an episodic novel, *Extra(Ordinary) People* melds and modifies the two major forms in Russ's fictional work. *The Zanzibar Cat* and *The Hidden Side of The Moon*, for instance, are collections of largely unrelated, autonomous short stories. Similarly, *The Adventures of Alyx* combines autonomous stories, but the main character, an extraordinary woman warrior and con-artist, provides a connecting theme.

Extra(Ordinary) People goes further in joining the individual stories together through several common themes and a narrative frame. Although the stories also stand on their own, this frame formally moves them closer to a novel. Filling the interstices between stories with comments that position them in an ironic history of utopian desires, the linking narrative echoes the scene of teaching that is one of the central themes in most of the stories. Staging a series of inter-actions between an anthropomorphic electronic tutor and an (ungen-dered) 'schoolkid', the frame narrative focuses on the desire for and impossibility of utopian visions. This scene of teaching also connects the text as a whole with the 'rescue of the female child' theme and the Sappho model in Russ's earlier writing.

However, here, the scene of teaching is also skewed, since the 'teacher' is a machine which the schoolkid controls. This electronic tutor presents the individual stories as 'history' lessons to the stu-dent, whose central question remains throughout *'Is that the way the world was saved?'* (161, italics in original). The laconic answer of the tutor is: 'If you believe that ... you'd believe anything!' (93). The inter-actions between the tutor and the schoolkid are reminiscent of the struggle between Alyx and Edarra in 'Bluestocking', with the signifi-cant exception that there is no emotional involvement between the kid and the tutor. After the tutor tells the story 'Bodies', the student temporarily turns it off; after 'What Did You Do During the Revolu-tion, Grandma', s/he finally says 'I don't believe you' (145). What the schoolkid presumably learns through listening to the stories is not to answer her/his question about the history of her/his society, but to question her/his own assumptions. The tutor's final answer after all the storytelling is another question: 'What makes you think the world's ever been saved?' (161)

The narrative layers introduced by the interactions between this frame narrative and the individual stories make the spectre of the fictional author herself unstable, endowing her with self-mocking cyborg qualities. The stories' common themes and character types, set in relation by the frame narrative, thus combine the individual stories with a destabilizing assemblage that refuses to pose as a unified whole. This framing narrative also creates a tension between the highly personal voices of the individual narrators and the depersonalized voice of the computer. The schoolkid as a character without depth or individuality also stands in tension with the highly individualized richly narrated characters in the stories. The computer tutor makes the process of learning infinitely reproducible in identical patterns. An infinite number of interchangeable schoolkids can ask the same questions and will essentially learn the same lesson. Consequently, the framing narrative runs counter to the utopian thrust of the stories and shatters a concept of history that depends on causal links between events.

Extra(Ordinary) People thus also foregrounds the disruption of a linear temporality as it is assumed in Marxist concepts of historical progression as well as in materialist feminism. *The Female Man*, as I demonstrated in Part One, still uses the notion of a dialectical movement towards utopia. *Extra(Ordinary) People* not only destabilizes the historical dialectic, but further shatters its logic, replacing the dialectic with an apparently loosely linked assemblage of separate stories. However, the revolution is still present, even if it moves to the background, disconnected from the utopia. Two of the stories, 'Souls' and 'The Mystery of the Young Gentleman', represent the utopian longing of individuals with telepathic powers; 'Bodies' is the story of a utopian society which realizes some of these visions. Yet the story of the supposedly transformative event, 'What Did You Do During the Revolution, Grandma?', only demonstrates that the revolution does not directly result in a historical change, but is no more than its expression. The final story, then, 'Everyday Depressions', is a sketch of a lesbian gothic novel in the form of a series of letters which relates the banal excitements of everyday life. Represented through the limited visions of the individual personal narrative voices in each story, utopia receives an ironic undertone, without, however, being invalidated as an idea. The 'revolution', central to the solution of the sex-class antagonism in materialist feminism, becomes an ironic yet necessary (im)possibility.

'What Did You Do During the Revolution, Grandma?' is a case in point. 'Grandma', in a self-mocking parody of historical causality, instead of focusing on the revolution in her narrative, indulges in telling the story of pleasurable erotic activities with a 13-year-old young woman. The story thus puts in place an ironic distance to the most elevated objectives of radical feminism, such as inspiring a world-changing revolution, saving young girls from compulsory heterosexuality, or creating stories that will transform the lives of women and the course of history. However, this ironic distance, rather than invalidating the political goals of feminism, makes them contingent, open and adaptable, transforming static utopian visions into powerfully transgressive thought-experiments. Foregrounding the sexual pleasure implicit in the 'rescue of the female child' theme, 'What Did You Do During the Revolution, Grandma?' also reconstitutes the character of the maternal 'rescuer'. Reminiscent of such characters as Janet in *The Female Man* or Miss Edward in 'Scenes from Domestic Life', the narrator in 'What Did You Do During the Revolution, Grandma?' is an older woman whose narrative laughs about her own desire and contributes to the discourses which aim to depoliticize sex.

This type of character, which works with fragmentary biographic allusions to the author, is one of the themes that hold *Extra(Ordinary) People* together. Earlier novels such as *The Female Man* and *The Two of Them* accompany such links between characters and the persona of a fictional author with a split in the narrative between a science fictional and a realistic story line. *Extra(Ordinary) People* abandons that split, integrating the allusions to the life of the fictional author in the science fiction or fantasy plot. For example, 'What Did You Do During the Revolution, Grandma?' is partially set in Washington State, where Joanna Russ lived when she wrote the story. The narrator/protagonist is a spy and among other things teaches self-defence classes. Similarly, the narrator in 'Everyday Depressions' is a lesbian college teacher and writer. What links these characters to quasi-autobiographic elements in Russ's earlier work is their privileged position in relation to the act of narration. These characters appear as primary protagonists and/or narrators in each of the stories in *Extra(Ordinary) People*, occupying positions of power and self-reflexive knowledge. Their disillusioned yet still hopeful voices again correspond to the central tension in the text between the impossibility and necessity of utopian, revolutionary thinking.

In the first story, 'Souls' (1982), which won the 1983 Hugo Award, such a character takes the shape of a medieval German abbess. Although the simple-minded male narrator Radulf refers to the abbess as a 'demon' because he is limited to the language of medieval Christianity, her 'alienness' links her to Haraway's cyborgs. Like the other 'cyborg' characters in Russ's fiction, such as Jael, the abbess's existence as both human and alien endows her with special power in the story. Even though she is not the narrator, she controls both the plot and the act of narration. Radulf purports to relate the events as they occurred: 'This is the tale of the Abbess Radegunde and what happened when the Norsemen came. I tell it not as it was told to me but as I saw it, for I was a child then and the Abbess had made a pet and errand-boy of me ...' (1). But the text contains direct speech, particularly one long monologue from the abbess, which, in its cultural criticism and analytical dimension, is clearly beyond the grasp of 'Happy Radulf', the narrator. Moreover, the ambiguities of the narrative itself are inconsistent with the self-image projected by the narrative voice. The abbess Radegunde's speech acts in some instances directly contradict what the narrator says. Installing a distinct tension between the simplicity and naiveté of the narrator and the complexity and sophistication of the narrative, the text opens a third space that remains beyond representation.

The particular power yielded by the abbess correlates once more with an act of androcide, which, however, the text's ambiguity releases from its direct link to the woman's agency. When one of the Norsemen, who had raped a young nun, breaks his neck after Radegunde had miraculously healed him from a fatal wound, the abbess says: 'To be plain: I have just broken Thorfinn's neck, for I find the change improves him' (50). Yet a little further on in the narrative, recalling the event itself, the narrator remarks without modifying comment: 'Young Thorfinn had gone out in the night to piss and had fallen over a stone in the dark and broken his neck ...' (51). Leaving the tension between the two versions of Thorfinn's death unresolved, the story partially disconnects androcide from the narratives of causality and agency which had informed Russ's earlier fiction.

Furthermore, these inconsistencies produce an unstable narrative voice similar to the voices of the multiple narrators in *The Female Man* or the ghost-narrators in other texts by Russ. The 'ghost' of the alien woman controls the narrator's speech acts, which reduces him to a mere medium. He recalls: 'And she said also: 'Remember me,' and thus I have, every little thing, although it all happened when I was the age my own grandson is now, and that is how I can tell you this tale today' (56).

The tale this narrator tells corresponds to the instabilities on the level of narrative. The story recalls a medieval German abbey in a moment of crisis, in the process of which the ambiguously non-human character who acts as the abbess breaks with this role as the saintly older woman. A group of invaders, Norsemen, sack the little German village after a futile attempt by Radegunde to prevent the violence. As it turns out, Radegunde thinks of herself as an intellectually superior being among 'puppies and kittens' who fight and kill each other over mere 'toys'. Hoping to end her suffering and intellectual deprivation, she desperately calls to outer space for help: 'I have looked in all directions: to the east, to the north and south, and to the west, but there is one place I have never looked and now I will: away from the ball, straight up. Let us see—' (46). Her encounter with the aliens is reminiscent of James Tiptree's parodic reversal of alien invasions in science fiction which she created in her classic short story 'The Women Men Don't See':

> Then I saw, ahead of us through the pelting rain, a kind of shining among the bare tree-trunks, and as we came nearer the shining became more clear until it was very plain to see, not a blazing thing like a fire at night but a mild and even brightness as though the sunlight were coming through the clouds pleasantly but without strength, as it often does at the beginning of the year.
>
> And then there were folk inside the brightness, both men and women, all dressed in white, and they held out their arms to us and the demon ran to them, crying out loudly and weeping ... ('Souls', 53)

The abbess, although she turns out to be an 'alien' herself, produces a superior performance of perfect humanness. The narrator describes her as 'a prodigy of female piety and learning' (3) and emphasizes that she 'was kind to everyone' (3). Indeed, her 'alien' qualities, for instance her ability to perceive events and people's thoughts telepathically, equip her to be more perfectly human. Julie Linden in her thesis on The Female Man and Extra(Ordinary) People points out that Radegunde 'is aware of and controls her own identity' (61). I agree, but the identity she assumes is also controlled by the historical moment and place in which she operates. She appears in a medieval German town and it is no coincidence that she chooses as her 'identity' the role of an abbess, a woman in a position of learning and power who does not have to directly submit to anyone. Since she is also an 'alien' to the human system of signification, she can use this system for her own purposes.

Like the vampire Martin Guevara in 'My Dear Emily', the woman who performs 'Radegunde' destabilizes both sex and gender. Since Radegunde is only a role she plays, the 'sex' of her 'true' body is irrelevant. When she drops Radegunde like a 'garment', she points out that there was only one way she could pass as a human woman in human society: 'I could stay here long years only as Radegunde ... none of us can remain here long as our proper selves or even in our true bodies' (54). The narrator's sparse representation of the telepathic aliens projects a utopian vision of a society in which neither race, class nor gender has symbolic meaning or economic function. Since in Radulf's system of reference an ungendered and unsexed humanity is unrepresentable, he can only represent the being that plays Radegunde as non-human.

'Bodies' (1984) further develops the idea of a utopian society in which sex and gender have become irrelevant in economic terms and merely function as pretexts for playful performances which seem campy from the perspective of the late twentieth century. As in 'Souls', the narrator does not fully understand the utopian society in her tale. The story is in the form of a long email message from one of two visitors to the utopia to the other. Rose Marie, the narrator, is an older woman who acts as a teacher to James, the recipient of her message. Consequently, she does not write for a large, anonymous audience, but directly addresses James in the intimate voice of a personal letter. Both central characters have been transported to the future world from the twentieth century, James from London in the 1930s and Rose Marie from the US in the 1970s. Both of their original lives were determined by their homosexuality, which exposed them to painful persecution and discrimination but also gave them a stable identity. Furthermore, both participated in the subversion of gender categories in their own cultures, but remain aliens to the culture which realizes the utopian dream of sexual non-suppression. Because sex, gender and sexuality are unrelated as well as unfixed in this utopian society, Rose Marie and James lose track of their sense of self which was based on their fixed position in oppression.

James, newly hatched from a machine which regrew his life-information picked up moments before his real death in the 1930s, initially despairs with bewilderment at these confusions. The utopian society's playful proliferation of gender-roles and its changed interactions between erotic fantasies and power both titillate and frustrate his desire for sexual exploration. When he considers flirting with Billie

Joe, a mechanic in overalls, and learns the person's 'true' sex, he is disappointed:

> 'Will he be at the party?'
> 'She.'
> 'Oh.' (100)

In addition to disrupting James's expectations concerning the correlation between gender and sex, the utopian society also disrupts his sexual fantasies. His erotic encounter with Harriet, 'six foot four of sunburnt blond cowboy in range clothes' (101–02) with a handlebar moustache, reduces James to tears because the object of his desires destroys his fantasy of submission to an act of brutal masculine dominance. Instead of acting out his role as Visigoth conqueror of Rome, Harriet puts on perfume and flowers, disrupting James's part as 'proud Roman patrician lad' (104).

An erotic encounter with the narrator, whose gender performance seems to approximate James's idea of masculinity most consistently, also falls flat because he cannot cope with the oddness of her female body. The text once again evokes the 'rescue of the female child' theme, but disrupts the correlation between sex and gender in both protagonists. Male and female do not necessarily correspond to masculine and feminine. Further transforming the 'rescue of the female child', the text produces another variation on the theme as a broken 'rescue of the deviant male child'. The letter is an extended apology and invitation to resume a friendly relationship after a traumatic separation in the wake of the failed sexual interaction. The narrator, 30 years James's senior, uses the narrative to give the 20-year-old involuntary time-traveller 'maternal' advice, further disrupting fixed links between sex, gender and sexuality: 'I too spent my first year out of the tank getting it on with anyone who would, first the women (of course) and then the men' (112). The underlying assumption of this utopia is that the specificity of lesbian and male gay desire, as soon as homosexuality is not stigmatized as unnatural, ceases to exist. The two twentieth-century characters' experience in a society that represents their own utopian longings are based on the idea that sexuality is historically and culturally specific rather than a natural given. 'James wants to be adored by a real man (thought I) and that will be hard on him in this world where the men and women all vanished years ago' (105).

On the whole, 'Bodies', like the other stories of *Extra(Ordinary) People*, destabilizes gendered narration as well as the gender, sex and sexuality of the characters, continuously disrupting the correlation between the protagonists' sexed body, gender performance and sexual desire. The utopian vision of 'Bodies' therefore responds to and goes beyond the earlier utopia in *The Female Man*. Whileaway preserves and repeats the categories of oppression, such as sex-class and deviant sexuality. 'Bodies', on the other hand, takes another step away from biological determinism, basing its dissolution of categories on disjunctive performances rather than on revolution. Since the utopian society in 'Bodies' is largely incomprehensible to the narrator, she can only represent it as a vague sketch herself, leaving room for a spectre of the unrepresentable. However, 'Bodies' does not attempt to envision a society completely without gender, which would inevitably reconfirm the system it negates. In proliferating gender instabilities as they already exist in twentieth-century gay cultures, 'Bodies' plays with and loosens but does not supersede the link between sex, gender and sexuality.

Impersonations and gender uncertainties thus affect all levels of *Extra(Ordinary) People*. The novel/collection further develops the deconstructive and self-reflective aspects that have always served to counterbalance the partial 'essentialism' in Russ's work. More thoroughly than earlier texts by Russ, *Extra(Ordinary) People* ruptures totalizing separatist strategies and identity politics without abandoning empowering women-only spaces. In other words, this most recent collection/novel puts the strongest emphasis on deconstruction and indeterminacy, although, as I have shown, on many levels it also intersects with the stabilizing discourses discussed in Parts One and Two. *Extra(Ordinary) People* picks up and develops the central themes in Russ's oeuvre, androcide, the Sappho model and specifically the 'rescue of the female child' plot, as well as narrative voice and authorship. Again, the development is marked not by a complete paradigm displacement, but rather by a slight yet distinct shift in emphasis.

These simultaneities have baffled and continue to baffle Russ scholarship. Sarah Lefanu in *In the Chinks of the World Machine*, for example, stresses the deconstructive moments in Russ's writing, dismissing her separatist utopia and largely ignoring her materialism:

> Russ is hailed as a feminist first and foremost for an aspect of her work that, in my view, is comparatively minor: her participation in the feminist utopian tradition with her creation of the planet Whileaway. This sub-genre of SF ... relies to a certain

extent for its feminism on an essentialist, unitary view of
women ... I would contend that Russ's feminism is to be found
not so much in her utopian creations as in her deconstruction
of gender identity, of masculine and feminine behaviour.
(174–75)

My readings suggest that it is precisely the tensions and contradictions between the 'essentialisms' and the deconstructive elements in
Russ's fiction which make up her most significant contribution to
feminism. Russ's speculative fiction utilizes the three feminist
moments identified by Kristeva to create open, unstable texts which
undermine existing dominant narratives. These texts are explicitly
political, yet do not provide monolithic, reductive conclusions.

Through my readings I have also delineated the development in
Russ's fictional writing beginning with her earliest short stories. This
delineation partially builds on the work by Samuel Delany and Marilyn Hacker, who distinguish between an early, 'pre-feminist' and a
mature, 'truly' feminist Russ (Hacker, 73; Delany, 'Orders of Chaos',
116). However, my interpretations stress a continuity of major concerns in Russ's work and suggest a third, critically feminist phase,
which most fully develops the indeterminacies that destabilize these
concerns. Thus, Russ's work before 'When It Changed', such as the
novels *Picnic on Paradise* and *And Chaos Died*, puts a central focus on the
critique of capitalism. The later short stories and novels move
towards a stronger, more explicit critique of patriarchy, without, however, giving up the interrogation of the capitalist economy. But even
her earliest stories such as 'My Dear Emily' or 'Life in a Furniture
Store' as well as her first two novels *Picnic on Paradise* and *And Chaos
Died* create defiant female characters who live up to the women in
Russ's later novels. *Extra(Ordinary) People*, then, gives shape to the
third phase in Russ's writing, which remains explicitly feminist but
self-critically shifts further towards instabilities and performative,
provisional identities.

Russ's fiction in all of these phases speaks with narrative voices
that demand attentive reading. Along with this demand comes an
urgent concern for authorship and the act of narration. Her writing
moves the 'public' form of genre fiction to more 'private' forms which
borrow from autobiography, diary and particularly letter. *Extra(Ordinary) People* completely abandons narrative omniscience. Four of the
five stories in the collection/novel use an epistolary form in which the
narrator addresses an audience of one specific person. The narrative

voice in all of the stories is distinctly sexed, even if the sex of 'Joe Smith' in 'The Mystery of the Young Gentleman' remains ambiguous. As I have demonstrated for representative stories from each of the previous phases in Russ's writing, this quasi-autobiographical narrative voice is also closely affiliated with the scene of teaching and the 'rescue of the female child', a combination which corresponds to Elaine Marks's Sappho model. Directly addressing a 'you' as intimate friend, *Extra(Ordinary) People*, in a similar way to the novel *Kittatinny*, also pulls the reader into this erotic pedagogy. In all of these short stories and novels, the maternal and the erotic between two characters of different generations become unstable liberatory spaces.

These liberatory spaces in the interstices of patriarchy are the sites where cultural transformation can occur. This transformation does not come in the shape of a monolithic, phallic universal revolution, which would inevitably revert to old structures of hierarchy and power distribution, but as an infinite number of possible revolutions and subversions on every level of human interaction. Effectively combining the political enthusiasm and thrust of the early 1970s with an anticipation of the distrust in monolothic concepts of reality of the 1980s and '90s, Joanna Russ's fiction is a challenge to feminist theory. In its radical vision, Russ's fiction goes far beyond even her own critical work. The generic possibilities of speculative fiction allow her texts to explore alternative possibilities simultaneously and to carry each of these possibilities to its radical conclusion. Materialism, feminist separatism and poststructuralism may fundamentally contradict each other, but their combination propels Russ's texts beyond the necessity to hold on to reductive concepts of power. Rereading and rewriting feminism, such texts can transform patriarchal discourses, possibly before the effects of these discourses have destroyed the last remnants of a liveable environment—a while away.

Notes

Introduction

1. For a detailed discussion of feminism and genre fiction cf. Anne Cranny-Francis, *Feminist Fiction: Feminist Uses of Generic Fiction* (1990).

Part One
Introduction to Part One

1. The collection first came out in 1976 under the title *Alyx* and contains stories first published individually from 1967 to 1970. The earlier edition contains an Introduction by Samuel Delany.

Chapter One

1. Mieke Bal in *Narratology. Introduction to the Theory of Narrative* gives a useful summary of the various approaches to these homologies (11–12).

2. I use the term *fictional author* to refer to the author-character inscribed in the text, e.g. through such phrases as 'I'm the spirit of the author and know all things' (*The Female Man* 166). As I will show in this and Part Two, the presence of such a fictional author, who is sometimes conflated with the narrator, gives the narration a sexed authority. The term is distinct from Wayne Booth's *implied author* which is an abstract construct.

3. Russ wrote the story in 1963 (Delany, 'Introduction', v) under the title 'The Adventuress' and it came out in 1967 in *Orbit Two*. Significantly, Russ renamed the story 'Bluestocking' when it was collected in *Alyx* (1976). My quotations are from 'Bluestocking' because it is more readily available than the first printing.

4. Delany's long introduction is one of the finest appreciations of the Alyx sequence to date. He locates the stories in relation to Russ's

predecessors in pulp sword-and-sorcery and science fiction as well as to her own later work up to 1975.

5. In her brilliant and insightful essay 'Lesbian Intertextuality', in which she explores the paradigm of women loving women in written texts by women and men, from Sappho to Wittig.

6. Kathleen Spencer in 'Rescuing the Female Child' (1990) makes a similar point: 'In a later story, this moment would most likely lead to a recognition of sexual attraction between the two women ...' (169).

7. This does not exclude potential references to such writers as Emily Dickinson and Charlotte Perkins Gilman, or to William Faulkner's short story 'A Rose for Emily'.

8. The page numbers of the quotes from 'What Can a Heroine Do?' refer to Russ's more recent collection of essays, *To Write Like a Woman* (1995).

9. Susan Lanser in *Fictions of Authority* explores the pervasiveness of this 'heterosexual writing plot', the origin of which she locates in the eighteenth-century with writers such as Daniel Defoe, Samuel Richardson and Jean-Jacques Rousseau (35).

Chapter Two

1. The story was reprinted in *Alyx* (1976) and in *The Aventures of Alyx* (1983) under the title 'I Thought She was Afeard Till She Stroked My Beard'. All further references are to the 1985 edition by the Women's Press.

2. Russ, introductory note to 'When it Changed' (9).

3. Russ, Afterword to 'When It Changed' in *Again, Dangerous Visions* (280–81) cited in Hacker's 'Science Fiction and Feminism' (73).

4. All references are to the reprint in *The Zanzibar Cat* (1984).

5. I will discuss intersections between the biblical story of Jael and Russ's rewriting in Part Two, 'Sexuality'.

6. The reference is to the 1995 reprint in *To Write Like a Woman*.

7. I will expand on this intimate nexus between sexuality and oppression and its relevance for Russ's novels as part of feminist discourse in Part Two.

8. Thelma J. Shinn also points this out in 'Worlds of Words and Swords: Suzette Haden Elgin and Joanna Russ at Work' (210). However, I do not fully agree with the linear development she sets up between Russ's female protagonists. Even though Irene shares superficial characteristics with Alyx, she is a profoundly different character,

whose story is a fundamental critique of precisely the assumptions that motivate Alyx's texts.

Chapter Three

1. If it had not been for my students who pointed me to Cal I would probably have overlooked the inconspicuous yet pitiful character as well. In a letter, Joanna Russ also reminded me of Cal.

2. Maggie Humm in *The Dictionary of Feminist Theory* defines 'femininism' as follows: 'A term used by cultural and essentialist feminists to describe the ideology of female superiority. Feminism, to writers like Hélène Cixous and Monique Wittig, represents a narrow bourgeois demand for egalitarianism. Femininism, on the other hand, can celebrate feminine plurality' (93).

3. In reference to but clearly distinct from Harold Bloom's 'anxiety of influence'.

Part Two
Introduction to Part Two

1. Feminist thinking in the late 1980s and the '90s, e.g. Dianna Fuss's *Essentially Speaking* (1989), has exposed this opposition between 'equality' and 'difference' as a theoretical trap. The move beyond this dualism will be the concern of Part Three.

2. In *Partial Visions: Feminism and Utopianism* in the 1970s, Angelica Bammer analyses the ways in which writers in the 1970s appropriated nineteenth-century American utopian writing by women. Bammer also criticizes the stark racism of these utopian visions.

Chapter Four

1. The story was reprinted in *The Hidden Side of the Moon* (1987). All further references are to the 1989 edition by the Women's Press.

2. Russ says in 1995: 'Unfortunately ... the book can be interpreted as anti-Arab. If I were going to write it again, I would stress that the folks on Ka'bah are not descendents of Arabs but fake Arabs, middle Americans from Iowa or whatever, who are trying to re-create their own fantasies about a society that was, after all, a real one' (Letter to

the author, 9 March 1995).

3. Joanna Russ in a letter criticizes scholarship for its neglect of the connection: '... nobody seems to recognize Irene Adler, *the* woman— I suppose literary educations don't include Conan Doyle and Sherlock Holmes' (Letter to the author, 9 March 1995).

4. Part Three, 'Indeterminacy', will further explore such subvertive refusals to identify one single, unified self as origin and utopian vision in Russ' fiction.

5. Although *On Strike Against God* was first published in 1980 by Out and Out Books, the manuscript was finished by 1977 (Hacker, 77).

Chapter Five

1. Russ later combined 'Daddy's Girl' with 'The Autobiography of My Mother' under the title 'Old Thoughts, Old Presences' in *The Hidden Side of the Moon* (as well as in the first edition of *The Zanzibar Cat*).

Chapter Six

1. Person is critical of tying 'female liberation' to sexuality: '... one ought not to dictate a tyranny of active sexuality as critical to female liberation' (624). However, as I have tried to demonstrate, the effectiveness of Russ's texts rests on the strategy to accept the premises of the oppressive system for the moment of liberation. After all, even the decision against an active sexuality depends on current concepts of sexuality.

Part Three
Chapter Eight

1. *We Who Are About To* ... was first published in parts in 1975, 1976 and 1977 in *Galaxy* magazine but came out as a novel in 1977 (cf. also Lefanu, 177).

Chapter Nine

1. Frederick Jackson Turner's essay 'The Significance of the Frontier in American History' (1893) inaugurated the study of the frontier

myth in American culture. Twentieth-century cultural historiography, beginning with Henry Nash Smith's *The Virgin Land,* has identified Turner's thesis as part of the myth-making process and elaborated the analysis of whose interests it served.

Bibliography

Primary Bibliography: Joanna Russ

A: Short fiction

'Nor Custom Stale'. *The Magazine of Fantasy and Science Fiction*, 17:3 (1959): 75–86. Repr. in Russ, *The Hidden Side of the Moon*: 124–137.

'My Dear Emily'. *The Magazine of Fantasy and Science Fiction* July 1962. Repr. in *The Zanzibar Cat*: 116–46; and in *The Dark Descent*, ed. David G. Hartwell. New York: Doherty Assoc., 1987.

'There is Another Shore, You Know, Upon the Other Side'. *The Magazine of Fantasy and Science Fiction* September 1963. Repr. in *The Zanzibar Cat*: 147–65.

'I Had Vacantly Crumpled It Into My Pocket ... But My God, Eliot, It was a Photograph from Life!' *The Magazine of Fantasy and Science Fiction* 27:2 (1964): 12–21. Repr. in *The Hidden Side of the Moon*: 53–63; and in *Cthulhu. A Lovecraftian Anthology*, ed. Jim Turner with illustrations by Bob Eggleton. Sauk City, WI: Arkham House, 1995.

'Come Closer'. *Magazine of Horror* 2:4 (1965). Rep.*The Hidden Side of the Moon*: 64–69.

'Life in a Furniture Store'. *Epoch* 15:1 (1965): 71–82. Repr. in *The Hidden Side of the Moon*: 162–74.

'Mr Wilde's Second Chance'. *The Magazine of Fantasy and Science Fiction* 31:3 (1966): 65–67. Repr. in *The Hidden Side of the Moon*: 71–73; in *100 Great Fantasy Short Stories*, ed. I. Asimov, T. Carr and M.H. Greenberg. New York: Doubleday, 1984; in *In Another Part of the Forest. An Anthology of Gay Short Fiction*, compiled by Alberto Manguel and Craig Stephenson. New York: Crown Trade Paperbacks, 1994; and in *Masterpieces of Terror and the Unknown*, selected by Marvin Kaye. New York: St Martin's Press, 1993.

'The New Men'. *The Magazine of Fantasy and Science Fiction* 31 (February 1966). Repr. in *The Zanzibar Cat*: 244–55.

'This Night, at My Fire'. *Epoch* 15:2 (Winter 1966): 99–104. Repr. in *The Hidden Side of the Moon*. 49–52.

'I Gave Her Sack and Sherry'. *Orbit 2*. New York: Berkley Books, 1967.

Repr. in *Best Stories from Orbit, Volumes 1–10*, ed. Damon Knight. New York: Putnam, 1975; and as 'I Thought She Was Afeard Till She Stroked My Beard', in *The Adventures of Alyx*: 29–45.

'The Adventuress'. *Orbit 2*. New York: Berkley Books, 1967. Repr. as 'Bluestocking', in *The Adventures of Alyx*: 9–28.

'Visiting'. *Manhattan Review* (Fall 1967). Repr. in *The Hidden Side of the Moon*: 197–99.

'Harry Longshanks'. *Fiction as Progress*, ed. Carl Hartmann and Hazard Adams. New York: Dodd and Mead, 1968.

'Scenes from Domestic Life'. *Consumption* 2:1 (Fall 1968): 22–33.

'The Barbarian'. *Orbit 3*. New York: Berkley Books, 1968. Repr. in *Another World: A Science Fiction Anthology*, ed. with an introduction and commentary by Gardner Dozois. Chicago: Follett, 1977; and in *The Adventures of Alyx*: 49–67.

'This Afternoon'. *Cimarron Review*. 6 (December 1968): 60–66. Repr. in *The Hidden Side of the Moon*: 42–48.

'A Short and Happy Life'. *The Magazine of Fantasy and Science Fiction* 36:6 (1969). Repr. in *The Hidden Side of the Moon*: 95–97.

'Oh! She Has a Lover'. *Kinesis I* (February 1969).

'The Throaways'. *Consumption* 2:3 (Spring 1969): 26–31. Repr. in *The Hidden Side of the Moon*: 98–102.

'What Really Happened'. *Just Friends I* (October 1969).

'Cap and Bells'. *Discourse* (Summer 1970).

'Not for Love'. *Arlington Quarterly* (Fall 1970): 63–89.

'Suffer a Sea-Change'. *The William and Mary Review* (Fall 1970).

'The Man Who Could Not See Devils'. *Alchemy and Academe*, ed. Anne McCaffrey. New York: Doubleday, 1970. Repr. in *The Zanzibar Cat*: 121–34; and in *Masterpieces of Fantasy and Enchantment*, compiled by D.G. Hartwell with the assistance of Kathryn Cramer. New York: St. Martin's Press, 1988.

'The Precious Object'. *The Red Clay Reader* 7 (November 1970). Repr. in *The Zanzibar Cat*: 222–43.

'The Second Inquisition'. *Orbit 6*. New York: Berkley Books, 1970. Repr. in *In Dreams Awake: A Historical-Critical Anthology of Science Fiction*, ed. L.A. Fiedler. New York: Dell, 1975; in *More Women of Wonder: Science Fiction Novelettes by Women About Women*, ed. with an introduction and notes by Pamela Sargent. New York: Vintage, 1976; and in *Adventures of Alyx*: 163–92.

'The View from this Window'. *Quark 1*, ed. Marilyn Hacker. New York: Paperback Library, Coronet, 1970. Repr. in *The Hidden Side of the Moon*: 175–94.

'The Wise Man'. *Cimarron Review* 13 (October 1970): 44–63.

'Visiting Day'. *South* 2:1 (Spring 1970). Repr. in *The Hidden Side of the Moon*: 200–05.

'Window Dressing'. *New World of Fantasy 2*. New York: Ace, 1970. Repr. in *The New Women's Theatre*, ed. Honor Moore. New York: Random House, 1977; and in *The Hidden Side of the Moon*. 74–80.

'Poor Man, Beggar Man'. *Universe 1*, ed. Terry Carr. Repr. in *Nebula Award Stories 6*, ed. D. Clifford. New York: Doubleday, 1971: and in *The Zanzibar Cat* (Arkham House edition).

'Foul Fowl'. *The Little Magazine* 5:1 (Spring 1971): 25–27. Repr. in *The Hidden Side of the Moon*: 91–94.

'Gleepsite'. *Orbit 9*, ed. Damon Knight. New York: Putmans, 1971. Repr. in *Best Stories from Orbit, Volumes 1–10*, ed. Damon Knight. New York: Putnam, 1975; and in *The Zanzibar Cat*: 84–92.

'The Zanzibar Cat'. *Quark 3*, ed. Samuel Delany and Marilyn Hacker. New York: Paperback Library, Coronet, 1971. Repr. in *The Zanzibar Cat*: 274–86.

'Dear Diary'. *Northwest Review* 12 (Fall 1972): 43–50.

'Nobody's Home'. *New Dimensions II*, ed. Robert Silverberg. New York: Doubleday, 1972. Repr. in *New Dimensions*, ed. Robert Silverberg. New York: Harper & Row, 1980; in *The Zanzibar Cat*: 93–115; in *The Arbor House Treasury of Science Fiction Masterpieces*, ed. R. Silverberg and M.H. Greenberg. New York: Arbor House, 1983; and in *Women of Wonder: The Classic Years: Science Fiction by Women from the 1940s to the 1970s*, ed. and with an introduction and notes by Pamela Sargent. San Diego, New York and London: Harcourt Brace & Company, 1995.

'Useful Phrases for the Tourist'. *Universe 2*, ed. Terry Carr. New York: Ace, 1972. Repr. in *Infinite Jests: The Lighter Side of Science Fiction*, ed. Robert Silverberg. Radnor, PA: Chilton Books, 1974; in *The Zanzibar Cat*: 192–97; and in *Microcosmic Tales: 100 Wondrous Science Fiction Short-Short Stories*, ed. I. Asimov, M.H. Greenberg and J.D. Olander.

'When It Changed'. *Again, Dangerous Visions*, ed. Harlan Ellison. New York: Doubleday, 1972. Repr. in *The New Women of Wonder*, ed. Pamela Sargent. New York: Vintage Books, 1978; in *The Zanzibar Cat*: 10–21; in *The Arbor House Treasury of Science Fiction Masterpieces*, ed. Robert Silverberg and M.H. Greenberg. New York: Arbor House, 1983; in *Kindred Spirits: An Anthology of Gay and Lesbian Science Fiction Stories*, ed. Jeffrey M. Elliot. Boston: Alyson Publications, 1984; in *The Norton Anthology of Literature by Women*, ed. Sandra M. Gilbert and Susan Gubar. New York: Norton, 1985: 2262–69; and in *The Best of the Nebulas*, ed. Ben Bova. New York: Doherty Assoc., 1989.

'Laura, The Camp, and That Terrible Thing'. *Monmouth Review* (Spring 1973).

'Old Pictures'. *The Little Magazine* 6:4 (Winter 1973): 49–50. Repr. in *The Hidden Side of the Moon*: 195–96.

'The Soul of a Servant'. *Showcase*, ed. Roger Elwood. New York: Harper & Row, 1973. Repr. in *The Zanzibar Cat*: 42–64.

'A Game of Vlet'. *The Magazine of Fantasy and Science Fiction* (February 1974). Repr. in *The Zanzibar Cat*: 256–73.

'An Old Fashioned Girl'. *Final Stage*, ed. Edward L. Ferman and Barry N. Malzberg. [N.p.]: [n.p.] 1974.

'Passages'. *Galaxies* (January 1974): 50–51.

'Reasonable People'. *Orbit 14*. New York: Harpers, 1974. Repr. in *The Hidden Side of the Moon*: 156–61.

'Innocence'. *The Magazine of Fantasy and Science Fiction* 26 (February 1975): 82–83. Repr. in *100 Great Science Fiction Short Stories*, ed. I. Asimov, M.H. Greenberg, and J.D. Olander.

'A Few Things I Know About Whileaway'. *The New Improved Sun*, ed. Thomas M. Disch. [N.p.]: [n. p.] 1975: 81–97. Repr. in *The Norton Book of Science Fiction. North American Science Fiction, 1960–1990*, ed. Ursula K. Le Guin and Brian Attebery. New York and London: Norton, 1993: 337–49. [Excerpts from *The Female Man*]

'Daddy's Little Girl'. *Epoch* 24:2 (Spring 1975). Repr. combined with 'The Autobiography of My Mother' under the title 'Old Thoughts, Old Presences', in *The Zanzibar Cat* (Arkham House edition); and in *The Hidden Side of the Moon*: 206–29.

'Existence'. *Epoch*, ed. Robert Silverberg and Roger Elwood. New York: Putnam's 1975. Repr. in *The Hidden Side of the Moon*: 81–90.

1975 'The Autobiography of My Mother'. *Epoch* 25:1 (Fall 1975). Repr. in *Prize Stories, 1977: The O. Henry Awards*, ed. and with an introduction by William Abrahams. New York: Doubleday, 1977; in *Between Mothers & Daughters: Stories Across a Generation*, ed. and with an introduction by Susan Koppelman. Old Westbury, NY: Feminist Press, 1985; and in *Ms.* (May/June 1991): 54–60. Repr. combined with 'Daddy's Little Girl' under the title 'Old Thoughts, Old Presences', in *The Zanzibar Cat* (Arkham House edition); and in *The Hidden Side of the Moon*: 206–29.

'The Clichés from Outer Space'. *The Witch and the Chameleon* (1 April 1975). A longer version repr. in *Women's Studies International Forum* 7:2 (1984): 121–24. Repr. in *Despatches from the Frontiers of the Female Mind*, ed. Jen Green and Sarah Lefanu. London: Women's Press,

1985: 27–34; and in *The Hidden Side of the Moon*: 103–11.

'The Experimenter'. *Galaxy* 26:9 (October 1975). Repr. in *The Hidden Side of the Moon*: 138–55.

'Corruption'. *Aurora: Beyond Equality*, ed. Susan Janice Anderson and Vonda N. McIntyre. Greenwich, CT: Fawcett, 1976. Repr. in *The Zanzibar Cat*: 205–21.

'My Boat'. *The Magazine of Fantasy and Science Fiction* (January 1976). Repr. in *The Best from Fantasy and Science Fiction*, 22nd ser., ed. Edward L. Ferman. New York: Doubleday Science Fiction, Doubleday, 1977; in *The Zanzibar Cat*; and in *Tales of The Cthulhu Mythos, by H.P. Lovecraft and Divers Hands*, with illustrations by Jeffrey K. Potter. Sauk City, WI: Arkham House, 1990.

'How Dorothy Kept Away the Spring'. *The Magazine of Fantasy and Science Fiction* 52:2 (February 1977). Repr. in *The Hidden Side of the Moon*: 33–41.

'Kit Meets the Dragon'. *Sinister Wisdom*. (Fall 1977): 9.

'Dragons and Dimwits or … Lord of the Royalties'. *The Magazine of Fantasy and Science Fiction* (December 1979). Repr. in *The Zanzibar Cat*: 198–204.

'The Extraordinary Voyages of Amélie Bertrand'. *The Magazine of Fantasy and Science Fiction* (September 1979). Repr. in *Nebula Winners, Fifteen*, ed. Frank Herbert. New York: Harper, 1981; and in *The Zanzibar Cat*: 22–41.

'It's Important to Believe'. *Sinister Wisdom* 14 (1980). Repr. in *The Hidden Side of the Moon*: 70.

'Little Tales from Nature.' *WomanSpace: Future and Fantasy Stories and Art by Women.*, ed. Claudia Laperti. Lebanon, NH: New Victoria Publications, 1981: 17–21.

'Russalka: or, The Seacoast of Bohemia'. *Don't Bet on the Prince: Contemporary Feminist Fairy Tales in North America and England*, ed. Jack Zipes. London: Methuen, 1981.

'Elf Hill'. *The Magazine of Fantasy and Science Fiction* 63:5 (November 1982). Repr. in *The Hidden Side of the Moon*: 112–23.

'Souls'. *The Magazine of Fantasy and Science Fiction* 62:1 (January 1982). Repr. in *The Nebula Awards # 18*; in *Souls*. [bound with 'Houston, Houston, do you Read?' by James Tiptree, Jr.]. New York: Tor SF, 1989; and in *Extra(Ordinary) People*: 1–62.

'The Little Dirty Girl'. *Elsewhere*, ed. Terry Windling and Mark Alan Arnold. Vol. 2. New York: Ace, 1982. Repr. in *The Hidden Side of the Moon*: 1–22; and in *What Did Miss Darrington See? An Anthology of Feminist Supernatural Fiction*, ed. Jessica Amanda Salmonson, with an introduction by Rosemary Jackson. Old Westbury, NY: Feminist Press, 1989.

'The Mystery of the Young Gentleman'. *Speculations*, ed. Isaac Asimov and Alice Laurance. New York: Houghton Mifflin, 1982. Repr. in *Extra(Ordinary) People*: 62–92; and in *Worlds Apart: An Anthology of Lesbian and Gay Science Fiction and Fantasy*, ed. Camilla Decarnin, Eric Garber and Lyn Paleo. Boston: Alyson Publications, 1986.

'Main Street: 1953'. *Sinister Wisdom* 24 (Fall 1983): 11–13. Repr. in *The Hidden Side of the Moon*: 29–32.

'Sword Blades and Poppy Seed with Homage to (Who Else) Amy Lowell'. *Heroic Visions*, ed. Jessica Amanda Salmonson. New York: Ace, 1983: 157–62. Repr. in *The Hidden Side of the Moon*: 23–28.

1983 'What Did You Do During the Revolution, Grandma?'. *The Seattle Review* 4:1 (Spring 1983). Repr. in *Extra(Ordinary) People*: 118–44.

'Bodies'. *Extra(Ordinary) People*: 95–114.

'Everyday Depressions'. *Extra(Ordinary) People*: 147–60.

'Let George Do It'. *Women's Studies International Forum* 7:2 (1984): 125–126.

'Invasion'. *Isaac Asimov's Science Fiction Magazine*. (Jan. 1996). Repr. in *Years Best Science Fiction* 2. Ed. by David G. Hartwell. New York: Harper-Prism, 1997: 124–130: 'Excerpts from a Forthcoming Novel'. *The Seattle Review* 9:1 (1986): 51–58.

B: Novels

Picnic on Paradise. New York: Ace, 1968. Repr. London: MacDonald, 1969. [included in *Alyx* and in *The Adventures of Alyx*]

And Chaos Died. New York: Ace, 1970. Repr. New York: Berkley, 1979.

The Female Man. New York: Bantam, 1975; London: Star, 1977. Repr. with a new introduction by Marilyn Hacker. Boston: Gregg Press, 1977; London: The Women's Press, 1985.

We Who Are About To ... New York: Dell, 1975. Repr. Boston: Gregg Press, 1978; London: Methuen, 1978; London: The Women's Press, 1987.

Kittatinny: A Tale of Magic. Illustrated by Loretta Li. New York: Daughters Press, 1978.

The Two of Them. New York: Berkley, 1978; London: The Women's Press, 1986.

On Strike Against God. Brooklyn, NY: Out & Out Books, 1980. Repr. Trumansburg, NY: The Crossing Press, 1985; London: The Women's Press, 1987.

Extra(Ordinary) People. New York: St Martins Press, 1984; London: The Women's Press, 1985.

C: Short Story Collections

Alyx. With an introduction by Samuel Delany. Boston: Gregg Press, 1976.

The Adventures of Alyx. New York: Pocket Books-Simon & Schuster, 1983; London: The Women's Press, 1985.

The Zanzibar Cat. New York: Baen, 1983. Also printed as a slightly different collection [contains 'How Dorothy Kept Away the Spring', 'Poor Man, Beggar Man,' and 'Old Thoughts, Old Presences'] with a foreword by Marge Piercy and drawings by Dennis Neal Smith. Sauk City, WI: Arkham House, 1984.

The Hidden Side of the Moon. New York: St Martin's Press, 1987; London: The Women's Press, 1989.

D: Plays

'Window Dressing'. *Confrontation* (Spring 1973): Repr. *The New Women's Theatre*, ed. Honor Moor. New York: Vintage Books, 1977.

E: Poems

'To R. L.'. *Epoch* 6 (1953/1955): 242.

'Family Snapshots—Botanical Gardens, A la mode'. *Epoch* 7 (1955/1957): 35.

F: Criticism

'Daydream Literature and Science Fiction'. *Extrapolation* 11:1 (December 1969): 6–14.

'Communiqué from the Front: Teaching and the State of Art'. *Colloquy* 4:5 (May 1971).

'Genre'. *Clarion*, ed. Robin Wilson. New York: Signet, 1971.

'The Image of Women in Science Fiction'. *The Red Clay Reader* [N.p.]: [n.p.], 1971. Repr. *Images of Women in Fiction: Feminist Perspectives*, ed. Susan Koppelman Cornillon. Bowling Green, OH: Bowling Green University Popular Press, 1972: 79–94; and *Vertex*. 1:6 (February 1974): 53–57.

'The Wearing Out of Genre Materials'. *College English* 31:1 (October 1971): 46–54.

'The He-Man Ethos in Science Fiction'. *Clarion* 2 (1972).

'What Can a Heroine Do? or Why Women Can't Write'. *Images of Women in Fiction: Feminist Perspectives*, ed. Susan Koppelman Cornillon. Bowling Green, OH: Bowling Green University Popular Press, 1972: 3–20. Repr. in *To Write Like a Woman*: 79–93.

'The New Misandry.' *The Village Voice* (12 October 1972).

'Setting'. *Those Who Can: A Science Fiction Reader*, ed. R.S. Wilson. New York: New American Library. Mentor, 1973: 149–54.

'Speculations: The Subjunctivity of Science Fiction'. *Extrapolation* 15:1 (December 1973): 51–59. Repr. in *To Write Like a Woman*: 15–25.

'Somebody's Trying to Kill Me and I Think It's My Husband: The Modern Gothic'. *Journal of Popular Culture* 6 (1973): 666–91. Repr. in *To Write Like a Woman*: 94–119.

'"What if …' Literature.' *The Contemporary Literary Scene 1973*, ed. Frank N. Magill. Englewood, New Jersey: Salem Press, 1974.

'Dear Colleague: I Am Not an Honorary Male'. *Colloquy: Education in Church and Society* 7:4 (April 1974).

1975 'Introduction'. *Tales and Stories*, by Mary W. Shelley. Facsimile of the 1881 Lippincott edition. Boston: Gregg Press, 1975, p. v–xviii. Repr. as 'On Mary Wollstonecraft Shelley' in *To Write Like a Woman*: 120–32.

'This is Your Life'. *Khatru 3 & 4. Symposium: Women in Science Fiction*, ed. Jeffrey D. Smith. First printing November 1975. Second printing with additional contemporary material, ed. Jeanne Gomoll, May 1993. Madison, WI: Obsessive Press, 1993. [Suzy McKee Charnas, Samuel R. Delany, Ursula K. Le Guin, Vonda N. McIntyre, Raylyn Moore, Joanna Russ, James Tiptree, Jr., Luise White, Kate Wilhelm, Chelsea Quinn Yarbro, Virginia Kidd.]

'On the Nature of Concrete Phenomena and Rhetorical Sleight-of-Hand'. *Khatru 3 & 4. Symposium: Women in Science Fiction.*

'Risk'. *The Magazine of Fantasy and Science Fiction* 26 (June 1975): 157.

'Towards an Aesthetic of Science Fiction'. *Science Fiction Studies* (July 1975): 112–119. Repr. in *To Write Like a Woman*: 3–14.

'The Scholar as Translator (Contra)'. *Translators and Translating: Selected Essays From the American Translators Association, Summer Workshops, 1974*, ed. T. Ellen, Crandell. Binghamton: State University of New York Press, 1975: 61–64.

'Outta Space: Women Write Science Fiction'. *Ms Magazine* (January 1976): 109+.

'Alien Monsters'. *Turning Points: Essays in the Art of Science Fiction*, ed. Damon Knight. New York: Harper, 1977: 132–43. [Philadelphia Science Fiction Convention speech delivered November 1968].

Comment on 'Prostitution and Medieval Canon Law'. *Signs: a Journal of Women in Culture and Society* 3:2 (Winter 1977).

Comment on '"The Exquisite Slave": the Role of Clothes in the Making of Victorian Women' and 'Dress Reform as Anti-feminism'.

Signs: a Journal of Women in Culture and Society 3:2 (1977).

'"Technology", The Immense Red Herring'. *Forum on Technology and the Literary Mind*, Proceedings of the MLA Convention, December 1977. [n.p.: n.p.], [n.d.]: 1–22.

'SF and Technology as Mystifications'. *Science Fiction Studies* (November 1978): 250–60. Repr. in *To Write Like a Woman*: 26–40.

Comment on Nacy Sahli's 'Smashing: Women's Relationships before the Fall' *Chrysalis* 8 (1979); *Chrysalis* 9 (1979).

'*Amor Vincit Foeminam*: The Battle of the Sexes in Science Fiction'. *Science Fiction Studies* (March 1980): 2–15. Repr. in *To Write Like a Woman*: 41–59.

'Women and Science Fiction'. *Science-Fiction Studies* 7:21.2 (1980).

'On the Fascination of Horror Stories, Including Lovecraft's.' *Science-Fiction Studies* 7:22.3 (1980). Repr. in *To Write Like a Woman*: 60–64.

'Not for Years but for Decades'. *The Coming Out Stories*, ed. Julia Penelope and Susan J. Wolfe. Watertown, MA: Persephone Press, 1980. Repr. in *Magic Mommas, Trembling Sisters, Puritans and Perverts*: 17–42.

'Recent Feminist Utopias'. *Future Females: A Critical Anthology*, ed. Marleen S. Barr. Bowling Green, OH: Bowling Green State University Popular Press, 1981: 71–75. Repr. in *To Write Like a Woman*: 133–48.

'Howard Philips Lovecraft'. *Twentieth Century Science Fiction Writers*, ed. Curtis C. Smith. New York: St Martins Press, 1981.

'Power and Helplessness in the Women's Movement.' *Sinister Wisdom* 18 (1981).

'How to Write Book Reviews'. *The Feminist Review/New Women's Times* (July–August 1982).

'Being Against Pornography'. *Thirteenth Moon* 6:1–2 (1983).

'Introduction'. *Uranian Worlds*, ed. Camilla Decarnin, Eric Garber and Lyn Paleo. Boston: G.K. Hall, 1983.

'To Write Like a Woman: Transformations of Identity in the Work of Willa Cather'. *Journal of Homosexuality* (Winter 1987).

'Introduction'. *The Penguin Book of Fantasy by Women*, ed. A. Susan Williams and Richard Glyn Jones. London: Penguin, 1995.

G: Books

How to Suppress Women's Writing. Austin: University of Texas Press, 1983.

Magic Mommas, Trembling Sisters, Puritans and Perverts: Feminist Essays. The Crossing Press Feminist Series. Trumansburg, NY: Crossing Press, 1985.

To Write Like a Woman. Essays in Feminism and Science Fiction. Bloomington and Indianapolis: Indiana University Press, 1995.

What Are We Fighting For? Sex, Race, Class, and the Future of Feminism. New York: St Martin's Press, 1998.

H: Book Reviews

College English 33:3 (December 1971).

The Village Voice 14 June 1973; 9 September 1971.

Frontiers 5:5 (Fall 1980); 4:2 (Summer 1979); 4:1 (Spring 1979); 3:3 (Fall 1978); 1:1 (Fall 1975).

The Magazine of Fantasy and Science Fiction 2 (1980); 11 (1979); 6 (1979); 2 (1979); 11 (1976); 4 (1975); 3 (1975); 1 (1975); 2 (1973); 12 (1972); 11 (1971); 4 (1971); 2 (1971); 2 (1971); 7 (1970); 1 (1970); 9 (1969); 4 (1969); 12 (1968); 7 (1968); 19 (1967); 12 (1966).

The Washington Post 10 May 1981; 24 February 1980; 27 January 1980; 9 May 1979; 1 April 1979; 21 January 1979.

Sinister Wisdom 12 (Winter 1980).

I: Interviews

'Reflections on Science Fiction: An Interview with Joanna Russ'. *Quest* 2 (1975): 40–49.

Walker, Paul. *Speaking of SF: The Paul Walker Interviews.* Oradel, NJ: Lima, 1978: 242–52.

Platt, Charles. *Dream Makers II.* Berkely, NY: [n.p.], 1983. [Contains biographical information and interview.]

Johnson, Charles. 'A Dialogue: Samuel Delany and Joanna Russ on Science Fiction'. *Callaloo: An Afro American and African Journal of the Arts and Letters* 7:3 (22) (1984): 27–35.

Shervington, Sharon. 'Letting all the voices speak. An interview with Joanna Russ'. *The New York Times Book Review* (31 January 1988): 16.

McCaffery, Larry. *Across the Wounded Galaxies: Interviews with Contemporary American Science Fiction Writers.* Urbana: University of Illinois Press, 1990.

Perry, Donna. *Backtalk: Women Writers Speak Out.* New Brunswick, NJ: Rutgers University Press, 1993: 287–311.

Brownworth, Victoria A. 'Battling Back'. *Lambda Book Report. A Review of Contemporary Gay and Lesbian Literature* 4:7 (1994): 6–7.

Secondary Bibliography

Alcoff, Linda. 'Cultural Feminism versus Post-Structuralism: The Identity Crisis in Feminist Theory'. *Signs* 13 (1988): 405–36.

Annas, Pamela J. 'New Worlds, New words: Androgyny in Feminist Science Fiction'. *Science Fiction Studies* 5 (1978): 143–56.

Atwood, Margaret. *The Handmaid's Tale* (1985). New York: Fawcett Crest-Ballantine, 1989.

Ayres, Susan. 'The "Straight Mind" in Russ's *The Female Man*'. *Science Fiction Studies* 22:1 (1995): 22–34.

Bal, Mieke. *Narratology: Introduction to the Theory of Narrative*. Toronto: University of Toronto Press, 1985.

Bammer, Angelika. *Partial Visions: Feminism and Utopianism in the 1970s*. London: Routledge, 1991.

Barbour, Douglas. 'Joanna Russ's *The Female Man*: An Appreciation'. *The Sphinx: A Magazine of Literature and Society* 4:1 (1981): 65–75.

Barr, Marleen S. *Alien to Femininity: Speculative Fiction and Feminist Theory*. Contributions to the Study of Science Fiction & Fantasy 27. New York: Greenwood, 1987.

—— *Feminist Fabulation: Space/Postmodern Fiction*. Iowa City: University of Iowa Press, 1992.

Barth, John. 'The Literature of Exhaustion'. *The Atlantic Monthly* 220:2 (1967): 29–34.

Bartkowski, Frances. *Feminist Utopias*. Lincoln: University of Nebraska Press, 1989.

Boston Women's Health Book Collective. *Our Bodies, Ourselves. A Book by and for Women* (1973). Second, revised and expanded edition. New York: Simon and Schuster, 1976.

Butler, Judith. *Gender Trouble: Feminism and the Subversion of Identity*. London: Routledge, 1990.

—— 'Against Proper Objects'. *differences*. 6:2+3 (1994): 1–26.

Byrne, Deirdre. 'The Postmodernization of Gender/The Gendering of Postmodernism: Joanna Russ's *Extra(Ordinary) People*'. *Unisa English Studies: Journal of the Department of English* 30:1 (1992): 47–52.

Charnas, Suzy McKee. *Walk to the End of the World* and *Motherlines* (1974; 1978). London: The Women's Press, 1995.

Cranny-Francis, Anne. *Feminist Fiction: Feminist Uses of Generic Fiction*. Cambridge: Polity Press, 1990.

Crowder, Diane Griffin. 'Separatism and Feminist Utopian Fiction'. *Sexual Practice, Textual Theory. Lesbian Cultural Criticism*, ed. Susan J. Wolfe and Julia Penelope. Cambridge, MA: Blackwell, 1993:

237–50.

Daly, Mary. *Gyn/Ecology: The Metaethics of Radical Feminism*. Boston, MA: Beacon, 1978.

—— *Pure Lust*: Elemental Feminist Philosophy. Boston, MA: Beacon Press, 1984.

Delany, Samuel R. Introduction. *Alyx*, by Joanna Russ. Boston: Gregg Press, 1976.

—— 'Orders of Chaos: The Science Fiction of Joanna Russ'. *Women Worldwalkers: New Dimensions of Science Fiction and Fantasy*, ed. Jane B. Weedman. Lubock: Texas Tech Press, 1985: 95–123.

Doyle, Sir Arthur Conan. *Selected Stories by Sir Arthur Conan Doyle*. The World's Classics. London: Oxford University Press, 1951: 206–35.

DuPlessis, Rachel Blau. 'The Feminist Apologues of Lessing, Piercy, and Russ'. *Frontiers* 4:1 (1979): 1–9.

—— 'The Pink Guitar'. *The Pink Guitar: Writing as Feminist Practice*. New York: Routledge, 1990. 157–174.

Dworkin, Andrea. *Pornography: Men Possessing Women*. New York: Perigree Books-G.P. Putnam's Sons, 1981.

Elgin, Suzette Haden. 'For the Sake of Grace'. *The Norton Book of Science Fiction*, ed. Ursula K. Le Guin and Brian Attebery. New York: Norton, 1993: 211–30.

Faderman, Lillian. *Odd Girls and Twilight Lovers: A History of Lesbian Life in Twentieth-Century America*. Between Men – Between Women. Harmondsworth: Penguin, 1991.

Firestone, Shulamith. *The Dialectic of Sex: The Case for Feminist Revolution*. (1970) New York: Quill, 1993.

Fitting, Peter. '"So We All Became Mothers": New Roles for Men in Recent Utopian Fiction'. *Science Fiction Studies*. 12 (1985): 156–83.

—— 'Reconsiderations of the Separatist Paradigm in Recent Feminist Science Fiction'. *Science Fiction Studies* 19 (1992): 32–48.

Fuller, Margaret. *Women in the Nineteenth Century* (1855). New York: Norton, 1971.

Fuss, Diana. *Essentially Speaking: Feminism, Nature & Difference*. London: Routledge, 1989.

Gardiner, Judith Kegan. 'Empathic Ways of Reading: Narcissism, Cultural Politics, and Russ's Female Man'. *Feminist Studies* 20:1 (1994): 87–111.

Gearhart, Sandy Miller. *The Wondergrand. Stories of the Hill Women* (1980). Boston, MA: Alyson Publications, 1984.

Gilbert, Sandra M. and Gubar, Susan. *The Madwoman in the Attic: The Woman Writer and the Nineteenth-Century Literary Imagination*. New

Haven, CT: Yale University Press, 1979.

Gilman, Charlotte Perkins. *Herland* (1915). New York: Pantheon Books, 1979.

—— 'The Yellow Wall-Paper'. *The Heath Anthdogy of American Literature*, vol. 2, second edition. Ed. Paul Lanter, *et al.* Lexington: Heath, 1994: 800–12.

Gomoll, Jeanne. 'An Open Letter to Joanna Russ'. *Aurora* 10.1 (1986–87): 7–10.

Greer, Germaine. *The Female Eunuch.* (1970) London: Paladin-Harper Collins, 1991.

Hacker, Marilyn. 'Science Fiction and Feminism: The Work of Joanna Russ'. *Chrysalis* 4 (1977): 67–79.

Haddawy, Husain. Introduction. *The Arabian Nights.* Trans. by Hussain Haddawy. New York: Norton, 1990.

Haraway, Donna. 'A Manifesto for Cyborgs: Science, Technology, and Socialist Feminism in the 1980s'. *Socialist Review* 80 (1985): 65–107.

Holt, Marilyn J. 'No Docile Daughters: A Study of Two Novels by Joanna Russ'. *Room of One's Own* 6:1–2 (1981): 92–99.

Humm, Maggie. *The Dictionary of Feminist Theory.* 2nd edn. Columbus, OH: Ohio State University Press, 1995.

Jagose, Annamarie. *Lesbian Utopics.* New York: Routledge, 1994.

Jones, Libby Falk and Goodwin, Sarah W. (editors). *Feminism, Utopia, and Narrative.* Tennessee Studies in Literature: Vol. 32. Knoxville: University of Tennessee Press, 1990.

King, Betty. *Women of the Future: The Female Main Character in Science Fiction.* Metuchen, NJ: Scarecrow, 1984.

Kristeva, Julia. 'Women's Time'. Trans. Alice Jardine and Harry Blake. *Signs* 7 (1981): 13–35.

Landon, Brooks. 'Eve at the End of the World: Sexuality and the Reversal of Expectations in Novels by Joanna Russ, Angela Carter, and Thomas Berger'. *Erotic Universe: Sexuality and Fantastic Literature*, ed. Donald Palumbo. New York: Greenwood, 1986: 61–74.

Landry, Donna and MacLean, Gerald. *Materialist Feminisms.* Cambridge, MA: Blackwell, 1993.

Lane, Mary E. Bradley. *Mizorah* (1980). Bosto, MA: Greg Press, 1975.

Lanser, Susan. 'Toward a Feminist Narratology'. *Feminisms. An Anthology of Literary Theory and Criticism*, ed. Robyn R. Warhol and Diane Price Herndl. New Brunswick, NJ: Rugers University Press, 1991.

—— *Fictions of Authority: Women Writers and Narrative Voice.* Ithaca and London: Cornell University Press, 1992.

Law, Richard. 'Joanna Russ and the "Literature of Exhaustion"'.

Extrapolation. 25 (1984): 146–56.

Le Guin, Ursula K. and Attebery, Brian (editors) *The Norton Book of Science Fiction.* New York: Norton, 1993.

Lefanu, Sarah. *In the Chinks of the World Machine: Feminism and Science Fiction.* London: The Women's Press, 1988.

Linden, Julie. 'From Woman to Human: A Radical Feminist Reading of Joanna Russ's *The Female Man* and *Extra(Ordinary) People*'. Master's Thesis, University of Connecticut, 1995.

McCaffery, Larry (editor). *Postmodern Fiction: A Bio-Bibliographical Guide.* Movements in the Arts, 2. New York: Greenwood, 1986.

McClenahan, Catherine. 'Textual Politics: The Uses of the Imagination in Joanna Russ's *The Female Man*'. *Transactions of the Wisconsin Academy of Sciences, Arts, and Letters* 70 (1982): 114–25.

Marcus, Laura. 'Feminism into Fiction: The Women's Press'. *The Times Literary Supplement* (27 September 1985): 1070.

Marks, Elaine. 'Lesbian Intertextuality'. *Sexual Practice, Textual Theory. Lesbian Cultural Criticism*, ed. Susan J. Wolfe and Julia Penelope. Cambridge, MA: Blackwell, 1993: 271–290.

Moers, Ellen. *Literary Women: The Great Writers.* New York: Doubleday, 1976.

Moi, Toril. *Sexual/Textual Politics: Feminist Literary Theory.* New Accents. London and New York: Routlege, 1985.

—— 'Representation of Patriarchy: Sexuality and Epistemology in Freud's Dora'. *Feminist Review* 9 (1981): 60–73. Repr. in *Contemporary Literary Cirticism: Literary and Cultural Studies*, ed. Robert Con Davis and Ronald Schleifer. New York: Longman, 1994: 388–99.

Morgan, Robin (editor). *Sisterhood is Powerful: An Anthology of Writings From the Women's Liberation Movement.* New York: Random House, 1970.

Moylan, Tom. *Demand the Impossible: Science Fiction and the Utopian Imagination.* New York: Methuen, 1986.

Murphy, Patrick D. "Gender Politics': Epithet or Accolade? Or, Feminist SF and the Case of Joanna Russ'. *New York Review of Science Fiction* 10 (1989): 3–5.

—— 'Suicide, Murder, Culture, and Catastrophe: Joanna Russ's *We Who Are About To...*'. *State of the Fantastic: Studies in the Theory and Practice of Fantastic Literature and Film*, ed. Nicholas Ruddick. Contributions to the Study of Science Fiction and Fantasy 50. Westport, CT : Greenwood, 1992: 121–31.

Notkin, Debbie and Wood, Susan. 'A Reader's Guide'. *Room of One's Own* 6:1–2 (1981): 124–39.

Palmer, Paulina. *Contemporary Women's Fiction: Narrative Practice and Feminist Theory.* Jackson: University Press of Mississippi, 1989.

Person, Ethel Spector. 'Sexuality as the Mainstay of Identity: Psychoanalytic Perspectives'. *Signs* 5:4 (1980): 605–30.

Pfaelzer, Jean. 'The Changing of the Avant Garde: The Feminist Utopia'. *Science Fiction Studies* 15 (1988): 282–94.

Review of *The Female Man*, by Joanna Russ. *The Library Journal* 113 (15 November 1988): 30.

Review of *The Female Man*, by Joanna Russ. *The Magazine of Fantasy and Science Fiction* 49:2 (1975): 50–52.

Rich, Adrienne. 'Compulsory Heterosexuality and Lesbian Existence'. *Signs: Journal of Women in Culture and Society* 5:4 (1980): 631–60.

—— *Of Woman Born. Motherhood as Experience and Institution* (1976).New York and London: Norton, 1995.

Roberts, Robin. 'Post-Modernism and Feminist Science Fiction'. *Science Fiction Studies* 17:2 (1990): 136–52.

—— *A New Species: Gender & Science in Science Fiction.* Urbana: University of Illinois Press, 1993.

Robinson, Sally. 'The 'Anti-Logos Weapon': Multiplicity in Women's Texts'. *Contemporary Literature.* 29:1 (1988): 105–24.

Rosinsky, Natalie M. 'A Female Man? The Medusan Humor of Joanna Russ'. *Extrapolation: A Journal of Science Fiction and Fantasy.* 23:1 (1982): 31–36.

—— *Feminist Futures: Contemporary Women's Speculative Fiction.* Ann Arbor: UMI Research Press, 1984.

Ruether, Rosemary Radford. *Gaia & God. An Ecofeminist Theology of Earth Healing.* San Francisco: Harper, 1994.

Russ, Joanna. Letter to the author (9 March 1995).

—— Letter to the author (21 September 1995).

Sauter-Bailliet, Theresia. 'Joanna Russ, *The Female Man*'. *Der Science-Fiction-Roman in der Angloamerikanischen Literatur: Interpretationen,* ed. Hartmut Heuermann. Düsseldorf: Bagel, 1986: 355–75.

Shelton, Robert. 'The Social Text as Body: Images of Health and Disease in Three Recent Feminist Utopias'. *Literature and Medicine* 12:2 (1993): 161–77.

Shinn, Thelma J. 'Worlds of Words and Swords: Suzette Haden Elgin and Joanna Russ at Work'. *Women Worldwalkers: New Dimensions of Science Fiction and Fantasy,* ed. Jane B. Weedman. Lubock: Texas Tech Press, 1985: 207–22.

Smith, Jeffrey D. (editor). *Khatru 3 & 4. Symposium: Women in Science Fiction.* First printing November 1975. Second printing with additional contemporary material, ed. Jeanne Gomoll May 1993. Madison, WI: Obsessive Press 1993. [Suzy McKee Charnas, Samuel R. Delany, Ursula K. Le Guin, Vonda N. McIntyre, Raylyn Moore, Joanna Russ, James Tiptree, Jr., Luise White, Kate Wilhelm, Chelsea Quinn Yarbro, Virginia Kidd.]

Spector, Judith A. 'Dr Jekyll and Mrs Hyde: Gender-Related Conflict in the Science Fiction of Joanna Russ'. *Extrapolation.* 24 (1983): 370–79.

—— 'The Functions of Sexuality in the Science Fiction of Russ, Piercy, and LeGuin'. *Erotic Universe: Sexuality and Fantastic Literature*, ed. Donald Palumbo. New York: Greenwood, 1986: 197–207.

Spencer, Kathleen L. 'Rescuing the Female Child: The Fiction of Joanna Russ'. *Science Fiction Studies* 17:2 (1990): 167–87.

Stableford, Brian, Lefanu, Sarah, Wolmark, Jenny *et. al.* 'Foundation Forum: Feminism and SF'. *Foundation: The Review of Science Fiction* 43 (1988): 63–77.

Tiptree, James, Jr. 'The Women Men Don't See'. *Women of Wonder. The Classic Years. Science Fiction by Women from the 1940s to the 1970s*, ed. and with an introduction and notes by Pamela Sargent. San Diego: Harcourt Brace, 1995.

Walker, Nancy A. *Feminist Alternatives: Irony and Fantasy in the Contemporary Novel by Women.* London: University Press of Mississippi, 1990.

Weedman, J. B. (editor) *Women Worldwalkers: New Dimensions of Science Fiction and Fantasy.* Lubbock, TX: Texas Tech Press, 1985.

Wittig, Monique. *Les Guérillères.* Trans. David Le Vay. Boston: Beacon Press. (French edition, Paris: Les Editions Miniut, 1969,)

—— 'One is Not Born a Woman'. in Wittig, *The Straight Mind and Other Essays.* Hemel Hempstead: Harvester Wheatsheaf, 1992: 11–20.

Wolmark, Jenny. *Aliens And Others: Science Fiction, Feminism and Postmodernism.* Iowa City: University of Iowa Press, 1994.

Zimmerman, Bonnie. 'Feminist Fiction and the Postmodern Challenge'. *Postmodern Fiction: A Bio-Bibliographical Guide*, ed. Larry McCaffery. Movements in the Arts, 2. New York and Westport, CN: Greenwood, 1986: 175–88.

Index of Names

Index of Novels and Short Stories by Joanna Russ